Housing the Poor:
The Case for Heroism

Housing the Poor:

The Case for Heroism

by
Alexander Polikoff

Ballinger Publishing Company ● **Cambridge, Massachusetts**
A Subsidiary of J.B. Lippincott Company

International Standard Book Number: 0–88410–665–9

Library of Congress Catalog Card Number: 77–11869

Printed in the United States of America

Library of Congress Cataloging in Publication Data

Polikoff, Alexander.
  Housing the poor.

  1. Housing policy—United States. 2. Discrimination in housing—United States.
I. Title.
HD7293.P55   301.5'40973   77–11869
ISBN 0–88410–665–9

Admittedly, it is all too easy to flinch in the face of necessary heroic measures. The question I would raise is: Is this degree of heroism [a housing dispersal policy] necessary? I have argued it is not, for integration of blacks is occurring, while a major public policy for the integration of the poor would be impossible to implement.

—Nathan Glazer

For Barbara

Contents

Acknowledgments

Thanks in fullest measure to my daughter Deborah and my son Daniel Polikoff for editorial assistance; to Len Rubinowitz for reading and criticism; to Sylvia Scheinfeld for providing a unique place to work (The Woodstock Center); to Elaine Oslakovic for typing endless drafts; to The Twentieth Century Fund for financial assistance; to the directors of BPI (Business and Professional People for the Public Interest) for releasing me part time for this project; and to my wife, Barbara Polikoff, for everything.

Preface

In April 1976, by a unanimous (8-0) vote, the U.S. Supreme Court decided the case of *Hills v. Gautreaux*. The Court ruled that federal judges could order the U.S. Department of Housing and Urban Development to administer federally subsidized housing programs throughout the six county Chicago metropolitan area to help remedy the effects of past racial bias in Chicago's public housing.

A "landmark," proclaimed the Baltimore Evening *Sun;* likely to be as important as the *Brown v. Board of Education* school case. "Tyranny," cried an outraged Pat Buchanan, erstwhile speechwriter for Richard Nixon; a little "rebellion" would be in order. Between these two extremes of reaction, most of the rest of the nation's press, including *Time, Newsweek, The New York Times*, and the *Christian Science Monitor*, viewed the decision as a small, albeit important, first step on the long road to housing desegregation.

Many readers of the news reports could identify Hills—she was the photogenic Carla Hills, secretary of the Department of Housing and Urban Development, the only woman in Gerald Ford's cabinet. Dorothy Gautreaux, on the other hand, was virtually unknown. She was a black woman, dead some six years now, whose unsuspected linkage to the Supreme Court had been forged over two decades earlier when, in 1953, seeking housing for her family of six (which was then living in a single bedroom), she obtained an apartment from the Chicago Housing Authority. Like most CHA housing, the project to which the Gautreaux family was assigned was in a black neighborhood. Dorothy Gautreaux knew that under CHA policies, which mirrored the racial pattern of the times, she would not be accepted in any of the handful of CHA projects in white neighborhoods. Those were reserved for whites.

Over the next decade, in education, in employment, in voting, in transportation, and in other public facilities and services, racial segregation diminished significantly. But not in housing. CHA's new projects were still confined to the black ghetto; if anything, residential segregation intensified across the land. If they wished to live in subsidized housing only one choice was afforded the Dorothy Gautreauxs of the country: they would have to live in virtually all-black neighborhoods.

In 1964, Congress passed a new civil rights law that outlawed discrimination in federally subsidized programs. Lyndon Johnson was saying, "We shall overcome." The time seemed ripe for change. But, despite protests, CHA racial policies remained firmly the same.

In 1965, Dorothy Gautreaux and other CHA tenants asked the American Civil Liberties Union to try to halt another massive CHA project proposed for Chicago's west side black ghetto and to force a change in CHA site location policies. The author, as volunteer head of an ACLU team of cooperating lawyers, took on the case. Thus began *Hills v. Gautreaux*, a battle that has continued for over a decade, has outlasted Dorothy Gautreaux, and at this writing is still not over. (Since 1970 the case has been carried on jointly by ACLU and BPI [Business and Professional People for the Public Interest], a public interest law firm of which the author is executive director.)

This book grows out of the author's experiences with the Gautreaux litigation, and with the broader issue of residential segregation to which it speaks. The book is dedicated to the Dorothy Gautreauxs of our land.

—Alexander Polikoff

Introduction

Separation—economic and racial—between central cities and suburbs has become deeply ingrained in our national life. The division persists and intensifies despite a substantial drop in the number of poor, a major improvement in the quality of the housing stock, an enormous increase in social welfare spending, an impressive array of antidiscrimination laws, and a remarkable rise in the level of racial tolerance.

The nation faces critical problems that arise in significant measure from this "concentration of persons of lower income in central cities."[1] Whenever a large concentration of poor people in urban communities persists, serious problems associated with poverty, such as unemployment, welfare, poor education, bad housing, and a high incidence of crime, are intensified. In addition, an inordinate burden is placed on central city taxpayers to provide costly public services. This burden drives industry and middle class families to the suburbs and thus saps the central city's tax base and its ability to provide needed jobs and services.[2] As the city's strength drains away, its problems compound, and the downward spiral accelerates. So long as massive concentrations of the poor remain intact, even temporarily successful efforts to deal with selected problems such as housing or crime are eroded and ultimately rendered fruitless by the vast scope and pervasive nature of the poverty-related problems that always remain.

But it is not simply the poor who are concentrated in central cities; preeminently it is the black poor. In 1974, although there were less than half as many blacks as whites among the poor (7.5

against 16.3 million according to federal government statistics), there were more than twice as many blacks as whites in the poverty areas of central cities, 2.8 million against 1.3.[3] Thus, the ghettos in most of our largest cities are black ghettos (even though a few exceptions exist, for example, concentrations of Puerto Ricans in New York City and of Spanish language minorities in cities of the Southwest). As long ago as the early 1960s, an editor of *Fortune* wrote that when city officials talked about "spreading slums," they were talking in the main about black areas.[4] Academicians seem to agree that when we refer to the urban slum we generally mean the "poor Negro ghetto."[5] A study of St. Louis, while arguing that poverty, not race, produces urban decay, said that statistically, in St. Louis, to be black was to be poor and to be poor was to be black. It concluded, "We must equate . . . black takeover of a neighborhood with ensuing blight. . . ."[6] As economics professor John F. Kain puts it, "Only when the city loses its monopoly on black poverty will it have a chance."[7]

This central city monopoly not only leads to economic and social deterioration but creates an enormous potential for violence as well. Nearly a decade ago, the National Advisory Commission on Civil Disorders—the Kerner Commission—reported to the nation about the "explosive mixture" that had been accumulating in American cities since the end of World War II and had finally erupted into rioting and turmoil. To paraphrase the commission's grim conclusions,

- America was moving toward two societies, one black and one white, the first largely confined by discrimination and poverty to the destructive environment of urban ghettos in our largest cities; the second, relatively more affluent, increasingly suburban, increasingly isolated from the first, physically, economically, and socially.

- Unless important changes in public policy were made, this division within the American community would deepen and ultimately threaten the destruction of basic democratic values.[8]

Through the 1970s, the Kerner Report's observations continue to hold true. Although violence on the 1960s scale has not been repeated, the "explosive mixture" remains.

It is the purpose of this book to examine how *public policies* have contributed, in two mutually reinforcing ways, to metropolitan economic and racial separation; first, by fostering the confinement of impoverished blacks within central cities; and second, by facilitating the exodus of middle class whites from them. The author contends that the city will not lose its monopoly on black poverty unless and until a housing policy is developed that enables and encourages the dispersal of a significant portion of the black ghetto population into suburban white middle class communities. That dispersal can only be achieved through federal, not local, initiative because it is contrary to the self-interest of most local communities to open their doors voluntarily to the central city minority poor.[9] ("Dispersal" is used in the sense of geographically scattered housing *opportunities* to be offered to prospective occupants to accept or reject at *their* option.)

Urban problems in general are therefore not the subject of this volume; traffic congestion, air pollution, and other undesirable characteristics of large cities would not cease to exist if metropolitan racial and economic separation were magically eliminated. Neither is housing, in its physical shelter sense, or land use planning the focus of the discussion. A vast literature describes and documents the individual and social costs of the nation's housing deficiencies, analyzes the economics of housing markets and the housing construction industry, and counsels on how we should avoid unsightly, energy-wasteful, ecologically destructive urban sprawl while meeting our housing needs—all with only fleeting mention of the problem of metropolitan apartheid.[10] If we accepted and implemented all that counsel, we would still be left with the "explosive mixture" and with what another presidential commission called the "most serious problem" of the American city, the poverty and isolation of minority groups in central cities.[11]

Of course no single policy initiative can cope successfully with the monumental problem of metropolitan racial and economic apartheid. The most enlightened range of employment, education, housing, income maintenance, and social service policies, instituted concurrently, would not assure success. No matter what is done, it is difficult to imagine significant amelioration of the problem in less than a generation; nothing short of the simultaneous employment of a variety of policies could produce substantial results even in that time span.[12] The author argues, however, that a dispersal initiative must be central to any public strategy that is to have a reasonable chance of dealing effectively with the apartheid condition.

Part I of this book describes the racial and economic residential segregation that spread throughout this country's metropolitan areas following World War II, and explains why efforts to combat it have been ineffective. It traces the relevant history up to the inauguration of Richard Nixon in January 1969; describes how, despite what for a short time thereafter appeared to be a serious effort to combat residential segregation, federal housing programs were then administered in ways that not only failed to ameliorate metropolitan apartheid but actually reinforced it; and explains why neither the new housing legislation enacted by Congress in 1974 nor the courts are able to deal effectively with the problem.

Part II, turning from narrative to analysis and argument, asks, What should we do now? The author argues that the isolation of the poor and minority groups in central cities should be addressed by affirmative government action in the form of a housing dispersal policy and lists the essential elements of such a policy, exploring its technical aspects, including dollar costs. Finally, the political question—is the nation ready for a serious, costly, and difficult effort to ameliorate metropolitan apartheid?—is considered. It is the author's contention that a new, responsible, national administration should accept the challenge.

The views set forth in this book do not command uniform support. For example, social scientist Edward C. Banfield argues that lower class ghetto dwellers are beyond the redemption of public policy because of their "present-orientedness," their exclusive focus on present rather than future goals and gratifications. In Banfield's opinion, nothing very useful can be done about the ghettos because their inhabitants are the way they are.[13] Others are pessimistic for different reasons. Disillusioned by what is seen to be the failure of the Great Society programs of the Johnson administration, they conclude that, in principle, such large-scale government interventions cannot work, that government lacks both the knowledge and the capability to respond effectively to the forces that have produced residential segregation.[14] Even among those who feel that government is not immobilized by the intractability of the problem or by its own limitations, there is a virtual consensus that housing dispersal is beyond the pale of political possibility.

This book does not assert that the nation *can* achieve significant dispersal, much less that it *will* do so. Rather the argument is: (1) a dispersal policy may be feasible—at least the technical and political arguments against it are inconclusive; and (2) dispersal ought therefore to be tried, at least experimentally, because it is in the interest of the American community as a whole to do so.

Throughout, the author's intention is to raise questions and stimulate discussion for a thoughtful general public. No attempt has been made to deal with legal, economic, sociological, or psychological issues in a formal, academic manner. However, some matters of terminology should be clarified.

"Apartheid" is a strong word. Although it has come generally to mean separation of the races, historically it meant the nearly complete political, economic, and social segregation imposed by law by the white minority upon the black majority of the Union of South Africa. Although the black experience in the United States has been unlike that in South Africa, the huge enclaves of black poor in many of America's largest cities are so separated by physical, economic, social, and psychological barriers from the mainstream of American society that the use of a term having South African roots seems appropriate.

The practice of calling a black neighborhood a "ghetto" and describing it as "segregated" may imply a degree of coercion that does not exist. According to one scholar, the ghetto may be, partly or wholly, the result of the circumstance that large numbers of unskilled blacks came all at once to live in the inner city and occupied all the low cost housing then available, or it may result largely from the blacks' own preference for living there.[15] While not denying those assertions, this books contends that ghettos are much more a function of public policies than that view suggests.

The term "metropolitan area," as defined by the Census Bureau, applies to a county or group of counties containing at least one city, or twin cities, having a population of 50,000 or more, plus adjacent counties that are economically and socially integrated with the "central city."[16] As of 1975, there were 272 such metropolitan areas in the United States, and they contained nearly three-quarters of the total U.S. population.[17] While their rate of growth was slowed, it is in metropolitan areas that the great majority of Americans now live and will continue to live for the foreseeable future. Resolving or failing to resolve the problems of metropolitan areas will determine the quality of the lives of most of the population of future generations, and it is those areas that therefore provide the geographic focus for this book.

Finally, the author is a lawyer for black plaintiffs in the *Gautreaux* case, an extended lawsuit trying to bring about dispersal of subsidized housing in the Chicago area. The reader should therefore know that this book comes from one whose profession is advocacy and who is himself personally embroiled in the dispersal issue. Though every effort has been made to state counterarguments fairly and to consider them objectively, the author's personal viewpoint is unconcealed. If some books merely clarify while others advocate, this volume is plainly of the second type. It is of course hoped that the reader will feel that clarification has also been provided.

Part I

 *Chapter One*

Policy Without Conscience

In 1944, while most Americans were still absorbed by the grim realities of World War II, Gunnar Myrdal's monumental discussion of blacks in America, *An American Dilemma*, foresaw the implications of residential segregation for American cities. As long as the city's black population was increasing, Myrdal wrote, it would be an impossible policy to try to "protect" white neighborhoods against black intrusion. The result of enforced segregation for blacks would be scandalous housing conditions, destruction of the family unit, juvenile delinquency, and other symptoms of social pathology. These would have a contagious influence upon adjoining white areas, and inevitably, the blacks would finally break through anyway. Myrdal concluded:

> After the War a great increase in private and public building is likely . . . . [I]t would be prudent not to overlook segregation and the abominable housing conditions for Negroes. Gross inequality in this field is not only a matter for democratic American conscience, but is also expensive in the end.[1]

When the war was over, however, we not only overlooked segregation and abominable housing conditions for blacks but employed public policies that actually fostered racial and economic residential segregation and helped bring about precisely the "expensive" consequences Myrdal had foreseen. Even when some racial barriers began to fall in the freedom movement of the 1960s, residential segregation remained rock-solid. Only after several years of urban rioting

3

and the assassination of Martin Luther King did it begin to appear
that the rock might be cracked.

THE PATTERN OF RESIDENTIAL
SEGREGATION

Twentieth century residential patterns in the United States are
sometimes described as having three major elements. The first is
what urbanologist Philip Hauser calls "population implosion"—the
accelerating urban concentration of America's growing population.
When the first census was taken in 1790, about 95 percent of Americans lived in rural areas.[2] A century later, the country was still two-
thirds rural; not until 1920 did a majority of the population become
urban residents. In the 1920s, however, Americans began flocking to
big city metropolitan areas. They paused in the stagnation of the
1930s, some even returning to farms and small towns. But with the
onset of World War II, they resumed their trek to metropolitan
centers, and in little more than a quarter of a century they turned
America into an overwhelmingly urban nation. By 1970, the urban
percentage of the population had risen to over two-thirds, and 80
percent of all Americans lived within commuting distance of a metropolitan area central city.[3]

The second major aspect of twentieth century American demography was the centrifugal migration from central city to suburbs that
occurred *within* metropolitan areas. In 1920, only 17 percent of
Americans were suburbanites. As the truck and automobile came
into more general use, dispersion into suburban areas increased.
Slowed by the Depression, the movement resumed on a large scale
following the war. By 1960, total population was about equally
divided among central cities, suburbs, and nonmetropolitan areas.[4]
By 1970, more Americans lived in the suburbs than lived either in
central cities or in nonmetropolitan areas.[5]

The distinctly racial character of these mass movements to cities
and suburbs was the third important aspect of the demography. Disproportionately to their numbers in the population as a whole, it was
blacks who moved into the cities and whites who moved out of them
to the suburbs. Early in the century, when 90 percent of American
blacks still lived in the South, a large black migration toward the increasing industrial employment opportunities of northern cities
began. Stemmed temporarily by the Depression, it resumed in response to the industrial needs of World War II. By the end of the
war, northern city slums were already heavily black, and the continuing agricultural revolution throughout the South fed the inmigration

during the rest of the 1940s and through the 1950s. Between 1910 and 1960, the rural-urban proportion of the nation's blacks completely reversed itself from 73 percent rural to 73 percent urban.[6]

This black influx to central cities began to be matched, especially as the suburban housing boom accelerated in the postwar years, by a massive exodus of more affluent whites to outlying city neighborhoods and to the rapidly burgeoning suburbs. As early as the mid-1950s, the developing situation was described this way:

> The white and non-white citizens of the U.S. are being sorted out in a new pattern of segregation. In each of the major urban centers the story is the same: the better-off white families are moving out of the central city into the suburbs; the ranks of the poor who remain are being swelled by Negroes from the South. This trend threatens to transform the cities into slums, largely inhabited by Negroes, ringed about with predominantly white suburbs.[7]

The threat materialized rapidly. By 1960, the 6.5 million blacks in central cities of ten years earlier had increased 50 percent to 9.7 million. In the same decade, the white population of central cities increased less than 5 percent, from 45.5 to 47.7 million, and by the beginning of the following decade had actually begun to diminish.[8] From 1960 to 1965, the white population of central cities decreased by 1.3 million, while the black population grew 2.3 million.[9] City after major city lost large numbers of whites, while the black population increased dramatically. One research report predicted that by 1985 three-quarters of all nonwhites in metropolitan areas would live in central cities, while nearly three-quarters (70 percent) of all whites in metropolitan areas would live in suburbs.[10]

These figures take no account of residential segregation *within* cities and suburbs. As increasing numbers of blacks moved north, racial residential segregation in northern cities grew more intense.[11] By the late 1960s, a U.S. Department of Health, Education, and Welfare pamphlet could say, simply, "There is an almost total segregation of Negroes in most American cities."[12]

NEIGHBORHOOD PRESERVATION

White neighborhoods were "protected" by a combination of strategies. Local realtors commonly practiced such techniques as the referral of customers according to race, the exclusion of black brokers from property-listing services, and the advertising of housing on a racial basis. For years, the code of ethics of the National Association of Real Estate Boards provided that a realtor "should never be instrumental in introducing into a neighborhood . . . members of any race or nationality whose presence will clearly be detrimental to property values. . . ."[13] The association itself was all white, and a separate black national association was not founded until the 1940s. (The two organizations are still racially separate.)

Local boards were vigilant in enforcing their ethical codes. For example, in 1955, the executive secretary of the St. Louis Real Estate Board reminded members of the board's long-standing rule that they could not sell to a black unless there were three "separate and distinct" buildings in the block already occupied by blacks. That, said the secretary's letter, was the St. Louis board's interpretation of the national association rule from which, in 1950, "race or nationality" had been excluded and which now simply prohibited introducing a detrimental "use" into a neighborhood. In 1958, the St. Louis interpretation was modified to allow sales to blacks in the city if a single black already lived on the block, but the minimum of three continued to be required for sales to blacks outside city boundaries.[14]

Wherever these marketing practices were not sufficient, they were supplemented by the activities of neighborhood "preservation" or "improvement" associations. Using a variety of methods, not excluding rocks and fire bombs, such groups saw to it that property in white neighborhoods was not occupied by blacks. Extreme measures were rarely required, however, for racially restrictive covenants (prohibitions written into property deeds against sales to racial minorities) rendered much property in white areas legally unavailable to blacks. Although in 1948 the Supreme Court outlawed judicial enforcement of such covenants, the practices associated with them continued long after the Court's decision.[15]

Local government officials tolerated and even encouraged these local real estate marketing and "self-help" techniques. In two ways, however, local laws themselves played a direct role in maintaining racial separation. Both helped determine where the urban poor, among whom blacks and other minorities were a disproportionately large fraction, would be allowed to live. The first way was through discriminatory enforcement of housing and building codes that established minimum standards for building maintenance, materials, and techniques. Such codes made older, deteriorated housing or newer, low quality housing illegal—except, that is, in central city ghettos where housing and building codes were generally not enforced and the poor were permitted, by the law's sufferance, to live in slum dwellings with loose wiring, broken windows, faulty plumbing, and inadequate heat. This dual law enforcement standard restricted low quality housing that the poor could afford to central city ghettos and a few minighettos in adjacent suburbs. Economist Anthony Downs summarized the consequences:

[L]aws against low quality housing units are rigorously enforced in new-growth areas, but virtually ignored in older, more central areas where poor households live. Consequently, the urban poor cannot live in any new-growth areas or most well kept older areas because of legally created high costs there. So they are concentrated in areas of low quality housing. Such concentration multiplies and reinforces the normal problems associated with poverty. This creates extremely undesirable neighborhood environments, from which most non-poor households depart if they can. The entire process results in excellent housing and neighborhoods for the wealthy; good housing and neighborhoods for the middle class; and poor housing (in relation to its cost) and disastrous neighborhoods for the very poor. *Most of the nation's urban 'housing problems' result directly from a combination of poverty per se and the way this process compels the poorest household to bear the social costs of creating desirable neighborhood environments for the upper two-thirds of the income distribution. . . .*[16]

Zoning and subdivision ordinances constituted the second type of local law that helped maintain residential segregation. Zoning ordinances generally prescribed how individual parcels or lots could be utilized, such as for dwellings, businesses, and industry in a number of categories (detached single family houses, apartment buildings, light or heavy industry, and so on). They also limited population density, for example, by specifying minimum required lot sizes or maximum numbers of families per acre. Subdivision regulations generally governed the ways in which landowners were permitted to create individual lots out of larger tracts. They frequently required the developer to provide site improvements, such as streets and drainage facilities, or demanded the dedication of land or the payment of cash for schools, parks, and other community facilities.

These and other land use control planning devices were all justified as an exercise of the police power of the state for the traditional purposes of protecting the health, safety, morals, and general welfare of the entire population. That theory led the Supreme Court to uphold the use of the zoning power in 1926[17] and to sustain zoning and other land controls over the years. By 1968, over 14,000 local governments, including more than 5,200 within metropolitan areas, possessed some form of land use control law.[18]

Like housing and building codes, most land use controls increase
the price of housing by requiring homes to be built on large lots, by
excluding apartments, and by a myriad of other restrictions. Land
use controls thus tend to keep out housing that the poor can afford;
indeed, they quite literally empower suburban officials to dictate the
minimum cost of new housing and thereby the income level of persons to be permitted to live in their communities.[19] An early judicial
critic of zoning called it a segregation scheme for classifying the
population of a city according to their means.[20] Forty-four years
later, reviewing the course of zoning history, one writer suggested
that the only area in which zoning had really been effective was in
excluding the poor, especially the black.[21]

In fact, excluding the poor for fiscal reasons ultimately came to be
the explicit aim of much zoning. Rightly or wrongly, communities
perceived that low income housing produced relatively low tax revenues, while the poor families who occupied the dwellings required
relatively large public expenditures for public services and facilities.
Since the effect would be to require either a lower level of public
services or higher tax bills, residents exercised their land use control
powers to exclude low income housing. Usually, nobody bothered to
ask where the excluded families should live.[22]

Eventually, "fiscal zoning" came under attack in the courts. Some
judges began to rule that the desire to avoid fiscal strain did not justify the exclusion of lower income families; the poor had to live
somewhere, and barring them from one community simply passed
the problem along to another. The decisions stressed that the
"general welfare" rationalization for upholding zoning powers required the welfare of the general population, poor as well as rich, to
be taken into account. In the wake of such rulings, many communities suddenly acquired an acute concern for the environment. New
development was halted or slowed because of inadequate sewer and
water facilities, the desire to preserve or provide for open space, and
the like. The result, of course, was the same: exclusion of lower
income housing, which generally meant the exclusion of blacks as
well as the poor.

There was another motivation for the omission of lower income
housing in suburban areas, perhaps the most powerful of all. Testifying before a Senate committee, Anthony Downs argued that exclusionary land use practices reflected the desire of middle class parents
for social homogeneity in their neighborhoods and schools. Screening
out the poor by making it impossible to build housing for them accomplished that result. The motivation was not specifically to keep
out blacks or to keep taxes down but an understandable desire to

keep neighborhoods free of such undesirable characteristics as high crime rates, juvenile delinquency, and drug addiction, which were statistically associated with low income people. This motivation, Downs felt, was as legitimate as the desire of low income families in the ghettos to escape to the suburban communities. In any event, both it and its consequences were predictable.[23]

GHETTO GATES SWING SHUT

Private citizens and local laws cannot be blamed exclusively for the residential segregation pattern of the postwar years. Beginning in the 1930s, when the federal government first became deeply involved in housing matters, federal policy made a significant, perhaps definitive, contribution. The story begins with public housing.

In the spring of 1933, the new administration of Franklin Roosevelt faced misery and fear across the land—fifteen million people were without work, eighteen million were on relief.[24] One of the earliest acts of the New Deal to provide jobs for the Depression's unemployed was to create the Public Works Administration (PWA) and to give the new agency the authority to carry out building programs, including "low-cost housing" and "slum-clearance."[25] As a by-product of providing jobs, it seemed to make good sense to replace slum housing with decent shelter that the poor could afford. In the next few years, the PWA public housing program built over 20,000 new housing units and demolished some 10,000 substandard homes and apartments.[26] Adhering to the racial views of the times, PWA used a "neighborhood composition" rule: public housing tenancy was to mirror, not alter, the racial composition of its neighborhood. Projects in black areas were for blacks, in white areas for whites.[27]

In 1935, a serious threat to the new program suddenly arose. Resisting federal condemnation of his property, a stubborn landowner persuaded a federal judge in Louisville, Kentucky, to rule that the federal government could not use its powers of eminent domain to acquire and clear slum property to build public housing. Housing private citizens, the judge held, even if they were poor, was not a "public purpose" for which public funds could be lawfully spent.[28]

In response, Roosevelt proposed, and Congress enacted, the Housing Act of 1937. To deal with the problem of the Louisville case, the new law restructured the fledgling public housing program in a fundamental way. Since state courts had permitted the states to do what the Louisville case had barred the federal government from doing, public housing was decentralized and turned over to state and local administration. The act provided for federal loans and annual payments to locally established housing agencies, called "authorities," which would build and operate housing for poor families.[29] The federal government would pay the capital costs—initial acquisition, development, and construction expenses—while rents would cover the costs of operation. The federal role was thus significantly reduced; public housing was now to be initiated at the option of, and administered by, local officials.

The new program began auspiciously, and by the following year projects in various stages of development were springing up in fifty cities across the country.[30] World War II soon interrupted the program, however; housing for defense workers became the priority task, and after the war, housing for returning veterans. When housing for the poor eventually reemerged as the primary goal, unfriendly congressional committees blocked action on public housing bills. For several years, the program sputtered along on the few droplets of appropriations still in the pipeline.

Finally, the Housing Act of 1949 provided a solid *housing* reason for a public housing program by proclaiming a national goal of a decent home for every American family. Yet the public housing sections of the act passed only after three cliffhanger votes in the House of Representatives: 136–135 for; 168–165 against; and finally, 209–204 for.[31] The underlying reasons for this congressional ambivalence foreshadowed public housing's eventual unhappy fate.

The first was an uncertainty about objectives. Was the goal of public housing slum clearance or decent housing for the poor? The primary concern of many supporters was housing for the needy that could be built on cheap, outlying vacant land, not in slum areas, where demolition costs had to be added to the cost of more expensive sites. Others had little interest in housing; their goal was to get rid of the eyesores of the slums. The predominant view of the 1930s had been that the socially destructive slum environment was caused by bad housing. Advocates of this theory pointed to the long list of supposed social benefits that would flow from replacing bad housing with good. One such list included: a diminished danger of epidemics; less crime, juvenile delinquency, and immorality; reduced costs of police and fire protection; lower accident rates; increased land values; and prevention of the cancerous spread of slums to uninfected areas.[32]

The 1937 act had resolved the debate between the "housers" and the "slumclearers" by a compromise requiring that each new public housing unit be matched by a demolished slum unit, a resolution that inevitably tied public housing to slum areas. The 1949 Housing Act produced another compromise: the slum demolition requirement was now limited to new urban public housing units. But by 1949, the slum clearance argument for public housing was beginning to come under heavy attack. An article published that year, "The Myths of Housing Reform," concluded that housing reform did not give rise to anticipated improvements in social welfare.[33] As it became evident that the slum problem was more complex than had been assumed and would not be "solved" by replacing slum tenements with new dwellings, support for public housing waned.

The second factor that made the 1949 votes so close was the changing character of the public housing family. Originally, as it was put in a 1938 U.S. Housing Authority pamphlet, the purpose of public housing was to raise the living standards of working families who had reasonably steady but inadequate income.[34] New Deal social welfare programs, among them public housing, had that constituency in view. Residents of public housing in the 1930s and through the World War II years were therefore mostly "good" tenants, self-supporting families accustomed to city living.[35] Only a small proportion were "problem" families. Most families with unpleasant social histories or living habits, families on welfare or otherwise not "normal," were denied admission or strictly limited in number.[36] Not surprisingly, and contrary to its later image, social welfare indexes gave public housing high marks.[37]

So, under those circumstances, did the communities in which projects were built. The slum demolition requirement of the 1937 act did not *require* public housing to be in the slums, and many projects —for whites—were built outside them, low rise projects on vacant land. It was possible during and immediately after the Depression to build public housing in "decent" places. In the late 1930s and early 1940s, attractive townhouse or row style projects were built in solid working or middle class neighborhoods, where single family homes were mixed with small two and three story apartments, lawns were mowed, streets were clean, garbage was collected, schools were good —where there was a solid sense of community in the all-white neighborhood. But those were the halcyon years. In the growing prosperity of the postwar years, the public housing constituency gradually became the "true poor." Increasingly, also, it became black. Neither development strengthened the political muscle of public housing supporters.

Finally, by 1949 Congress had begun to detect the problem of race mixing. Would a federal housing program somehow impinge on local custom in race matters? Opponents were assured it would not. Local control had been the keystone of the program ever since the 1937 act had turned the direct construction and management role over to local housing authorities, created by local governments. In addition, the 1937 act required that no individual project could proceed until the authority and the local municipal government entered into a "cooperation agreement" under which the local government agreed to exempt the project from taxes and provide it with municipal services. By simply refusing to make such a contract, local officials could veto a proposed project. Local governments, therefore, had the power to decide whether public housing was to be built at all in their communities and could retain control, project by proposed project, over the place and pace of development.[38] Congressional concern was also allayed by the rigid segregation of most public housing projects; the neighborhood composition rule of the PWA had been followed by virtually all local authorities.

Yet the war years had brought some changes in racial matters. The armed forces were being desegregated. Fair employment practices had become a significant issue. Human relations commissions were formed in many localities in the postwar years to deal with a variety of race problems. The 1948 Supreme Court decision ending court enforcement of restrictive racial covenants could be viewed as an ominous portent of things to come. A few states even began to pass laws against discrimination in housing.[39] Some far-sighted congressional segregationists were not happy about the prospects for public housing.

Nonetheless, despite the loss of its broad constituency and the spectre of race mixing, public housing scraped through by a margin of three votes. Moreover, the 1949 bill was generous. Whereas fewer than 200,000 housing units had been built in the more than a dozen years since the inception of the public housing program, the 1949 act authorized over four times that number in less than half the time—810,000 housing units at the rate of 135,000 units a year over a six year period.

But the joy of public housing supporters was short-lived. Events soon returned the program to the limbo from which the 1949 act had presumably rescued it. First, demands of the Korean War emergency forced President Truman, a public housing supporter, to cut back construction to a low level. Then a hostile House Appropriations Committee drastically limited new construction appropriations. Finally, an equally unfriendly Eisenhower administration, essentially trying to find a way to kill public housing altogether, kept the same low lid on production for the rest of the decade. By the end of the 1950s, only 322,000 of the 1949 act's 810,000 units had been authorized, only 270,000 completed.[40]

More important, hardly any of the completed units were built in white neighborhoods. Rising land prices and stringent federal cost limitations forced more and more high rise construction in the large cities, leading to monoliths of concentrated poverty. As the law began to turn against segregation and it became evident that blacks could no longer be kept out of public housing projects in white neighborhoods, those neighborhoods became unavailable to housing authorities. Also, housing authority commissioners, generally appointed by the mayor, were predominantly white, middle class business and professional people.[41] They were not likely to propose building housing for the truly poor—generally black as well—in outlying white neighborhoods of the city—especially not the newer high rise buildings. Suburban areas were, of course, unavailable to central city housing authorities; the local cooperation agreement requirement assured that the suburbs could ignore central city housing needs with impunity.[42] Thus, if public housing was to continue to be built in the 1950s, there was a clear choice: allow blacks into projects in white neighborhoods or build only in black communities. The resolution of that issue was never in doubt. "The great ghetto gates swung shut," said one observer. "The wall of white hostility forced Negroes into ghettos. Negro public housing followed them into the ghettos. There is has essentially remained."[43]

In 1961, the Kennedy administration brought political support back to public housing. The month before his election, Kennedy blasted the Eisenhower-Nixon housing record. Calling slums and blight the "shame of the nation," he said the country faced a critical shortage of decent housing for low and middle income families and urged that housing production be increased by 50 percent. Public housing projects should be smaller, he said, and should blend with the neighborhood; housing opportunities should be created for minority groups in "attractive neighborhoods."[44] The new Congress responded generously. The 1961 Housing Act picked up all the unused public housing authorizations of the 1949 act. In addition, Kennedy chose as public housing commissioner Marie McGuire, an enthusiastic public housing supporter who had spent nineteen years in the program.

Yet construction increased little. In the first half of the 1960s, the average number of public housing starts was actually below the 1960 level.[45] Instead of concentrating on building new units, Marie McGuire focused on what could be done to improve the lot of the tenant population in existing projects. The idea was that helping "problem" families would help repair the badly damaged image of public housing. As a step toward that aim, a joint task force with the Department of Health, Education, and Welfare (HEW) was established to develop showpieces of supportive social services in a few selected localities.

McGuire's focus was understandable. Public housing tenancy now reflected the confinement of urban public housing to slums that were growing increasingly black. In 1952, nonwhites (largely blacks) occupied 38 percent of public housing units. By 1961, the percentage was up to 46. In 1965, it was 51 percent and rising.[46] These are national figures; in major metropolitan areas the percentages were higher. By 1965, for example, over 83 percent of the tenants in public housing in St. Louis were black.[47]

The number of "problem" families had also begun to increase. The percentage of families on welfare grew steadily after rent requirements were relaxed to admit welfare families who in the early days would have been rejected. By 1963, 39 percent of new public housing families were receiving assistance or benefits. In big cities the proportion was higher—50 percent in St. Louis, over 62 percent in Detroit.[48] The number of children also increased, as did the percentage of broken families. In addition, families displaced by urban renewal or highway projects were given priority for admission to public housing by the 1949 act; but the more stable families were likely to make their own arrangements elsewhere, leaving the problem families with nowhere else to turn. Little wonder then that Marie McGuire's effort to improve the lot of public housing tenants and the image of the program was a failure. The task force with HEW lasted four years and sponsored four projects. None succeeded, and the social services initiative never came close to achieving its rejuvenation goals.[49]

The central problem of site selection had been recognized and carefully avoided. Kennedy's preelection housing statement had platitudinously circled the issue, saying, "creating decent housing opportunities in attractive neighborhoods for all our citizens can constitute a dramatic advance in civil rights and equal opportunities for all."[50] Although Marie McGuire told the U.S. Commission on Civil Rights in 1961 that the Public Housing Administration had "long been aware that the selection of sites in areas of predominant occupancy by one race or another makes for de facto segregation,"[51] in fact, PHA did nothing about the concentration of public housing in inner city ghettos except provide money to continue the pattern.

Thus, by the middle of the 1960s, urban public housing had become a largely ghettoized repository for the poorest and most troubled of society's black families. The "good" tenant, the independent, self-supporting householder, had long since been replaced by a black welfare family, headed by a female, living in housing that had come to symbolize concentrations of social pathology—destructive, drug-addicted, crime-oriented, uneducable youth, and unemployed adults living in decaying surroundings without hope of improvement. In an often reprinted passage, Harrison Salisbury, fresh from years in Russia, described what he saw in New York City's public housing,

> . . . the broken windows, the missing light bulbs, the plaster cracking from the walls, the pilfered hardware, the cold, drafty corridors, the doors on sagging hinges, the acid smell of sweat and cabbage, the ragged children, the plaintive women, the playgrounds that are seas of muddy clay, the bruised and battered trees, the ragged clumps of grass, the planned absence of art, beauty or taste, the gigantic masses of brick, of concrete, of asphalt, the inhuman genius with which our know-how has been perverted to create human cesspools worse than those of yesterday.[52]

The creation of cesspools had gone on steadily, it seemed, ever since the 1949 Housing Act had barely kept public housing alive to play its part in the development of American apartheid.

NEGRO REMOVAL

The 1949 Housing Act exacerbated residential segregation in yet another way. Urban renewal, a new name for slum clearance, was designed to tear down slums and replace them with rejuvenated neighborhoods. Under the new program, local governments could buy and clear land in blighted areas and then resell it at low prices to private developers. The federal government would share not only in the "write-down" of land costs but also in the cost of site improvements and public facilities for the redevelopment project. The principal purposes of the new program were to speed up slum clearance, to facilitate the replacement of slum dwellings with decent housing and the attendant public and private support facilities, and to afford private enterprise a maximum opportunity to participate in the redevelopment process.[53]

Since most of the slums to be cleared contained rundown dwellings that housed the poor, most urban renewal projects should have been geared to building new low income housing. That expectation never was fulfilled. The law was flexible enough to permit local officials and private builders to concentrate principally on developing commercial properties and erecting middle class and luxury apartments rather than on rehousing the poor whose dwellings were bulldozed to provide raw land for the renewal projects. Thus, the typical urban renewal project of the 1950s and early 1960s followed this pattern: take a blighted neighborhood inhabited largely by the poor or near poor, close to the central business district or other valuable commercial property; demolish much of the existing housing while paying little attention to the relocation needs of the inhabitants; then replace it with commercial properties and apartments whose rent levels preclude the return of any of the former residents. Eighteen years after its inception, urban renewal had destroyed over 400,000 homes and apartments, most of which housed the poor, while only about one-tenth that number of units had been completed for low and moderate income families on urban renewal sites.[54] In addition, most of the replacement units were designed for families in the upper ranges of the moderate income category; only one-quarter were public housing.[55] The poor who were evicted moved to other slum areas, where they frequently had to pay higher rents.[56] Many were blacks—two-thirds of the cleared urban renewal units were black occupied—who were then forced to crowd into other black ghettos. "Negro removal" came to be a bitter synonym for urban renewal. In too many cities, said one commentator, that was the point.[57]

By the mid-1960s, however, outcries against the urban renewal program led to a reconsideration of policies, and in 1967, corrective action was finally taken: future urban renewal projects would be required to provide primarily housing for the poor.[58] But so many projects were in the pipeline, and urban renewal projects generally took so long to complete (frequently from twelve to fifteen years), that it would be many years before the new policy could have any significant effect. (Even that long-term possibility was never to be realized because the urban renewal program was terminated before it could provide any quantity of decent housing for the poor.)

SEPARATE FOR WHITES, NOTHING
FOR BLACKS

While public housing, and to some extent urban renewal, were contributing to the confinement of urban blacks to the racial ghettos of the cities, three other federal programs and policies were helping to fashion a largely white, middle class suburban society. The first of these was the mortgage insurance program of the Federal Housing Administration (FHA). The FHA was created in 1934 to expand the flow of money into home mortgages, thereby to increase employment in the then moribund housing construction industry. Its method was to provide insurance against default on home loans made by private lending institutions (primarily savings and loan associations and banks). This not only increased the supply of mortgage money but also encouraged lending on much more favorable terms, such as lower down payments and longer loan life, then had been traditional in the industry.

The program was remarkably successful; since 1935, more than seven million homes and apartments have been built with FHA-insured mortgages, about one-fifth of all privately financed nonfarm units built in the United States.[59] Moreover, that impressive figure does not include about thirty million home improvement loans, many of which would not have been made without government insurance.

But intensified racial and economic separation was the unfortunate by-product of FHA's success. Most FHA-insured new homes, particularly in the postwar years, were built in the suburbs to meet the needs of a growing middle class. Since the most profitable residential development opportunities were to be found in the burgeoning suburbs, it was natural for FHA, which had been created to aid the industry, to follow its patient from the city to the outlying areas. Also, FHA took the position that insuring homes in city neighborhoods presented higher risks than in the newer suburban areas. Its property evaluators were told to consider whether properties were protected from "adverse influences," which FHA defined to include "lower class occupancy."[60] Until the late 1960s, therefore, when FHA policy finally changed, FHA rarely insured mortgages on homes in slum or adjacent areas. The result was that 90 percent of FHA's borrowers were middle class or young, upwardly mobile families; the poor and those on the fringes of poverty were largely excluded from FHA benefits.[61]

Since most blacks were too poor to take advantage of suburban, middle class housing opportunities, FHA policies would have produced a predominantly white clientele even if FHA programs had been administered in a racially neutral fashion. But they were not. FHA required and promoted the use of racial restrictive covenants: it was, as a presidential commission later said, a "powerful enforcer" of them.[62] In addition, the FHA Underwriting Manual, which has been called "one of those decisive but little-known bureaucratic documents which help form American civilization,"[63] warned that the "infiltration of . . . inharmonious racial groups" would contribute to declining property values.[64] One FHA manual urged investigation of all areas in which FHA insurance was sought to assure that they were not likely to be "invaded" by "incompatible social and racial groups."[65]

FHA therefore not only withheld insurance from new or existing housing in integrated areas, but even shunned some white middle class residential districts in central cities for fear that they, too, might turn black. As HUD Secretary George Romney later acknowledged, in addition to preventing minorities from gaining access to new housing, these FHA practices—generally called "red-lining"—involved clear understandings with the private lending institutions that neighborhoods that were or might be occupied by minority groups had an unfavorable economic future and were to be treated accordingly.[66]

The effects of FHA's restrictive covenant policies survived long past the Supreme Court's 1948 decision banning their judicial enforcement. Two years later, when FHA finally announced that it would no longer insure properties with "new" covenants (meaning written after 1950), it also advised that it would continue to provide insurance on properties carrying covenants entered into before 1950. In addition, it was made clear to realtors that the agency did not object to so-called gentlemen's agreements or other arrangements requiring the approval of sales by neighbors or the board of a community group.[67] FHA "red-lining" did not formally cease until 1965, and it was 1968 before FHA took any effective action to make mortgage insurance available in the red-lined areas.[68] As late as 1966, a representative of the Civil Rights Commission, who had spent weeks with FHA appraisers to learn what went into FHA decision-making in the Chicago area, concluded that there were three types of houses the FHA absolutely would not insure: (1) a house immediately adjacent to a factory; (2) a house built on cedar posts; and (3) a house in a white neighborhood into which a black proposed to move.[69]

The impact of these FHA policies and practices, described by one observer as "separate for whites and nothing for blacks,"[70] was enormous. Looking back on FHA policies from the perspective of 1967, the Civil Rights Commission concluded that segregated housing patterns were "due in large part to racially discriminatory FHA policies in effect during the post World War II housing boom." The FHA and the Veterans Administration (VA) together, it said, had financed more than $117 billion of new housing since World War II. Less than 2 percent of that housing had been available to nonwhite families, and much of the 2 percent was on a strictly segregated basis.[71]

It may be argued that this description overstates the federal contribution to racial residential segregation because in the late 1940s and throughout the 1950s, the peak years of FHA and VA activity, two out of three homes built in the United States were financed without any direct federal involvement at all.[72] That argument, however, ignores the pervasive FHA influence on the housing and real estate industries and the significance of the moral sanction FHA policies gave to private racial discrimination practices. One writer has explained the point this way:

> As the dominant economic force in the housing and home finance industries after the early 1930s, the government underwrote the industries and reshaped the way they operated. Governmental standards not only influenced that part of the market directly participating in federal programs, but also profoundly affected the way the rest of the business worked. In a highly fragmented industry dependent on federal support with many thousands of builders, realtors, lenders, salesmen, and rental agents, federal standards had a powerful national impact. The record . . . can only be read as a powerful and persistent use of public power to segregate American cities.[73]

The argument also overlooks another important fact: the savings and loan associations and banks, which supplied the "conventional" (not insured by FHA or VA) financing for home purchases, were supervised by federal agencies that adhered to the industry view that considering race in making loans was sound business. For example, the Federal Home Loan Bank Board had its own policy favoring racial homogeneity.[74] And even after they abandoned their own discriminatory policies, the federal agencies still overlooked discrimination by their member institutions. By 1961, only one of the four federal agencies that regulated conventional lenders had so much as adopted a resolution condemning discrimination in mortgage lending.[75] When President Kennedy issued an executive order in 1962 against racial discrimination in federally assisted housing, the order carefully excluded housing that was conventionally financed by federally supervised mortgage lenders.[76]

HIGHWAYS AND TAXES

Two other federal policies also significantly aided in the development of the white, middle class suburbia of the post-war years. The first was the vast, heavily subsidized highway building program that made central city commercial centers accessible to white collar suburban residents while at the same time permitting the spread of industry and blue collar jobs to suburban areas.[77] The dispersal of the blue collar jobs was a disaster for central city minorities, many of whom lacked information about suburban job opportunities or found the jobs difficult or expensive to reach because they did not own automobiles or could not afford the commuting costs.[78] "There is no question," said George Romney to a congressional committee, "but what the freeway program in our cities has permitted the jobs . . .

and also . . . the people to move out at an accelerated pace [leading to] patterns now of separation based on economic levels as well as racial backgrounds. . . ."[79]

The second, perhaps equally important, federal policy was the tax subsidy that provided benefits worth tens of billions of dollars to homeowners during the post-World War II housing boom. If the homeowner were taxed like other investors, he would report the rent he could have obtained on his house as gross income; would be allowed deductions for property taxes, mortgage interest, maintenance, and depreciation; and would be taxed on the difference. Instead, he is not required to treat the "imputed" rent as income; yet he is permitted to deduct the amount of his property tax and mortgage interest from other income on which he does pay taxes. In effect, says a Brookings Institution study, the tax treatment of home ownership is equivalent to the government issuing vouchers to homeowners to pay part of their housing costs, the vouchers being more valuable to high income than to low income taxpayers. The study doubted that if Congress were confronted with a proposal for such an expenditure program, a single vote could be found for "so bizarre a scheme."[80]

Since home ownership is less widespread among the poor than among the more affluent, the homeowners' subsidy benefits primarily middle and upper income taxpayers. In addition, the poor who do own homes have inexpensive ones that provide the least opportunity for tax savings, and because of lower tax rates, they receive less benefit from the same amount of deduction than more affluent taxpayers. This relative exclusion of the poor was only a minor inequity before World War II, when income tax rates were low and the homeowner tax subsidy was therefore relatively small. But in the postwar years, homeowner deductions quickly became the largest housing subsidy of all by a wide margin. For example, in 1962, when the federal government was spending $820 million to subsidize housing for the poor, income tax deductions for homeowners with middle incomes or higher (not including the revenue that might have been obtained by taxing imputed rent) amounted to $2.9 billion.[81] In other words, the federal government was providing to the relatively prosperous, including the whites moving to the suburbs, housing subsidies worth more than three and a half times those provided for the poor.

ANOTHER VIEW

This description places a heavy responsibility on government policies for the apartheid residential pattern that developed in the years following World War II. There is a different view, however, or at least a different emphasis. Edward Banfield writes of the "logic of metropolitan growth" as if it were a purely natural phenomenon, affected only marginally by the laws of men. As the population of the city grew, he says, the city needed to expand, and as it expanded, it was inevitable that the more outlying areas would be occupied by the wealthy.

[I]f the distribution of wealth and income is such that some can afford new housing and the time and money to commute considerable distances to work while others cannot, the expanding periphery of the city must be occupied by the first group (the "well-off") while the older, inner parts of the city, where most of the jobs for the unskilled are, must be occupied by the second group (the "not well-off").[82]

This "economic imperative" had its roots in land prices. The well-off sold their homes close in to the commercial center of the city because land there became valuable and "only the very rich could afford to forego the advantage of much cheaper land on the outskirts."[83] The close in homes of the well-off were then converted to smaller apartments or rooming houses and rented to the not well-off (those who could not afford new houses or the time and money to travel relatively long distances to work), thereby increasing the return from the land. The entire process resulted in the wealthy moving outward and the poor being concentrated inward.

The description is probably accurate for the last century and the early part of this one. But then a number of other factors entered the picture: the automobile and truck came into wide use beginning in the 1920s; the federal government entered the housing business in the 1930s; and, with the end of wartime restrictions in the 1940s, factories and residences began to shift to the suburbs in unprecedented numbers. Thus, the "logic" of metropolitan growth became a function of government policies as well as of land prices and technological developments. Even Banfield acknowledges that FHA activities gave the outward expansion of the well-off a further push.

Had it been disposed to do so, FHA might have stimulated the renovation of existing housing and thus the refurbishing of the central cities. If it had done this, it would have assisted many of the not well-off, a category that included most Negroes as well as other minority group members. In fact, it did the opposite: it subsidized the well-off who wanted to leave the central city, while (by setting neighborhood and property standards that they could not meet) refusing to help the not well-off to renovate their central city houses.[84]

That, of course, is only part of the story. Had it been disposed to do so, the federal government could also have attempted to assist many of the "not well-off," particularly minorities, by providing subsidized housing in places that would have allowed them to participate in the outward expansion.

In 1972, the president's annual housing report stated: "[F]ederal housing programs over the years have contributed to rapid suburbanization and unplanned urban sprawl, to growing residential separation of the races, and to the concentration of the poor and minorities in decaying central cities." The report also said, "While housing programs have *contributed* to these problems and in many cases intensified them, it is important to emphasize that they did not *cause* them. The causes stem from the complex interaction of population migration, community attitudes and prejudices, consumer preferences, local government fragmentation, and the impact of other federal programs such as urban renewal and the highway programs."[85] The summary is reasonably accurate. One is tempted only to add, for emphasis, that at least since the courts' approval of local land use controls in the 1920s and the entry of the federal government in the housing field in the 1930s, the outward expansion of the "well-off" and the inward concentration of the "not well-off" took place at *every* stage within a governmental framework that fostered, rather than deterred, racial and economic apartheid.

IN THE EYE OF THE STORM

Despite the fact that the postwar years did produce some antisegregation developments, none had much impact on housing. The 1948 Supreme Court decision outlawing judicial enforcement of restrictive covenants was followed six years later by the unanimous *Brown v. Board of Education* ruling in which the Court declared segregation in public schools (and by implication in all public facilites) unlawful.[86] In 1961, a second housing subsidy program was enacted to provide lower than market rate mortgages (under FHA) for nonprofit and limited dividend sponsors of new housing.[87] In 1962, President Kennedy issued an executive order against housing discrimination in federally supported programs.[88] Lyndon Johnson declared war on poverty in 1964. The same year, a new civil rights act outlawed discrimination in any program receiving federal aid.[89] The 1965 Housing Act established two new housing subsidy programs, rent supplements and leasing, that for the first time authorized subsidies for poor families living in privately owned housing.[90] The next year the Model Cities program began.[91]

In the years following the 1954 *Brown* decision, some of the varied activity by all three branches of the federal government led to significant progress in combating racial segregation. Although gains were sometimes achieved only after strife, changes did occur in schools, in transportation, in voting, and in employment.

Not so in housing. If anything, despite the civil rights efforts, residential segregation intensified. The flow of whites to the suburbs in the 1950s and 1960s did not abate. The black ghetto in the inner cities remained concentrated, although to accommodate its swelling population it expanded at its edges to absorb adjoining white neighborhoods. None of the housing measures of the early 1960s was adequate to deal with the problem.

The 1961 FHA program produced housing for moderate, not low income, families, and precious little of that—by 1968 only about 50,000 units had been built.[92] President Kennedy's 1962 executive order applied only to future, not existing, federally assisted housing, and excluded conventionally financed housing completely. The result was that only 20 percent of the new housing market and less than 1 percent of the existing housing stock were covered.[93] The 1964 Civil Rights Act expressly exempted FHA and VA insurance and guaranty programs and had virtually no impact on the way the public housing program was administered. Both the rent supplement and the leasing program were hamstrung by local government approval requirements that made it unlikely that they could be used to gain entry for poor and minority families to middle class and suburban communities.[94] The Model Cities program soon ran afoul of politics. It was designed to show that real improvements in the urban environment could be made if massive amounts of aid were focused upon small areas within a few "model" cities. But the political difficulties of concentrating large amounts of money in a few places soon dictated spreading the funds among many more cities than originally contemplated and eliminating the emphasis on particular neighborhoods. As the money was spread more thinly, any chance of truly revitalizing an entire inner city community vanished. Model Cities became just another federal program producing spotty results.

Most importantly of all, the Vietnam War siphoned away administration energies. In spite of the country's awareness of racial injustice, public housing, FHA and VA programs, and the lending activities of federally supervised institutions were still being handled in the same old way. In 1964, the high point of the federal commitment to civil rights, when the nation's first southern president in a century was saying "We shall overcome" and secured an overwhelming bipartisan congressional endorsement of a civil rights bill, the

National Committee Against Discrimination in Housing said, "Today, in the very eye of the storm of the Negro revolution the ghetto stands—largely unassailed—as the rock upon which rests segregated living patterns which pervade and vitiate almost every phase of Negro life and Negro-white relationships."[95]

This persistent intractability of housing segregation in the midst of all civil rights efforts of the early 1960s was perhaps most dramatically—and poignantly—highlighted by what happened to Martin Luther King, Jr., in Chicago in 1966 and 1967. On a hot July day in 1966, King, already a national leader, held a rally in Soldiers Field to propose steps to turn Chicago into a "racially open city."[96] Upwards of 50,000 people sat through five hours of entertainment and speeches in 100 degree heat. "Open housing" demands directed to real estate boards and brokers, banks and government agencies, were enthusiastically approved. Included were these for the Chicago Housing Authority:

> No more public housing construction in the ghetto until a substantial number of units are started outside the ghetto.
>
> A program to increase vastly the supply of low-cost housing on a scattered basis.[97]

King then led thousands of his followers to the Loop, where the demands were posted on the city hall doors. Grudgingly, Mayor Richard Daley agreed to a meeting, but after an unsuccessful conference, King announced that he would begin a series of marches to dramatize the open housing demands.

The first Chicago march took place on July 17, in the all-white Gage Park section of the city. Two hundred King followers held a prayer vigil outside a real estate firm, demanding that listings in white areas be made available to blacks. At this first confrontation, white onlookers merely heckled and jeered at the marchers. However, the steady stream of marches that followed soon produced violence. On July 30, seven persons were injured when a crowd assaulted the marchers. The next day, a mob of 4,000 whites overturned cars belonging to the marchers and dumped them into a park lagoon. Thirty-seven people were hurt. On August 5, Dr. King was knocked to the ground by a rock; the mob shouted, "Kill him, kill him."[98]

The deteriorating situation soon led to a "summit meeting" among Mayor Daley, King, and seventy-four religious, business, labor, government, and community leaders. On August 26, accord was reached on a ten point statement that come to be known as the "Summit

Agreement." It included promises from the Chicago Commission on Human Relations to enforce the city's fair housing ordinance against real estate brokers, from the Chicago Real Estate Board to support the principle of open housing, from the Department of Public Aid to seek housing for welfare recipients throughout the city and metropolitan area, and commitments from business and religious leaders to form a new organization that would undertake the education and action programs necessary to achieve fair housing. It also included this promise from the Chicago Housing Authority:

> It [CHA] recognizes that heavy concentrations of public housing should not again be built in the City of Chicago. . . . In the future, it will seek scattered sites for public housing and will limit the height of new public housing structures in high density areas to eight stories, with housing for families with children limited to the first two stories. Wherever possible, smaller units will be built.[99]

For his part, King agreed to end the marches and move on to other battles. The Chicago establishment, as it had promised, formed the Leadership Council for Metropolitan Open Communities, whose board of directors included presidents of banks, utilities and other corporations, and labor unions as well as the cardinal of the Chicago archdiocese. However, while larded with statements of good intention, the Summit Agreement was short on specific commitments. The Public Aid Department would make a "renewed and persistent effort" to find good housing regardless of location. The Mortgage Bankers Association "affirmed" that the policy of its members was to lend mortgage money without discrimination. The Chicago Housing Authority would "seek" scattered sites for public housing. But as for federal deposit insurance vital to financial institutions found guilty of racial discrimination, "the matter is a complex one [but] will be diligently pursued." The Real Estate Board remained free to pursue its appeal attacking the validity of the city's fair housing ordinance. Nor was CHA called upon to withdraw its pending proposals for thousands of new public housing units in the ghetto even though construction had not yet begun.

Under these circumstances, the Leadership Council understandably failed to achieve King's basic goal of opening white neighborhoods to poor blacks. Illustrative was its failure even to try to require CHA to perform its promise to scatter public housing, a promise CHA ignored. The following year, 1967, King let it be known that he might return to Chicago to try to achieve the promise of the Summit Agreement. The response was immediate. He was criticized violently by the mayor, by the United Auto Workers, by a group of black clergymen who accused him of creating hatred with his marches and urged him "to keep the hell out of Chicago," and even by the head of the Leadership Council.[100] Faced with this hostility, King issued a statement praising the Leadership Council for its hard work and said there would be no repetition of his open housing marches as long as "progress" continued.[101] On that ignominious note ended Martin Luther King's efforts to deal with residential segregation in Chicago.

The "progress" King had referred to was hard to find, in Chicago or elsewhere. In 1967, the National Committee on Discrimination in Housing issued a pamphlet summarizing the housing situation. Seventeen charges detailed the way in which the federal government was "primarily responsible for undergirding a ghetto system that dominates, distorts, and despoils every aspect of life in the United States today."[102] Specifically, it charged that HUD had not used its powers under the 1964 law; HUD continued to approve public housing projects that reinforced ghettoization; urban renewal programs continued to uproot black communities and to countenance segregated relocation patterns; FHA required no open occupancy commitments in its insured developments; federally supervised lending institutions were not required to eliminate discriminatory lending practices; HUD continued to make loans and grants to communities that practiced racial and economic exclusion; and so on.

A year later, after widespread urban, largely racial, rioting had frightened the nation into a formal examination of what was happening in its cities, the Kerner Report essentially restated these charges:

> Federal housing programs must be given a new thrust aimed at overcoming the prevailing patterns of racial segregation. If this is not done, those programs will continue to concentrate the most impoverished and dependent segments of the population into the central-city ghettos where there is already a critical gap between the needs of the population and the public resources to deal with them. This can only continue to compound the conditions of failure and hopelessness which lead to crime, civil disorder and social disorganization.[103]

CIVIL RIGHTS AND MAGNA CARTA

In April 1968, Martin Luther King's message of brotherhood and nonviolence brought him to Memphis and as assassin's bullet. Shame and outrage swept the nation. One week after the Memphis tragedy, open housing legislation, filibustered to death in the Senate two years earlier, was enacted. Discrimination in the sale, rental, or financing of roughly 80 percent of the housing in the land would eventually be outlawed.[104]

Title VIII of the 1968 Civil Rights Act—the "Fair Housing Act," as the new law was called—contained four elements. The first was the major symbolic step of expressly declaring housing discrimination, by private citizens as well as by government, to be unlawful. The *Brown* school desegration decision had dealt with *public* schools; the Fair Housing Act outlawed discrimination in private as well as in government subsidized housing. Second, the law provided remedies for discriminatory acts. Persons discriminated against could sue for possession of the home or apartment that had been denied them (if it was still available) and for money damages as well or could file administrative complaints with the Department of Housing and Urban Development, which was then obligated to investigate and try to resolve the dispute by conciliation. Third, the attorney general was authorized to sue on behalf of the United States to stop "patterns" of discrimination.

Finally, and most importantly, the law declared it to be national policy to provide for "fair housing" throughout the land and directed HUD and all other executive departments and agencies to administer their housing and urban development programs and activities "in a manner affirmatively to further" fair housing policy. The language was suggestively vague. The key phrase, "fair housing," was left undefined, an invitation to HUD to formulate its own definition. The courts had said that administrative interpretations of vague legislative language were entitled to great weight and that civil rights laws were to be read "expansively" to fulfill their purposes.[105] There was no telling what could be wrought with a "fair housing" mandate.

Two months later, in June, the Supreme Court ruling in a major housing case further limited discrimination. A moribund 1866 civil rights law, enacted to enforce the antislavery amendment to the Constitution, provided that blacks should have the same right as whites to purchase and lease property. In *Jones v. Mayer*—Jones was a black to whom Mayer, owner of a new housing development in suburban St. Louis county, had refused to sell a house—the Supreme Court now said the century-old law forbade all racial discrimination in housing transactions, private as well as governmental, because such discrimination interfered with the right to purchase and lease property and was therefore a " relic of slavery" to which the old law applied.[106] Although the Fair Housing Act now already prohibited most discrimination in housing sales, and the principal practical effect of the *Jones* case was to close some loopholes in the new law, the decision had the important psychological effect of linking efforts to combat housing discrimination to that most fundamental of human rights.

Congress acted again later that summer and passed a comprehensive housing subsidy law. As he signed the 1968 Housing and Urban Development Act on August 1, President Johnson grandly called it "a Magna Carta to liberate our cities." The law reiterated the national goal, first stated in the 1949 Housing Act, of a decent home in a suitable environment for every American family. For the first time, however, it quantified that goal—twenty-six million units of new and rehabilitated housing were to be provided over the next ten years, twenty million by the private sector and six million by federally subsidized programs.[107]

Public housing was dealt with handsomely; authority was provided for financing more than 300,000 new units over three years, a figure that amounted to nearly half the units built in the thirty year life of the public housing program. Two new programs, sections 235 and 236, were designed to involve private developers for the first time on any significant scale in the construction and ownership of subsidized housing.[108] The section 235 program for home ownership was intended to permit one million lower income families to own their own homes by 1978. It provided subsidies to builders (monthly payments to reduce interest costs to as low as 1 percent on FHA-insured home mortgages) to enable them to sell new or rehabilitated single family homes at prices the poor or near-poor could afford. The section 236 program was a rental housing counterpart of section 235 that provided similar subsidies on FHA-insured apartment mortgages. Although the new programs were geared to families with incomes somewhat higher than those of the very poor who were eligible for public housing, they represented a substantial commitment of federal aid for new housing for many relatively poor families. Moreover, neither of the two new programs required local government approval. Under sections 235 and 236, HUD could enter into contracts directly with private developers to provide the new types of subsidized housing, and local governments had no veto powers of the sort that had hampered earlier public housing and rent supplement programs.

The new law also dealt with FHA's history of favoring suburban, middle class areas by authorizing FHA to insure properties of "acceptable risk" as distinguished from the traditionally higher FHA standard of "economic soundness." The plain purpose of the law was to have FHA insure mortgages on properties that formerly would have been rejected because of their location.[109] It appeared, therefore, that FHA would no longer be permitted to focus exclusively on the middle class and the suburbs. Thus, while "Magna Carta" may have been an exaggeration, the 1968 act was the biggest and most imaginative housing program ever adopted.

THE MOST EXPLOSIVE PROBLEM

Finally, in December 1968, two separate presidential task forces delivered their reports to the White House. One, the President's Committee on Urban Housing, was headed by industrialist Edgar F. Kaiser. The other, the National Commission on Urban Problems, was chaired by former U.S. Senator Paul H. Douglas. Though their assignments overlapped somewhat, the Kaiser Committee was to explore the process of housing construction to find out how costs could be reduced and production increased, especially for low income housing, while the Douglas Commission's task was to examine federal and local laws and policies bearing on slum and urban growth problems and to make recommendations on those subjects.

The Kaiser Committee report, *A Decent Home*, contained a number of technical recommendations to help the construction industry increase the supply of housing. It enthusiastically endorsed the goal of the 1968 HUD act to build twenty-six million new and rehabilitated housing units in ten years and expressed its belief that reliance on the existing subsidy programs plus the new section 235 and 236 programs would enable the country to meet the subsidized housing portion of the goal. However, if these failed to do the job, the committee "would then foresee the necessity for massive federal intervention with the federal government becoming the nation's houser of last resort."[110] The committee's report also pointed out that previous subsidized housing programs had offered recipients little choice except to continue to live in deteriorating slum conditions. Merely enforcing the antidiscrimination provisions of the new Fair Housing Act would not change that pattern; the committee report warned that new subsidized low income housing "should not be concentrated in the present slums but scattered throughout the metropolitan areas."[111] Where necessary to accomplish that purpose the committee recommended that the federal government be empowered to preempt local zoning ordinances, subject only to a veto by the governor of the state. Although it was reluctant to suggest reducing local powers, the committee was "convinced . . . that widespread abuses of zoning techniques and their inherent defects as a land-use control make it necessary for local prerogatives to yield to the greater common good."[112]

The Douglas Commission report, *Building the American City*, concluded that of all the aspects of the urban problem it had explored, the most potentially "explosive" problem was the "almost unyielding pattern of [residential] segregation."[113] The overwhelming majority of future nonwhite population growth was likely to be concentrated in the social and economic disaster areas of central city slums unless there were major changes in public policies. That concentration would be accompanied by increasing tension and violence, repressive measures, further polarization of blacks and whites, the flight of more and more businesses and jobs from the city. The "suicidal consequences" of those possibilities were not, the commission thought, pleasant to contemplate.[114] It stressed that a massive amount of new housing was a national necessity, housing programs had to focus on the poor, and housing the poor and eliminating housing segregation were of such supreme national importance that if all else failed, the federal government should become the builder of last resort.[115]

The men who served with Kaiser and Douglas were all moderates; indeed, most Kaiser Committee members came from big business. Of Lyndon Johnson's appointments to the Kerner Commission, Tom Wicker of the *New York Times* observed that had the commission included militants, it could not have spoken with a voice so sure to be heard. What had to be said had been said at last, he wrote, not by radicals or militants but by representatives of white, moderate, responsible America.[116] By the end of 1968 such representatives had said it twice more. And they had said it as a time when the new Nixon administration, due to assume office in a matter of days, would be possessed of an unprecedented array of legal tools and congressional appropriations to respond to the urgent calls to action. It appeared that for the first time it might be possible to mount a serious effort to deal with the apartheid conditions that had settled upon so many of the nation's metropolitan areas in the quarter century following Myrdal's prescient warning.

✳ *Chapter Two*

Aspirin for Cancer

In the early days of the Nixon administration there were indications that the federal government would use its new powers to attempt to alleviate metropolitan apartheid. Nixon's secretary of housing and urban development, former Michigan Governor George Romney, began to formulate an "open communities" policy to provide subsidized housing for the poor and for minority families in the suburbs. At the first sign of opposition, however, the president halted open communities activities and issued a policy statement that severely limited the role of the federal government in combating racial and economic residential segregation. In addition, the 1968 housing subsidy programs were administered in ways that produced shoddy housing at high cost, rocked HUD with scandal, and actually exacerbated the segregation problem. With housing policy in disarray, Nixon summarily ended all the subsidized programs at the end of 1972. Thus, four years after the hopeful moment of 1968, the promise of the new housing laws remained unfulfilled and metropolitan apartheid had intensified.

ROMNEY—IN LIKE A LION . . . .

Shortly after assuming office, Romney announced that building the large number of dwelling units authorized by the 1968 Housing and Urban Development Act was the way to overcome the country's domestic crisis. Doing so would ease racial tensions and bring millions of poor people, "neglected Americans," into the mainstream of American life. It could save the cities. It was the nation's number one economic opportunity, and it would be Romney's number one priority.[1]

True to Romney's pledge, by the end of 1969 HUD had broken every previous record for building subsidized housing and was proposing still further major increases in the pace of new construction.[2] In April 1970, the president himself announced administration plans for a sharp acceleration in production in order to meet the nation's "increasingly urgent housing needs."[3] But with the construction of housing for poor people suddenly at record levels and rising, the question of where to put all the new housing became a problem. Available land in central cities was in short supply and expensive, and the courts were beginning to develop a doctrine that precluded confining subsidized housing to black neighborhoods.

Romney confronted the location issue with characteristic fervor. In January 1970, he argued that it was vital for subsidized housing to be dispersed more broadly than in the past.[4] His deputy, Undersecretary Richard Van Dusen, soon referred publicly, albeit vaguely, to HUD plans to expand suburban housing opportunities for low income minority families.[5] In April, Jerris Leonard, head of the Civil Rights Division of the Justice Department, said that past policy had sometimes made government a partner in perpetuating racial discrimination in housing. The Nixon administration, Leonard forecast, would soon unveil significant policy changes to prevent further construction of public housing in all-black or overcrowded areas and to encourage suburban locations. "There is no reason," he was quoted as saying, "why the suburbs cannot set aside areas for public and publicly supported housing."[6]

Through the *President's Second Annual Report on National Housing Goals*, issued in April 1970,[7] Nixon lent his support to the emerging new policy. Population growth, the report said, would require enlarging the housing supply beyond the crowded centers of the cities. That had to be accomplished without making the cities "islands of decay, tenated mainly by lower income families and stripped of adequate public services for the lack of a sufficient tax base." Though sufficient land was available in metropolitan—particularly suburban—areas for building the needed housing, one of the most serious problems in finding sites for housing the poor was opposition from middle class, white communities, opposition stemming from both racial and economic discrimination. "There must be an end," the report insisted, "to the concentration of the poor in land-short central cities, and the inaccessibility to the growth of employment opportunities in suburban areas." The opposition of middle class communities had to be overcome if opportunities for families to live where they wished were to be maximized, particularly in suburban areas where land was easily collected for development. Otherwise, no low or moderate income housing would be built, or it would be built only in the inner city, "thus heightening the tendency for racial polarization in our society."[8]

The president said that the objective was to achieve "open communities," that is, communities that provided jobs and housing for families of all income levels and racial characteristics. To that end, legislation would soon be proposed to prohibit local governments from discriminating against federally subsidized housing and to eliminate some restrictions on its use. Though such steps would not meet all the problems, they were realistic measures that would help broaden the range of housing opportunities for poor, particularly minority, families.[9]

Soon after the report was issued, Romney sent to the House Subcommittee on Housing a proposal to empower the federal government to override local zoning ordinances that excluded subsidized low income housing projects. Testifying in support of the proposal, Romney said that its adoption was a "necessary first step in ending the ominous trend toward stratification of our society by race and by income."[10]

Thus, in the first half of 1970, a steady stream of rhetoric, a strong presidential statement, and a legislative proposal all suggested that a serious initiative to break the ghetto site pattern might be in the offing. In a few short months, however, the initiative was aborted. The HUD legislative proposal was defeated in subcommittee and abandoned. The remaining legislation the president had described was never even submitted to Congress. A new federal policy that placed the burden of dispersal almost exclusively on local officials and severely restricted the role of the federal government was prepared and issued as a major policy statement. All references to racial polarization and overcoming white middle class opposition to dispersed housing for the poor were omitted from the following year's presidential report on housing. This sudden turnabout was the result of events that began in Chicago three years earlier.

CONFRONTATION

In 1967, Francis Fisher, a Chicago lawyer turned government official, was appointed regional administrator of HUD's ten state midwest region. He hired Edward Levin, a Chicago zoning lawyer, as his special assistant and gave him broad responsibility for administering a variety of programs. The assignment was something of an innovation;

Fisher's objective was to coordinate housing, urban renewal, Model Cities, and other HUD programs that had traditionally been administered by various department heads working independently. Fisher, who was in full sympathy with the 1968 Fair Housing Act, also persuaded a black lawyer, Robert Tucker, to become his assistant regional administrator for equal opportunity. Fisher, Levin, and Tucker played a central role in the rise and sudden fall of the open communities policy in the Nixon administration.

In the fall of 1968, the sprawling Detroit suburb of Warren submitted to Fisher's office a million dollar urban renewal application. Warren also submitted its "workable program," a plan outlining Warren's slum and community development problems and its plans for dealing with them, including its plans for meeting the housing needs of low and moderate income families. Under HUD regulations, approval of a workable program was required for an urban renewal application to be accepted.[11]

Warren was an economically diversified city with a population of about 180,000, a large industrial base, and a wide range of housing. Yet a grand total of only twenty-eight black families lived in the city, all but five on federally owned land, even though the population of neighboring Detroit was over 40 percent black, and 30 percent of the worker's in Warren's own Chevrolet, Dodge, Chrysler, and other plants were also black. It would have been hard to imagine a more appropriate place to apply the Fair Housing Act directive requiring HUD to affirmatively administer its program to achieve fair housing. As Levin later observed,

> Detroit and its suburbs present an unparalleled opportunity for the application of a fair housing strategy. . . . [P]erhaps nowhere else in the country, is there the combination of a large central city with a substantial black population (over 40 percent) surrounded by predominantly white large suburbs which use many HUD programs, in which there is extensive black employment, and with a great deal of housing for lower middle income families (suggesting racial rather than economic exclusion).[12]

Tucker's equal opportunity authority led him to focus on the Detroit area and its "sundown communities," such as Warren, where blacks worked during the day but, because housing near their jobs was unavailable to them, returned at sundown to their own neighborhoods. Tucker's staff began to make inquiries about the leverage HUD might have in the Detroit area to force some fair housing steps to be taken, and eventually advised rejecting the Warren workable program. Under the new civil rights law, it was argued, HUD could not approve a million dollar urban renewal program in an all-white city without getting some specific commitments to provide housing for the many black workers who had to make long trips to and from their jobs in Warren each day. Since HUD had not previously required such commitments as a condition of approval, Fisher felt Warren was entitled to some warning that the rules of the game were about to be changed. He approved the Warren urban renewal and workable program plans effective January 1, 1969, for one year, but sent a HUD team to Warren to explain the new situation. In February, the team was assured by Warren officials that affirmative equal housing opportunity steps would be taken in the coming year.

The following December, Warren's applications for the next year of its workable program, and for $3 million more urban renewal aid, were submitted to the HUD regional office. The same team was still there to receive them, Fisher having survived the January 1969 change in national administrations. Little if anything had been done, it appeared, to carry out the vague assurances of the previous February. Indeed, in September, plans for a 100 unit public housing project within one of Warren's urban renewal areas had been canceled by the Warren City Council because nearby residents feared a black "invasion." In a memo to Fisher, Levin proposed that the Warren application be disapproved.[13]

Instead of outright disapproval, Fisher wrote to Warren's Mayor Ted Bates, extending the urban renewal funding for a short time, suggesting various steps that might permit HUD to approve a normal extension for a full year, and appointing a HUD team, headed by Levin, to work with Warren officials "in achieving our mutual goal in increased housing opportunities for minorities in Warren."[14]

In April, Levin wrote a comprehensive memorandum to Fisher setting out the overall HUD strategy of which the Warren efforts were a part. Entitled "Strategy for Administering HUD Programs to Increase Suburban Minority Housing Opportunities," the memorandum advocated a general policy similar to that employed in Warren: by threatening to disapprove local applications, HUD might "persuade" local authorities to build some subsidized housing to which blacks would have access, or at least to pass open housing laws and appoint human relations commissions that would help to open up the existing housing stock to black families.[15]

The approach so impressed HUD Assistant Secretary Sam Jackson that he promptly sent some of the HUD-Warren correspondence to all regional administrators and encouraged them to "utilize similar approaches whenever appropriate."[16]

But Warren officials were not so taken with the regional office's approach as was Sam Jackson. It had become clear to them that Fisher's people were not going to abandon their insistence on some tangible expression of support for open housing as a condition of approving Warren's workable program and urban renewal applications. They decided to arrange a meeting with Romney in Washington.

On May 7, Mayor Bates and a group of about ten city officials were ushered into Romney's large, wood-paneled conference room by Van Dusen.[17] Fisher and Levin were already there, and Romney arrived shortly.

Van Dusen suggested that Bates explain his views. The mayor began, saying that Warren was not against open housing or minorities, that it was now an "open city." "We have our colored in Warren. We have no problems there. . . ." At this point, Romney leaned forward and said, "Mr. Mayor, you do have a problem or you would not be here."

Taken aback, Bates tried another tack. He explained that Warren had spent $75,000 on police protection for a racially mixed couple that had moved into the city in 1967. Again Romney cut in: "Mayor Bates, I was governor of Michigan when the Bailey family moved in and I had to send the state police in there to protect them because the local officials would not fulfill their responsibilities."

The silence was tense. Romney continued:

> You can try to hermetically seal Warren off from the surrounding areas if you want, but you won't do it with federal money. You will find it will be impossible to do. We are living in a nation now where everybody is interdependent. Black people have as much right to equal opportunities as we do. God knows, they have suffered so much they may have more right. Inexorably, there is going to be a change, so you might as well face up to it now and agree to these requirements.

In defense, a councilman said that they were trying to do their best, but there was considerable pressure against open housing in Warren. Was Romney talking about integration? He replied that he was. Said a councilwoman, "Well, what you're asking us to do is give up our jobs."

Then Fisher explained that he only wanted a commitment to progress, such as the appointment of a human relations committee, and that Warren did not have to show any actual open housing accomplishments to receive its money. Bates argued that integration should be a "natural happening," that the community should "wait for nature to take its course." Romney then spoke a final time:

The youth of this nation, the minorities of this nation, the discriminated against of this nation are not going to wait for "nature to take its course." What is really at issue here is responsibility—moral responsibility. This problem is the most important one that America has ever faced, is now facing and will ever face, bar none. It must be solved and we, the citizens, must solve it.

As the meeting ended, Bates said he now understood better how Romney felt, and he would go back home and discuss the situation.

During the six weeks following the May 7 meeting, there were more intense negotiations between the Chicago HUD office and Warren. Finally, on June 16, by a 5–4 vote, the Warren City Council approved a compromise Levin and Bates had worked out—a limited open housing ordinance and a resolution authorizing the mayor to appoint a community fair housing board. The papers were flown to Chicago the following morning. By afternoon, the regional office had recommended approval of the workable program and urban renewal applications; they were flown to Washington the next morning. Warren's check would be written as soon as Mayor Bates appointed the fifteen members of the Warren fair housing board.[18] Levin wrote a comprehensive memorandum of the Warren story which began by referring to the Warren City Council actions and the approval of Warren's applications as a "happy ending to a critical opening chapter in our efforts."[19]

But the joy in the regional office lasted for only five weeks. Mayor Bates was still assembling his list of appointees to the fair housing board when, on July 21, the Detroit *News* published the first of a series of explosive stories on the Warren-HUD negotiations. It was, as a Warren councilman later said, like dropping a bomb each day for seven days in a row.[20] "U.S. Picks Warren as Prime Target in Move to Integrate All Suburbs," read the headline of the first article. Weeks of effort, the *News* proclaimed, had enabled it to piece together the full story of how the federal government "intends to use its vast power to force integration of America's white suburbs—and it is using the Detroit suburbs as a key starting point."[21] Quoting liberally from Levin's memorandum to Fisher, in which Detroit and its suburbs were presented as offering an unparalleled opportunity for applying a fair housing strategy, the *News* promised a step-by-step account of the Warren story on succeeding days throughout the week.

Bates professed outrage. "I won't tolerate Warren being used as a guinea pig for integration experiments, even if it means losing urban renewal," he was quoted as saying in the next day's Detroit *News*. He charged that HUD had "lied about their intentions in wanting open housing guarantees from us," saying that HUD had told Warren it would not push "forced integration." The headline for the day was, "Warren Charges HUD Deceit."[22]

And so it went for the rest of the week. "How Warren Became Integration Test City," and "Warren Was Given Romney Ultimatum," were the headlines on succeeding days. Romney's concern about the increasing separation of the races was mentioned, as was the "dilemma that has plagued America since its founding," but the thrust of the week's articles was fairly reflected by the headlines.[23]

Romney felt compelled to respond to the charges and quickly arranged for a public meeting to be held on July 27 in the auditorium of Warren's Fitzgerald High School. The meeting lasted two and a half hours. Inside the auditorium were about 100 officials from Warren and other Detroit suburbs, as well as Fisher and Levin from the HUD regional office. Outside, a crowd of about 300 whites milled around, carrying signs with such sentiments as, "Romney is a HUDache" and "Get rid of the dud at Hud."[24]

Romney's prepared statement was conciliatory. There was no policy of "forced integration." Warren was not a testing place. In other cities as well as in Warren, HUD's general policies were to enforce laws against disrcimination in housing and to encourage *voluntary* action to provide more low and moderate income housing for the poor. The Detroit *News* headlines were "unjustified."[25]

In the heated questioning that followed, Romney retreated still further. He said that although Levin's suburban strategy memorandum did "reach" HUD files in Washington, it had "no relationship" to HUD policy, and "those responsible for policy were not aware of it."[26] (The truth was that Levin had sent Van Dusen a copy on April 16 and had delivered another copy to him on May 4, when Van Dusen came to the Chicago regional office for a briefing.[27]) In the face of persistent questioning from one Warren councilwoman, Romney continued to insist on the word "voluntary" as a means to develop more housing for the poor. But it was clear to everyone in the auditorium that what the word really meant was that Warren could "voluntarily" forego urban renewal dollars if it refused to appoint the fair housing board HUD was insisting upon. "Romney's speech was just a play on words," the Warren councilwoman was later quoted as saying, and she was clearly right.[28]

As he left the meeting Romney was booed, and the police had to clear a path for him through the milling throng. Mayor Bates had similar trouble when he departed. The crowd pounded on his car and shouted, "Bates is a nigger lover."[29]

The denouement was predictable. Two days after Romney's visit, petitions were circulated for a referendum to abolish the Warren urban renewal program. Within ten days, nearly 15,000 signatures had been obtained. In November 1970, Warren voted overwhelmingly to kill its urban renewal plan. Warren would forego the millions of federal dollars being held in readiness for it rather than take even a small step—well short of actually providing any housing for the poor—in the direction of an open housing community.

RACE-MIXING SHROUD

Romney was evidently chastened by his Warren experience. A few weeks later, testifying before a Senate committee investigating the relationship between de facto school segregation and housing discrimination, Romney hedged about supporting a policy of housing dispersal. He now sounded quite unlike the George Romney who had earlier said the nation could not wait for nature to take its course and that what was really at issue was moral responsibility. He was uncertain, he said, about the extent of HUD's power under the Civil Rights Law. There was also the question "of how far you go from the standpoint of pushing things forward without setting things back as a result of pushing too hard too fast."[30]

There were also portents of trouble with the White House. Early in the summer, John Ehrlichman had inquired about HUD's reported new intitatives. He hoped that HUD was not embarking on a new policy without consulting the White House. As the Warren debacle evolved, White House anxiety increased.

Then in October 1970, two and a half weeks before election day, a seriously embarrassing situation developed. To inquiries about its open communities activities, HUD had been routinely responding by saying that open communities policies were still in the formative stage. In communications to the White House, HUD insisted that it had not embarked upon a scheme to "force integration" on the suburbs and that White House concerns were without foundation. Meanwhile, some HUD officials had been talking candidly with writers for a periodical, *The National Journal*, about their hopes for open communities. They thought that the *Journal's* piece on housing would not be published before the election. In fact, however, the article appeared on October 17. Entitled "Romney Faces Political Perils with Plan to Integrate Suburbs," its lead sentence announced that Romney was in the final planning stage of a full-scale effort "to disperse largely black and poor populations of center-city ghettos into largely white and affluent suburbs."[31] Quoting an unnamed HUD official, the article continued, "The Secretary is dead serious about giving low-income people a credible opportunity to live where the jobs are—which often means in the suburbs." A confidential HUD memorandum was also quoted as saying that the decision to build low-income housing in the suburbs reflected the "need for a major change in past policies whereby HUD funds have been concentrated in the core cities; instead, this Department must now put *greatly increased resources where the solutions are, not where the problems are.*"[32]

The approach, the *Journal* said, was to be essentially the one employed in Warren. But the emphasis was not to be on terminating funds for programs already begun, as with Warren's ongoing urban renewal program; instead, new projects would be approved in accordance with priorities determined in part by a community's willingness to accept low income housing. The *Journal* article did describe HUD as reluctant to talk openly because of the Warren events and the upcoming November elections. Romney was supposed to have even prohibited official discussions of open communities policy until after the voting. But a HUD official, who asked not to be named, was nonetheless quoted as saying, "We've been doing our thing quietly, but we really plan to fly after the November election."[33]

If HUD was embarrassed by the *National Journal* article, the White House was angry. Harsh words were exchanged. One HUD official described the White House attitude about the incident as "paranoid." HUD promptly sent Ehrlichman an analysis of its open communities position, which said that the subject of suburban integration had been sensationalized in the press, that HUD's position-in-formation was not one of "forced integration," that HUD's ideas were soundly based in law, and that the White House was unduly concerned.

Amidst all the furor, the administration decided the time had come to develop a formal position on housing policy. It was made clear to HUD that any major new initiatives should await the definitive policy statement. A front page story in the *New York Times* reported that Attorney General Mitchell visited Romney and ordered him to drop his program initiatives until an official administration position on housing desegregation could be formulated.[34]

In December, the blow fell. The definitive administration policy paper was still six months away, but in a televised news conference, the president told the country, "I believe that forced integration of the suburbs is not in the national interest."[35] By selecting the phrase "forced integration," said the *Wall Street Journal*, the president had knocked the props out from under George Romney and had "draped the dreaded race-mixing shroud over the entire Romney effort to move subsidized housing beyond city limits."[36]

GESTURE OF FAITH

John Ehrlichman, special White House counsel Leonard Garment, and speechwriter Ray Price of the White House staff, as well as Romney, Van Dusen, and various Justice Department lawyers, were all involved in developing the administration's formal housing policy statement. When the "Statement by the President on Federal Policies Relative to Equal Housing Opportunity" was finally issued on Friday, June 11, 1971, it was with the fanfare appropriate to a major presidential pronouncement—Ehrlichman and Garment held a press conference in the presidential briefing room, and on the following Monday, Romney and Mitchell issued their own separate statements and held a joint press conference.[37]

The Nixon statement[38] first outlined the problem. In the nation's sixty-six largest metropolitan areas, which accounted for more than half of the country's population, the central cities were growing increasingly black, while the suburbs remained overwhelmingly white. During the decade of the 1960s alone, the white population of these metropolitan areas had declined by about two million, while the black population increased almost three million. During the same decade, the suburban white population had increased by twelve and a half million, the black by less than one million. In city after city, the president said, the story was the same; the facts revealed by the 1970 census were "compelling." Such a degree of racial separation engendered mistrust, hostility, and fear; wasted human resources by denying human opportunity; and exacted a direct dollar cost in lost wages when minority families could not find housing near suburban jobs for which they could qualify.

In light of the racial concentration problem, the Nixon statement continued, the administration had developed a three part housing policy. First, the federal government would be vigorous in enforcing all laws against racial discrimination. Second, the government would administer federal housing and urban development programs in ways that would encourage the expansion of housing opportunities. However, the federal role was secondary and reactive. Sites for HUD-assisted housing had to be selected and acquired by local public or private developers; HUD's role was confined to approval or disapproval. Priority would be given to proposed projects that would open up nonsegregated housing opportunities, but it was a "basic principle" that a municipality that did not want federally assisted housing "should not have it imposed from Washington by bureaucratic fiat."

Third, local authorities should press forward with "innovative and positive approaches," and local communities would be encouraged in their own voluntary efforts to make housing more widely available and to reduce the extent of racial concentration. The emphasis, though, was on the "voluntary" nature of local efforts. The federal government would not interfere, directly or indirectly, with local land use policies, such as zoning laws, except where those policies demonstrably cloaked racial discrimination. Local officials were entrusted with the initial, and often the final, determinations as to how much low and moderate income housing was to be built, how well it was to be built, and where it was to be built. It was not appropriate, the president emphasized, for the federal government to become involved in the "infinitely varied individual questions that arise as our thousands of local governments hammer out their individual local land use policies." His administration would offer leadership in encouraging local governments to address those questions "creatively and imaginatively," but the choices involved were essentially local.

From this three part policy emerged the administration's approach to the 1968 Civil Rights Act's imprecise term, "fair housing," and its response to the act's directive that housing and urban development programs should be administered to further that purpose. In approaching a definition of "fair housing," one had to distinguish between racial and economic discrimination. The former was clearly unlawful. But "black" and "poor" were not interchangeable. Although a higher percentage of blacks than of whites were below the poverty line, poor whites far outnumbered poor blacks. When predominantly poor members of a racial minority were concentrated in a particular area of a central city, the question of where to build housing for them was not easily answered. Concentrating the housing in the existing black area could reinforce racial separation. But apart from race, residents of outlying areas also objected to subsidized housing for the poor because they feared it would result in lower property values, increased taxes, and the "contagion" of crime, violence, and drugs. The question was to what extent did the 1968 law call upon the federal government to go beyond enforcement of laws against overt racial discrimination and use its program money leverage either to promote economic integration or break up racial concentrations.

As to the former, the answer was clear: not at all. "We will not seek to impose economic integration." To emphasize that imperative, the president defined "equal housing opportunity" to mean the opportunity for individuals "of similar income levels" to gain access to housing regardless of race; citizens must be able to choose housing locations "within their economic means." (Whereas the *President's Second Annual Report on National Housing Goals* in 1970 had said, "Community opposition to low and moderate income housing involves both racial and economic discrimination,"[39] in the June 1971 presidential statement, the term "economic discrimination" did not appear.)

With respect to the goal of breaking up racial concentrations, there was room for a federal role, but a very limited one. In selecting among applications for federal subsidies, preference would be given to communities that were interested in building federally assisted low and moderate income housing outside areas of racial concentration. In addition, policies relating to marketing practices would be developed to assure nondiscrimination in the purchase or rental of federally assisted housing. The federal government would "encourage" communities to accept well-conceived housing developments—always within the community's capacity to assimilate the families who would live in them. But, for emphasis, "This administration will not attempt to impose federally assisted housing upon any community."[40]

The presidential message closed with a section entitled, "A Free and Open Society." One way or another, it stated, the challenge of how to provide fair, open, and adequate housing was a challenge essentially addressed, not to the federal government, but to the people and institutions of American's local communities. The challenge was theirs. "[T]hey," the president said, "must live with their success or failure."[41]

Viewed pragmatically, Nixon's three-pronged housing policy seemed unlikely to be effective. The first prong—vigorous enforcement of laws against racial discrimination—was likely to be blunted by the Nixon distinction between economic and racial discrimination. It was true, of course, as the president had said, that "poor" and "black" were not interchangeable terms. But the distinction was largely irrelevant within the massive poor *and* black ghettos of central cities. If the poor could be legitimately barred from nonghetto communities by exclusionary zoning and other land use controls, as Nixon's firm distinction between racial and economic discrimination seemed to imply, the most vigorous enforcement of laws against racial discrimination might have little impact on central city ghettos.

The second prong of the federal response—giving priority in funding to communities that would provide housing for the poor outside areas of racial concentration—meant the rejection of any affirmative federal action to change housing development patterns. A year earlier, George Romney had acknowledged that residential segregation was so deeply rooted in the nation that neither enforcement of anti-discrimination laws nor rhetorical exhortations would break the racial separation pattern. What was required, he said, was to rearrange the segregated housing pattern through new housing construction, meaning that some way had to be found to get new federally subsidized housing into stable, relatively well-to-do white neighborhoods that did not want it.[42] Brutally high housing costs assured that in no other way could the inner city minority poor gain access to housing in communities beyond the fringe of the ghetto. Congressman Thomas Ashley of Ohio, one of the most knowledgeable members of the House Subcommittee on Housing, put the point succinctly: "Historically we have taken the view that people should live where they can afford to live; now we are having to change that view. . . . [P]eople will have to live where they cannot afford to live."[43]

The president himself, in a 1970 statement on school segregation, had defined "freedom" as having two essential elements, "the *right* to choose, and the *ability* to choose." Strikingly, the illustration of his definition that the president offered had to do with housing: "The right to move out of a mid-city slum . . . means little without the means of doing so."[44]

Several proposals had previously been made for an affirmative federal response to the problem of how to disperse subsidized housing. Both the Kaiser Committee and the Douglas Commission had recommended that if all else failed the federal government should become the builder or houser of last resort. Short of this, suggestions had been made for the use of federal "leverage." For example, the Reverend Theodore M. Hesburgh, chairman of the U.S. Commission of Civil Rights, argued that the affirmative administration provision of the 1968 civil rights law would permit federal agencies to insist that every suburb receiving federal assistance of any sort join in a plan for reversing racial and economic polarization.[45]

By the 1970s, it would be a rare American community that could maintain, let alone improve, its quality of life without continued federal assistance and participation. There was little doubt that if federal transportation programs, health, education, and welfare programs, environmental programs, defense department programs, and so on, as well as HUD programs, were made contingent on the development of local housing dispersal plans, the resulting leverage would be enough to do the job. Shortly after release of the Nixon statement, the U.S. Conference of Mayors proposed just such an approach. The conference adopted a resolution condemning Nixon's statement and calling upon the federal government "to advise all communities that the future availability of all federal funds depends on the applicant community's commitment to provide low and moderate income housing opportunities."[46]

Nixon's housing policy statement flatly rejected the leverage approach. "[P]rogram money leverage" would not be used to require local communities to subordinate land use policies to the goal of breaking up racial concentrations. "This Administration will not attempt to impose federally assisted housing upon any community." Instead, priority in funding would be given to those communities that opened up unsegregated housing opportunities.[47]

But priority in funding as a means of achieving desegregated housing was almost certainly doomed to failure. Funding criteria could not *compel* the building of housing for the minority poor where local land use controls prevented it. In his press conference of June 14, Romney said that most HUD programs had more applications than money.[48] Yet the rejection of urban renewal in the Warren referendum showed that many communities would forego federal funding, even for nonhousing programs, rather than open their doors to the minority poor.

Finally, the third prong of the president's policy—encouraging local governments to deal "creatively and imaginatively" with the problem of racial and economic division—was almost certain to come to naught. A few days after the release of Nixon's statement, David Trubek, then a Yale Law School professor, testified before the United Stated Civil Rights Commission. At the commission's request, Trubek had examined court decisions and state legislation on land use over the previous ten years. His paper to the commission, entitled "Will State Courts and Legislatures Eliminate Exclusionary Land Use Controls?", in effect dealt with the possibilities for local creativity and imagination.[49]

Examining the role of the courts, Trubek concluded that the judges were extremely unlikely to frame and implement a policy designed to counteract exclusionary land controls.[50] A strong judicial tradition supported land use powers. To provide housing for the poor, local courts would, in effect, be required to confront divisive social and economic issues by assuming planning powers over their jurisdictions. Trubek felt local courts would be extremely reluctant to take such an activist approach. Trubek also pointed out that even after a loss in court (a few recent cases in Pennsylvania had given some observers hope that a major shift in judicial attitudes was imminent), local officials would so delay and hamper a developer that court victories would only rarely be turned into brick and mortar housing.[51] In one of the major Pennsylvania decisions relied upon by the optimists, involving a four acre minimum lot size requirement, the court said that a zoning ordinance whose primary purpose was to prevent the entrance of newcomers to the community could not be upheld. After losing the case, the town rezoned the land for two acre lots.[52] In another decision, the Pennsylvania Supreme Court said that an ordinance that failed to permit apartment houses was unconstitutional. The town responded by zoning a quarry for apartment uses.[53] Trubek also noted that the "favorable" cases were mostly from Pennsylvania, which, uniquely among the states, traditionally construed zoning laws restrictively; moreover, they involved luxury, not low income, housing.[54]

Trubek's pessimistic appraisal of the judicial situation led him to consider the possibilities of corrective action by state legislatures. Here, too, his forecast was grim. Although state legislatures had ample power to deal with the exclusionary land use control problem, few had been willing, because of political pressures, to exercise those powers, and Trubek doubted that they would do so in the future. Trubek's general conclusion was that our land use control system works to keep the poor and minority groups bottled up in urban ghettos and that the situation would not be changed by local institutions.[55]

Several years earlier, the Douglas Commission had likewise pointed out that the employment of land use controls to exclude low income housing was inevitable. Each locality viewed itself as an "orphan in the fiscal storm"; ignoring its self-interest in order to assist in solving metropolitan housing problems might prove disastrous for the local budget.[56]

Trubek, the Douglas Commission—and common sense—thus made it clear that individual local communities would not act contrary to their own perceived self-interest to encourage housing for the very poor. It seemed an inescapable conclusion that low income housing would continue to be excluded from middle class communities in the suburbs and outlying areas notwithstanding the rhetorical encouragement that constituted the third prong of the president's policy.

In sum, having identified racial and economic concentration as an issue of serious national concern, Nixon's housing policy declined to break new ground in attempting to confront the problem. It ignored the Kaiser and Douglas proposals, turned its back on the new thrust called for by the Kerner Report, and refused to accept the "leverage" interpretation of the 1968 Civil Rights Act. For these rejected approaches, the president substituted no federal commitment that was likely to overcome or avoid local land use control obstacles to nonghetto housing for inner city ghetto dwellers. Instead, the president's rhetoric sanctified and thereby strengthened those very obstacles. The presidential message to local communities in essence was: It would be helpful if you would accept some of the ghetto poor, but the law does not require you to do so and, so long as you avoid overt racial discrimination, preserving your local land use decisionmaking prerogatives is a more important value than racial and economic deconcentration.

New Federalism—by now a dominant theme of the Nixon administration—could be relied upon for philosophical justification of the housing policy statement. As early as April, 1969, Nixon had begun to talk about sharing federal revenues with local and state governments.[57] In August of that year, when he first mentioned the phrase "New Federalism," the president said: "After a third of a century of power flowing from the people and the states to Washington, it is time for a New Federalism in which power, funds and responsibility will flow from Washington to the states and to the people."[58] His revenue-sharing proposals, he added, would be a gesture of faith in this country's state and local governments and in the principle of democractic self-government. During the next several years, Nixon sent a steady stream of revenue-sharing proposals to Congress and stressed New Federalism in almost every major speech he gave.

But the new philosophy was not likely to change the old reality. As Congressman Thomas Ashley of Ohio put it, some national goals could be achieved only with national leverage. The carrot and stick approach, he said, was a fact of life. "We can't leave it up to local communities to decide whether to ignore or adhere to what Congress has reiterated for twenty years—the need for a balanced growth policy for America."[59]

To Vernon Jordan of the Urban League, the New Federalism approach of putting money, and therefore power, into state houses and city halls was not the way to deal with the problems of blacks. "To black Americans," he said, "who historically had no choice but to look to the federal government to correct the abuses of state and local governments, that is very much like hiring the wolf to guard the sheep."[60] Nixon's own state of the union message the year before had said that "the violent and decayed central cities of our great metropolitan complexes are the most conspicuous areas of failure in American life today." Although the Nixon housing policy was thoroughly consistent with New Federalism, it gave no promise of responding meaningfully to that most conspicuous failure. As public interest organizations commenting on the president's statement said, the president had "diagnosed a cancer and prescribed aspirin as the remedy."[61]

EYEWASH

The remaining eighteen months of the first Nixon administration suggested no revision of the aspirin-for-cancer analysis of the president's three part housing policy. It was not possible to discern the "vigor" the president had promised in the enforcement of laws against racial discrimination. The administration of federal programs to expand equal housing opportunities produced much administration and little expansion. The "innovative and positive approaches" to land use questions with which Nixon had said local officials should press forward were virtually nonexistent.

Under the 1968 Civil Rights Act, the Department of Justice and HUD shared enforcement responsibility. It was the duty of the Justice Department to combat discriminatory housing practices through lawsuits brought by the attorney general, while HUD was assigned the tasks of dealing with individual complaints of discrimination, carrying out studies of discriminatory practices, and coordinating the approach to fair housing among all executive departments and agencies.[62]

In the important area of challenging the discriminatory employment of local land use controls, the Justice Department's record was dismal. The department had joined one such suit in 1969, when it intervened to support a developer and some low income blacks against the town of Lackawanna, New York. The suit involved the withholding of building permits to block a proposed section 235 development in a predominantly white residential area. The court eventually ruled in favor of the plaintiffs and ordered Lackawanna to issue the permits.[63] Two years then elapsed before the Justice Department filed a case of its own attacking land use controls. In this suit, the department challenged the rezoning of a tract of land from multiple to single family dwellings by the virtually all-white town of Black Jack, Missouri, claiming that the rezoning was designed to exclude a proposed interracial section 236 project.[64] Two more years passed before the Justice Department initiated its third suit aimed at a local land use practice, an ordinance enacted by the Cleveland suburb of Parma that subjected all zoning changes to a referendum.[65]

This record of less than vigorous activity was not for lack of opportunity. On a number of occasions, Civil Rights Division lawyers recommended attacking local exclusionary practices only to have their recommendations overruled at higher levels. For example, in

January 1972 they prepared a suit against Cleveland, whose black population was concentrated in a small area east of the Cuyahoga River (referred to locally as the Mason-Dixon line). Less than 1 percent of the population on the west side of the river was black; most public housing was on the east side. However, in a rare instance of a central city housing authority moving toward a "balanced" location policy, the local housing authority had recently sought and obtained HUD approval for the construction of 297 single family homes, 127 on sites in black areas and 170 in white. Construction proceeded without difficulty on the sites in the black areas and with 38 of those in the white areas until, in November 1971, Cleveland revoked the construction permits for the other 132 white area sites.

Civil Rights Division lawyers recommended that a Justice Department suit be filed as soon as possible, arguing that future housing authority plans would be undermined if the revocation by the city of building permits for the 132 white area sites were allowed to stand. Historically, they said, public housing authorities and local city officials had worked together in operating discriminatory housing programs. Although this had earlier been the case in Cleveland, it now appeared that the housing authority was attempting to implement a dispersal policy. The lawyers contended that a Justice Department suit would put local officials on notice that the federal government was prepared to support such efforts and would serve to strengthen HUD's hand in dealing with similar problems around the country.[66] The recommendation was rejected, and the case was not filed.

Even in the less sensitive—and less important—area of discrimination suits against private persons, Justice Department activity was restricted. A small staff limited the department's ability to discover and eliminate patterns of housing discrimination,[67] and the number of such suits actually dropped off following Nixon's promise of vigorous enforcement—from almost forty in 1971 to only fifteen in 1972.

HUD's performance was similarly restrained. An examination of enforcement activity under the 1968 Civil Rights Act conducted by the Civil Rights Commission concluded that the HUD staff for dealing with discrimination complaints was "grossly inadequate" and that the staff's activities consisted almost exclusively of handling individual complaints of discrimination. Although the Civil Rights Act directed all executive departments and agencies to cooperate with HUD to further the goal of fair housing, the commission said that HUD had done little to bring about a cooperative effort among federal agencies. HUD acknowledged that it had a duty under the act to carry out investigations to identify patterns of housing discrimination, but it apparently lacked any plans for fulfilling that duty.[68]

Part two of Nixon's housing policy was to develop equal opportunity criteria for deciding who could participate in HUD programs. Under that approach, if the Warrens of the country failed to meet equal housing opportunity requirements, their HUD program applications would presumably not receive funding. The instrumentality for this approach was to be HUD's "project selection criteria," supplemented by its "affirmative marketing regulations."

The project selection criteria, which became effective in final form in February 1972 (although HUD began employing them informally the previous July), were a complicated set of eight standards to be used in deciding which of the housing proposals submitted to HUD should be funded. Proposed housing projects were to be evaluated and assigned "grades" of superior, adequate, or poor on each of the eight categories. Unless a proposal scored at least "adequate" on all eight, it was ineligible for financing. Those with the best grades would get the money.[69]

Seven of the criteria dealt with the need for low income housing, the amount of subsidized housing already in the area, relationships to orderly growth and development and to the physical environment, the potential for minority employment, and the ability of the applicant to build and manage the proposed project. The remaining criterion, "Minority Housing Opportunities," focused on the extent to which a proposed project would open up nonsegregated housing opportunities. A superior rating on that criterion would be given a project that would provide minority housing opportunities outside areas that presently had minority concentrations or that were already racially mixed, or to a project inside such an area if there were "sufficient, comparable opportunities" for minorities outside racially concentrated or mixed areas. An adequate rating on criterion two would be given to a project within a minority concentration area if necessary "to meet overriding housing needs."[70]

There were several serious problems with the project selection criteria. First, they were not really designed to assure that projects tending to promote dispersal would be approved. For example, a proposal that involved dispersal might receive a superior rating under one criterion but be barred by a poor rating under another having nothing to do with dispersal. On the other hand, proposals that were only adequate under the minority concentration criterion and did not promote dispersal could pass under the remaining criteria and be funded.

Second, the criteria could not assure that any proposals involving dispersal would be submitted in the first place. They afforded no way of overcoming local option vetoes of public housing or local exclusionary land use policies.

Finally, there was the matter of tenant selection, or owner selection in the section 235 home ownership program. Even if low income housing were constructed outside ghetto areas, there was no assurance that ghetto dwellers would ever have access to it. A study conducted by the Civil Rights Commission showed that most new units built under the section 235 program were being located in suburban areas and were being purchased largely by white buyers, while existing units were in inner city ghetto areas or in changing neighborhoods and were being purchased largely by minorities. The commission concluded that, instead of reversing the trend toward racial separation, the section 235 program was "contributing toward perpetuating and intensifying the familiar pattern of racially separate and unequal housing."[71]

Yet the administration was not unaware of what was happening. As early as the middle of 1970, the director of the section 235 program was quoted as saying that preliminary reports indicated that most black families using the section 235 subsidies were buying older homes in inner city areas, while whites appeared to be using them to buy new homes in the suburbs. He even acknowledged that some builders in suburban areas were promoting homes designed for the subsidy program in such a way as to attract only whites.[72]

Problems of this sort were supposed to be dealt with by the affirmative marketing regulations, a companion set of requirements to the project selection criteria. First published in draft form in June 1971 and in final form seven months later, the marketing regulations were designed to assure that minority groups were informed about HUD-assisted housing projects and given access to them. To accomplish this, they required all developers who were seeking FHA assistance in the form of subsidies or mortgage insurance to prepare an "affirmative fair housing marketing plan." The plan was supposed to spell out how the developer intended to execute an affirmative program to attract minority buyers or renters to his project through advertising, contacts with community fair housing groups and employers, hiring minroity persons as salesmen, and so forth.[73]

Like the project selection criteria, the marketing regulations contained major weaknesses. First, they did not require any goals or timetables. Second, they did not apply at all to existing housing. The more than 1.5 million homes and apartments FHA had already insured since 1934 were simply not covered by the new regulations. Neither did they apply to public housing. Although HUD did insist on a first-come first-served waiting list method of selecting public housing tenants, the requirement applied separately to each individual housing authority. Inner city residents on the waiting list of a central city housing authority were therefore not offered access to public housing projects that might be built by county or suburban authorities. Finally, only the applicant—that is, the owner or developer—was required to submit an affirmative marketing plan. The people who were frequently the prime forces in the marketing process, the brokers and real estate agents, were not obliged to submit plans or make any commitments. At best, their activities were covered only indirectly by the developer's plan.

HUD enforcement of the regulations was also inadequate. The conclusion by a HUD division director that the affirmative marketing program "has experienced a difficult history of development" was a paragon of understatement. HUD's monitoring also was totally inadequate. It was generally acknowledged in the housing field that the affirmative marketing regulations could be ignored with impunity. Nearly two years after the regulations become effective, HUD had received only about a third of the reports the regulations called for, and most of those were either incorrectly or only partially filled out. Sanctions for noncompliance, in the rare instances where noncompliance was brought to HUD's attention, were nonexistent. A check in the Chicago area, for example, showed that over half of the plans for the six county Chicago metropolitan area filed with HUD and approved by it did not even conform on paper to HUD regulations. Field inspections disclosed that over three-quarters of the developments lacked site signs and other advertising material called for by the regulations, none had their affirmative marketing plan available as the regulations specified, few of the sales and rental personnel (5 percent of those interviewed) had been given any instructions at all in implementing the affirmative marketing plan, and only one of the more than thirty community groups listed by developers had actually been contacted by a developer for referrals.[74]

The president had promised that his administration would carry out its program in a way that would be as helpful as possible to communities that were receptive to the expansion of housing opportunities. As administered, the affirmative-marketing regulations did virtually nothing to assure that HUD-assisted housing built in non-ghetto areas would be offered to ghetto residents. At best, the project selection criteria could be described as theoretically "helpful," but in practice hardly enough to persuade communities to be "receptive." Connecticut senator Abraham Ribicoff put it more bluntly—"eyewash" was his term. "The big problem," he said, "is precisely that the suburbs do not want the HUD programs—putting further conditions on the programs isn't going to change that fact of life."[75] The presidential promise that federal programs would be administered in ways that expanded equal housing opportunities thus turned out to be as empty as the promise of vigorous enforcement of anti-discrimination laws.[76]

The third and final part of the Nixon housing policy—relying upon and encouraging local communities to be creative and imaginative in making low income housing more widely available—was likewise a failure. Pointing out how difficult it was to attack traditional land use controls on the ground that they excluded the poor and minorities, David Trubek had, in effect, forecast "innovative negativism." Some months after Trubek delivered his analysis to the Civil Rights Commission, an important new weapon was added to the arsenal of exclusionary devices: controlling the *time* allowed for developing land even for a sanctioned purpose.

On May 3, 1972, the New York Court of Appeals, the highest court in the state and one of the most respected state courts in the land, upheld the legality of a "development timing" or "controlled growth" ordinance of the township of Ramapo.[77] Situated across the Hudson River a few miles north of the upper tip of Manhattan, Ramapo was a part of one of the wealthiest counties in the United States. The township, which included several incorporated villages and about sixty square miles of unincorporated land, had amended its zoning ordinance to prevent the development of any of its unincorporated land for new development unless the developer first received a special permit. The special permit would be granted only if the land to be developed had a minimum level of public facilities, such as sewers, parks, roads, and firehouses. These facilities were to be provided in accordance with a capital improvement program spread over eighteen years. In effect, the ordinance prevented the use of any particular parcel of land for new housing until the surrounding area had been provided with the needed facilities—which might take as long as eighteen years.[78]

The court of appeals opinion upholding the validity of the Ramapo ordinance acknowledged that a community's effort to control its own development could not ignore the rights of people in search of a place to live and that a scheme like Ramapo's, which restricted that search, was "inherently suspect." Nevertheless, the opinion held it was a reasonable device aimed not at exclusion but at "population assimilation." It was a legitimate way to provide for phased growth on a predetermined, rational basis.[79]

A time control ordinance is, of course, likely to have the same sort of impact on proposed low income housing developments as more traditional restrictions. As a dissenting opinion in the case pointed out, Ramapo's ordinance amounted to a substantial moratorium on growth and development for as much as a generation. Its exclusionary effect was therefore clear. It was a device, said the dissenting judge, that if adopted by a few more towns like Ramapo would result in "destroying the economy and channelling the demographic course of the State to suit their own insular interests."[80]

The *Ramapo* decision seemed to be a fulfillment of Trubek's prophecy about the role state courts would play in combating exclusionary land practices. If traditional land use controls were overthrown as too exclusionary, and if reducing lot size requirements from four to two acres or rezoning quarries for apartment use did not satisfy the courts or frustrate a proposed low income project, timed development ordinances could be enacted as still another line of defense against housing for the poor.

Later events similarly bore out Trubek's gloomy predictions about legislative initiatives. In 1969, Massachusetts had passed a law designed to open the suburbs to the poor. It gave the state a limited power to review local zoning decisions and, after hearings, to authorize housing projects for the poor even if local land control laws would be violated. Yet according to a survey by the *Wall Street Journal*, by the end of 1972 no housing had been provided under the law. The statute called for public or private developers to initiate challenges to local land control decisions, but, the *Journal* concluded, the suburbs had "managed to completely frustrate" those challenges by lengthy hearings, condemnation of land for parks, and other tactics.[81]

In New York, in the wake of the assassination of Martin Luther King in 1968, Governor Nelson Rockefeller had supported a law that authorized the New York Urban Development Corporation (UDC) to raise money to build low income housing and to override local zoning ordinances where necessary to do so. For three years, the UDC refrained from using its zoning override powers, building 95 percent of its housing in cities rather than in the suburbs. Finally, in 1971, the UDC proposed to construct housing over local opposition—a modest plan to build 100 apartment units in each of nine Westchester County towns. (Under UDC practice, only twenty apartments in each town would have been for the use of low income families and ten for the elderly.) The New York legislature promptly passed a bill to deprive the UDC of its zoning override power. Although Rockefeller was able to veto it in 1972, by the following year the political storm had grown too furious. The override power was withdrawn, and the Westchester County units were never built.

As a Republican state politician put it, the governor couldn't ride any longer with the UDC monkey on his back.[82]

Here and there throughout the country, a local legislature—a county board, for example—would pass a law requiring private developers to include a specified percentage of low income housing units in their proposals as a condition of receiving zoning or subdivision approval. But the prospects for this "inclusionary" approach were at best uncertain. One such ordinance, passed in 1971 in Fairfax County, Virginia, was later struck down by the supreme court of Virginia as invalid "socioeconomic zoning."[83] Moreover, the number of county boards or city councils that would pass such laws was not likely to be any larger, proportionately, than the number of "liberal" state legislatures, such as those in Massachusetts and New York, that could be persuaded to deal with the exclusionary problem, however tentatively, through state legislation.

THE REAL CITY

If the Nixon housing policy was having no discernible impact on residential segregation patterns, neither was it—or any other administration policy—responding in an effective way to the rapidly advancing deterioration of the inner city. In the 1960s, both landlords and tenants began to abandon some central city dwelling units, which more often than not were then promptly ravaged by vandals until nothing remained but empty hulks. By the end of the decade, the abandonment process was rampant. Hard figures were difficult to come by, but 1972 estimates ran as high as 100,000 abandoned dwellings in New York City alone and tens of thousands in other cities.[84] An article on abandonment in HUD's own house organ spoke of "entire cities . . . slipping into an apparent morass of irreversible poverty, crime, and hopelessness."[85] An NBC documentary, reporting that abandoned dwellings amounted to 6 percent of all the housing in St. Louis, foresaw the urban future as characterized by vast, fenced-in ghost towns within towns.

Romney had commissioned several studies on the causes of abandonment, and when the experts reported they appeared to be in general agreement. None was really certain about exactly why and how the abandonment process began, but the triggering event appeared to be an outmigration of white middle income or working class residents from a neighborhood, usually on the perimeter of a black ghetto. They were pulled by the attractions of outlying city areas or the suburbs, repelled by the fear of an expanding ghetto, or both. The homes and apartments that became available through this outward movement were in turn occupied by ghetto residents who moved into the better accommodations now available to them. But many were unable to pay the higher rents or to make mortgage payments sufficient to maintain the housing. The number of low-skilled jobs available in most central cities was dwindling due to technological change and the shift of jobs to the suburbs; low income minority persons, who had historically filled those jobs, now found their means of livelihood slipping away. Particularly in the latter part of the 1960s, as inflation rapidly raised maintenance costs, landlords found it more and more difficult to develop returns on their investments in properties whose tenants were now unable to pay adequate rents. "Red-lining" and "disinvestment"—the withdrawal of investment capital from a neighborhood thought to be deteriorating—inevitably preceded or accompanied the process. Maintenance then suffered, and physical deterioration began or accelerated.[86]

A key stage in the typical abandonment process was reached when the demand for any but low cost housing vanished. As whites who could afford better housing departed from what were still physically sound neighborhoods, middle class blacks began to move in, accelerating the departure of the remaining whites. Usually there were not enough middle income blacks to occupy all the vacant units, which were then sold or rented to the very poor, precipitating the departure of the middle income blacks, too. Neighborhoods being vacated by whites were thus soon overwhelmed by the demand for low cost housing by poor blacks. One of the HUD-sponsored studies said that in every case where high abandonment was found, a "crisis ghetto," which has experienced rapid change from white to black, was also found. "Crisis ghetto" was defined as a slum in which the residents were both poor and members of a minority group, population density was excessive, housing was deteriorating, incomes were declining, and indexes of social pathology were high or rising rapidly.[87]

Ironically, abandonment and neighborhood deterioration were aggravated by the special risk program enacted in 1968 to enable FHA to insure mortgages in inner city areas that had always been off limits to FHA insurance programs. Instead of interpreting the new law as providing authority to do away with location criteria only, FHA lowered its standards generally. Appraisers were now told that a property was to be rejected for insurance only where it had so deteriorated or was subject to such "hazards, noxious odors, grossly offensive sights or excessive noises that the livability of the property or the health and safety of its occupants are seriously affected."[88] Whereas FHA had previously refused to insure any property, however sound, in what were viewed as questionable neighborhoods, now

FHA would insure *every* property that was not in such condition or location that its "livability" or the health and safety of its occupants was "seriously" affected.

What ensued is what one would have expected: the special risk insurance program was abused by real estate speculators, who bought unsound houses cheaply, made quick cosmetic repairs, and resold them with FHA insurance at substantial markups to poor families unable to pay the costs of maintenance.[89] Abandonment or eventual default and foreclosure of the mortgage frequently ensued.[90]

Similar problems plagued the section 235 program where it had been applied to existing housing in the inner city rather than to new homes in the suburbs. A 1971 HUD report severely criticized administration of the program on a number of grounds, particularly the attitude of HUD employees that as long as poor people were getting better housing than they had had, the doctrine of "buyer beware" would be allowed to prevail. Normal FHA inspection requirements were ignored or relaxed, with the result that homes in poor condition were appraised at unjustifiably high values, producing high monthly mortgage payment figures for purchasers who would soon be confronted with large repair bills.

Many of the high appraisals under both the special risk and 235 programs resulted from a series of payoffs to FHA appraisers. The scandal made big headlines all across the country, put a number of FHA employees in jail, and blackened FHA's previously solid reputation for integrity. For example, a House committee staff report concluded that FHA had virtually ignored real estate speculation of the worst type and was insuring section 235 homes of such poor quality that there was no possibility that they could survive the life of the mortgage.[91]

Summing up FHA's role in congressional hearings and speeches, Romney said that rapid changes in FHA's mandate had thrust the agency into the inner city housing market without sufficient preparation at a time when that market consisted largely of older, physically deteriorating housing whose owners were increasingly unable or unwilling to invest heavily in maintenance. It was also a time when the value of inner city housing was dropping because of the departure of whites and the expansion of the ghetto. Moving FHA into the inner city was an effort to buck these trends. The hope was that providing home ownership opportunities could help stop advancing decay and slow outmigration, perhaps even lure private investment back. But by temporarily pumping up the value of properties that were declining in a conventional market sense, FHA actually stimulated blockbusting and helped spread the ghetto to adjoining neighborhoods.[92]

Moreover, Romney acknowledged, the intensified use of FHA programs in the inner city accelerated the flight to the suburbs instead of stemming it. Previously, FHA had only financed the purchase of a suburban home; now it was financing the purchaser's sale of his inner city home as well.[93] Without FHA's new inner city mortgage insurance programs, many whites who wished to move out of the central city might not so readily have found buyers for the homes they wanted to leave.[94] Without FHA's low down payment terms, many black buyers who were ill-equipped to deal with real estate speculators and unforeseen maintenance costs—and would soon be victims of deteriorating neighborhoods and abandonment— would have been unable to make the higher down payments required by conventional lenders. (One journal asserted that FHA was "financing the collapse of large residential areas of the center cities."[95])

Whatever the full explanation of the abandonment process, HUD began to be confronted with neighborhoods that looked as if they had been bombed out in an air raid. In addition, HUD was finding itself the repossessing owner (after FHA-insured mortgages had been defaulted) of vast numbers of slum properties. There were wry comments about HUD becoming a larger landowner than the Interior Department. Stung by criticism that under his administration FHA had poured federal credit into inner city areas and would end up with repossessed, vandalized structures, Romney said he had to decide "whether I am going to tell twenty cities in this country, 'there are certain areas of your city we are not going to put any more money in because it will be wasted, because the social conditions and other conditions do not justify it.'" He would be accused, he said, of dictating the death of those central city areas, but he was telling the Congress that "they are not viable and they are not areas of acceptable risk."[96]

Public housing was encountering similarly intractable problems in the inner city. The very poor who now dominated the rent rolls were unable to pay even public housing rents. In 1969, Congress had taken account of the change in tenancy by passing the so-called Brooke Amendment (named after its principal sponsor, Massachusetts Senator Edward Brooke), which limited public housing rents to one-fourth of the tenant's income and authorized federal operating subsidies to cover the resulting housing authority deficits. But because of the large subsidies such an approach required, the Office of Management and Budget (OMB) was soon unwilling to release funds appropriated for the purpose. A House committee staff report said the Brooke Amendment had helped turn public housing into a welfare program by undermining its principle of providing low rent housing on a businesslike basis; it estimated that one-seventh of public housing tenants were paying no rent at all.[97] Making clear his displeasure with the results of the Brooke Amendment, the president requested only $170 million in operating subsidies for fiscal 1973 against an anticipated need of $325 million. Caught in a squeeze between the rent ceilings imposed by Congress and inflation-fueled operating deficits the OMB refused to pay, public housing authorities soon began to use up their reserves and head toward bankruptcy.

In addition to financial difficulties, the social problems public housing had been facing continued to worsen. High vacancy rates— virtual abandonment in some cases—became prevalent. The situation was epitomized dramatically in March 1972, when, in an effort to ameliorate problems by reducing population density, an eleven story, structurally sound, high rise building in St. Louis's Pruitt-Igoe project was dynamited to the ground. The project had won architectural awards when it was built fewer than twenty years earlier, but its thirty-three buildings, housing over 10,000 people, had become a disastrous concentration of very poor, troubled families whose needs and problems had simply overwhelmed the capability of government to maintain a viable environment. In a report accompanying pictures showing the huge, barren-looking structure crumbling into rubble, the *National Journal* summarized the Pruitt-Igoe story this way:

> As the very poor began to dominate the rent rolls and the social services began to collapse, the working poor began to leave the project in droves. Into the vacuum poured a host of the worst urban ills—violence, vandalism and drug addiction—all on a scale so great that the local government could not even maintain law and order.[98]

It was not surprising that public housing was no longer being built in any significant amounts in the central city. The project selection criteria now precluded locating new public housing exclusively in the ghetto, while opposition to sites in outlying neighborhoods could most easily be overcome if the projects were designed for the elderly (objections to which had always been less intense than to projects designed to house poor families). New public housing in the central city was now principally for the elderly; for the rest, public housing had become mostly a program for small towns.

It was thus rapidly becoming apparent that HUD's housing programs, the newer ones of the late 1960s as well as public housing, were not only failing to cure the festering disease afflicting the central cities but in some ways were actually contributing to it. Yet in

testifying before a House subcommittee, Romney maintained housing was not the cause of the problem:

> The forces that cause abandonment and decline in our central cities are
> not primarily physical, but are primarily human, social, and governmen-
> tal. ... FHA housing programs did not start block busting. Housing didn't
> take the jobs away. Housing didn't reduce the population. Housing didn't
> reduce the public services. Housing didn't destroy the quality of educa-
> tion in the schools. Housing didn't bring the drug addiction in. Deep
> social changes are at work that have little if anything to do with hous-
> ing. ... [I]f we had been able to avoid all of the mistakes that have
> occurred, we would still be up against the larger tragedy—the growing
> "critical mass" of people with problems in our central cities.[99]

At the time of the president's housing policy statement, Romney
had talked about the project selection criteria as a means of achieving
"meaningful progress." Now, facing the "critical mass" problem,
Romney's theme became the "real city"—a Romney phrase for the
central city and its surrounding urbanized area—and the need for
metropolitanwide solutions to "real city" problems. Romney began
to criss-cross the country with the message that central city housing
problems resulted from all the social, economic, and physical problems afflicting urban areas; that multiple, autonomous governments
prevented the development of metropolitan solutions for what were
really metropolitan problems; and that the powers of the states,
which were responsible for the creation and supervision of local governments, had to be exercised to overcome the "Balkanization" of
the metropolitan community.[100] Housing was "*the* single most
important question when you're dealing with community development," but the problem of housing could not be solved in the city.
"An effective solution will only come about when various jurisdictions and individuals within a metropolitan area determine through
careful, objective planning the best approach to the equitable dispersal of housing."[101] "[I]t is time to recognize that the effort to
meet central city needs separately from suburban needs is as futile as
it would have been for the United States to have tried to continue as
a Nation under the articles of confederation."[102]

Romney's metropolitan theme was not new. As long ago as 1965,
President Johnson had told the Congress that its first task was to
recognize that the city and its suburbs constituted a single metropolitan area, and he suggested that Congress could require metropolitan
planning as a condition for federal aid.[103]

In 1971, the Housing Subcommittee of the House Committee on
Banking and Currency, the seedbed for housing legislation in the

House of Representatives, had begun to develop new legislation designed to promote metropolitanwide dispersal plans. The idea, pushed most strongly by Congressman Ashley, was to restructure the delivery of federal housing subsidies. Money would go to metropolitan housing agencies, which would then allocate the funds to public and private developers in accordance with a plan the agencies were to prepare for low and moderate income housing. Monetary incentives would encourage the states to pass laws establishing such metropolitan agencies. Suburbs would be encouraged to participate in the plan by a grant of up to $3,000 per unit of subsidized housing.[104]

Still, the Ashley proposal was extremely limited. It did not require a local community to accept a project called for by a metropolitan plan. Neither could the metropolitan agencies themselves move beyond planning into the actual development of housing. The plan might be metropolitan in scope, but local autonomy over implementation remained. And if the metropolitan agency was not created in the first place, the only federal recourse was a denial of funds. Because of these limitations, some civil rights organizations actually opposed the Ashley bill, even though it was at least a small step in the direction of involving the suburbs in the racial and economic problems oppressing the cities.

Romney opposed it too. Testifying before the subcommittee in August 1971, he commended its recognition "of the essentiality of metropolitan action in meeting housing and other community needs."[105] But he could not support the subcommittee's proposal.[106] The problem was that the Ashley bill was not revenue sharing—it employed the traditional grant mechanism that required applicants to meet federal guidelines to receive federal money. Since such an approach could not be squared with the administration's New Federalism philosophy and its related revenue-sharing proposals, Romney could not favor it.

ROMNEY—OUT LIKE A LAMB

What then was to be done? Romney's answer was not new legislation, or even a new administrative initiative to empower HUD and state and local governments to deal with community needs on a metropolitan basis, but persuasion. In January 1972, Romney announced that he was going to convene meetings in Boston, Detroit, Philadelphia, St. Louis, and Wilmington. He would call together the major local government and civic leaders in each of those communities to attend "TOP" meetings. "TOP" stood for The Option Process, and at the TOP meetings, Romney would present the local leaders with an option: Did they want to utilize federal programs on a real city, metropolitanwide basis, or did they want to continue to use the existing network of fragmented local government bodies? The choice, Romney would urge, was between racial and economic polarization that would pit the central city against the suburbs, and a united effort to build a real city, a human community of opportunity for all.[107]

TOP was of course as foredoomed to failure as the president's call of the previous year for local "creativity and imagination" in dealing with racial and economic division. For the practical political problems Romney had confronted in Warren, TOP had nothing to offer but good intentions and the prospect of some more federal dollars for "good" communities—the same dollars Romney had seen Warren reject.

Nevertheless Romney played out his role. The rhetoric of the real city and the option process blurred into the rhetoric of New Federalism and revenue sharing, which in turn—as the summer wore on—became the rhetoric of the 1972 reelection campaign. Romney, stumping for real city solutions, soon became Romney stumping for Nixon's reelection. It was clear that Romney would not be part of the new administration. During his remaining two months after the election, while Nixon fired Father Hesburgh and selected a new HUD secretary, he prepared a summary of the accomplishments of his four years in office that described HUD's achievements in housing production, the issuance of the project selection criteria, and a miscellany of other matters. The Option Process was not mentioned.[108] Everything was now New Federalism, revenue sharing, and turning over to local government all manner of problems, including the problem of racial polarization. Indeed, a virtue was made of failure. HUD's failure proved that the federal government could not do the job, that only local government could be successful, and that the right course was New Federalism and revenue sharing.

To prepare for the new way, the old way first had to be discarded. The job was given to Romney. On January 7, 1973, at the Astrodome in Houston, before the annual convention of the association of home builders, George Romney delivered the funeral oration for the subsidized housing programs—and for good measure some of the community development programs—he had been administering for four years. A "moratorium" had been placed on new commitments for all four of the subsidized housing programs: public housing, section 235, section 236, and rent supplements. There would also be a "holding action" on community development programs (such as urban renewal, Model Cities, and water and sewer grants) until they were incorporated into a revenue-sharing bill. The time had come "to pause, to re-evaluate, and to seek out better ways."[109] Public housing had become a menace to the neighborhoods in which it was located. The section 235 and 236 programs were too frequently abused. Central cities were becoming concentration points for problem families, while stable families moved to the outskirts or to the suburbs. Housing programs, by themselves, were not the solution. "We need a new, integrated system of housing and social service at the local level, which only State, local and private agencies will ever be able to accomplish."[110] That was why the "urgent emphasis" in the Nixon administration on strengthening local effort was of such "historic" importance. Somehow New Federalism would help us face one of the great traumas of our time—what was happening to American cities.

It was also essential, however, to enlighten the people concerning that trauma. That was what George Romney wanted now to do, as he had told the president. As soon as his successor was confirmed he would organize a citizens' movement to help in the educational task. Thus did George Romney end his service as secretary of housing and urban development by terminating the subsidized housing programs that four years earlier he had said could ease racial tensions, bring millions of neglected Americans into the mainstream of American life, and save America's cities.[111]

※ *Chapter Three*

Legislative Pottage

Although Watergate would force a premature termination
of his second administration, Richard Nixon remained in
office long enough to bring about a drastic change in the
nation's housing policy. The administration's new housing proposal
involved a shift from subsidizing the construction of new housing to
subsidizing rents. If the poor were given the financial means to increase their purchasing power for housing, the administration theo-
rized, they would then be able to secure their own housing from the
private sector and not have to rely on relatively more expensive
subsidized new construction. Following intense bargaining with
Congress, the administration essentially got its way, and in August
1974, a new Housing and Community Development Act—the last
major piece of legislation to emerge from the now discredited Nixon
administration—was enacted. Perhaps the "most noteworthy domestic triumph of the Nixon philosophy," one observer called it. Despite
some positive innovations, however, the new law seemed unlikely to
be effective in combating metropolitan apartheid.

PRELUDE

The audacity of the Nixon administration's order suspending subsidized housing programs was stunning. Nearly forty years of national
policy to subsidize the construction of new housing for the poor was
simply wiped out by presidential fiat because the president did not
think the programs were working well. When exercised on such a
scale and for such reasons, the unilateral impoundment of funds

authorized by Congress cut deeply into the constitutional system of checks and balances. If a president could simply refuse unilaterally to spend congressionally appropriated funds, he would in effect be possessed of an absolute veto not conferred by the Constitution.[1]

Notwithstanding these concerns, few congressmen chose to make a major issue of the president's power to terminate the housing programs. In the hearings on the nomination of James T. Lynn as Romney's successor, Senator William Proxmire argued that if the Senate confirmed Lynn, it would be tacitly approving a usurpation of its constitutional prerogatives.[2] But most senators apparently felt that Lynn's nomination should be considered on the nominee's own merits, and so at the end of January, Lynn was confirmed by a voice vote on the Senate floor. The president had won handily the first round in his effort to shape a new housing policy.

Soon the advantage was pressed. In a radio address in March, the president announced that the urban crisis was over; crime statistics were improving and civil disorders had abated: "The ship of state is back on an even keel, and we can put behind us the fear of capsizing." In that context, Nixon made two announcements. First, it was time for a new declaration of independence for state and local governments; revenue sharing would give "grassroots governments a new chance to stand on their own feet." A good first step was the general revenue-sharing bill signed into law the preceding October, providing state and local governments with $30 billion over a five year period to use as they wished. Now the time was ripe to move on to special revenue sharing. The administration would therefore shortly propose several special revenue-sharing programs, including one for community development that would replace seven "outmoded" urban development programs, among them urban renewal and Model Cities.

Second, wasteful and obsolete federal housing programs had to be replaced with programs that would work. There were too many basic defects in the existing legislation. Too often the needy were not the primary beneficiaries; the programs were riddled with inequities; costs per unit of housing were too high. The administration would therefore continue the moratorium on section 235, section 236, public housing, and rent supplements—the four "ineffective" subsidy programs. Meanwhile, it would be one of the president's highest domestic priorities during the year to develop new housing policies. Under the direction of Lynn a major HUD study was already underway. Within six months the president would submit his housing policy recommendations to Congress based on the results of that study.[3]

Railing against the administration's "meat ax" approach, Senator Proxmire insisted that the HUD study was a facade because the administration had already made up its mind to kill the housing subsidy programs.[4] But in March hearings on the moratorium[5] a House subcommittee failed to recommend legislation to resume the suspended programs. In May, the House extended legal authority for the section 235 and 236 programs, again without requiring resumption,[6] and in June, the HUD appropriations bill was passed with no mention of resumption.[7] Again, the administration had won; Congress would await HUD's study and the president's recommendations.[8]

Six months later, in September 1973, the president announced[9] that, based on HUD's now completed study of federal housing policy—a long, detailed volume called *Housing in the Seventies*[10]—he was now ready to make his housing recommendations. In spite of the "proud record" of achievement in recent decades, the president said, the housing subsidy programs were "failures.": First, they produced poor quality housing. Although some public housing projects were impressive, too many were monstrous and depressing, concentrating poor people in one place, isolating them from the mainstream of American life. Second, subsidized housing programs were inequitable because they arbitrarily selected only a few of the eligible low income families to live in federally supported housing projects. Third, subsidizing the production of new dwellings was wasteful because it concentrated on new construction—the most expensive means of housing the poor—while ignoring the potential for using good existing housing. Finally, the president criticized the lack of choice under current subsidy programs. Housing was offered on a "take-it-or-leave-it" basis, in effect depriving families of the right to choose where they wished to live.

The main flaw in the old approach, the president said, was its underlying assumption that the basic problem of the poor was a lack of housing rather than a lack of income. The government had been attacking the housing problem by subsidizing builders directly and the poor only indirectly; it had not been treating the root cause—the inability to pay for housing. In place of that old approach, many had suggested direct cash assistance to the poor in the form of a housing payment that would enable poor families to select their own homes and apartments in the private market. Such a dollar payment would make up the difference between the rent a poor family could afford to pay and the market cost of decent housing. The new HUD housing policy study indicated that such an approach might be the most promising way to achieve decent housing for all poor families. It was an approach, the president said, that would eventually "get the Federal Government out of the housing business."

However, one had to proceed with caution, the president went on, seeking answers to a number of critical questions. Could a direct cash assistance program be put into practical operation? What relationship should it have to welfare payments? What would be its impact on inflation? These and other issues required close examination. What was really needed was more study. Some of the needed information would come from the results of the continuing "housing allowance" experiments authorized by Congress in 1970. (A "housing allowance" was a form of cash assistance that restricted the use of the subsidy to rent or home ownership payments.[11]) By late 1974 or early 1975, the president believed, the information needed to make a final decision on the direct cash assistance approach would be in hand.

Meanwhile, the need to provide housing for the poor remained, and in some places, there would simply not be a sufficient supply of housing for the forseeable future. Therefore, the president would authorize a limited amount of new subsidized construction during the remainder of fiscal year 1974 under the section 23 leasing program. With certain revisions, this program could be administered in a way that employed some of the principles of direct cash assistance.

Section 23 had been added to the public housing law in 1965 to authorize housing authorities to lease apartments in privately owned buildings at market rents, and then to sublease the apartments at lower rents to poor families.[12] The subsidy, which the federal government paid to the housing authority, was the difference between the rent paid by the authority to the private landlord and the lower rent it charged to the tenant. Later, HUD had stretched the language of the section by creating a "construction for leasing" program that Congress ratified by an amendment to section 23 that allowed housing authorities to lease apartments in newly constructed privately owned buildings for up to twenty years.[13] (The prospect of long-term leases was supposed to stimulate private construction.) The section 23 construction program thus meshed nicely with the principles of direct cash assistance because it did not involve outright construction subsidies.[14]

Racial and economic separation and housing dispersal were not discussed by the president. The closest his message came to those subjects was the statement that housing policy could not be considered separately from other economic, social, and physical aspects of community development. Those "crucial relationships," the president said, would be addressed in a report on urban growth to be submitted to Congress some time the following year. (Watergate intervened, and Nixon never did submit the promised report.)

Congressional critics protested vehemently the president's decision to continue studying housing policy while essentially continuing the moratorium. The administration had labored and brought forth not a mouse but the promise of a mouse, said Representative Henry Reuss of the Housing Subcommittee. Senator Proxmire called it a "sad, brutal fact" that the historic pledge of a decent home in a suitable environment had been abandoned.[15] But such rhetoric did not produce a congressional majority to resume the old subsidy programs.

Soon after the president's September 1973 message, the administration's housing proposal was sent to Congress. It would eliminate all construction subsidies except a modified section 23 leasing program and would expand housing allowance experiments. Pending the results of these experiments, section 23 would be employed as the sole vehicle for housing subsidies. Among other section 23 changes, the local housing authority would be eliminated as a lessee, and new construction would be allowed only where HUD determined that there was an inadequate supply of existing housing. The bill asserted that the suspended housing subsidy programs were "wasteful and inequitable," and it elminated the goal of twenty-six million housing units established by the Housing and Urban Development Act of 1968.[16]

DEMOCRATIC CHALLENGE

Earlier, Senate Democrats had introduced their own housing and community development bills. Essentially, the democratic-sponsored housing bill would continue existing construction subsidy programs, although with some important changes. The proposed community development bill adopted what had come to be called the "block grant" approach, transforming the separate urban development programs into a single community development program that gave the recipient community great flexibility in deciding how to spend its federal money. Unlike revenue sharing, however, the funds had to be applied for, and some federal program requirements were imposed. Significantly, the funding application had to describe not only the community's development plans but also the actions to be taken to meet *housing* needs, particularly of low or moderate income families—including those "who may reasonably be expected to seek housing in the community."[17]

In September, a combined community development and housing bill was introduced in the House. Known as the Barrett-Ashley bill after its two principal sponsors, Congressmen William Barrett of Pennsylvania and Thomas Ashley of Ohio, it scrapped all existing programs and used the block grant approach for both housing and community development. A modified section 23 leasing program would be the major form of housing subsidy. Like the proposed Senate bill, Barrett-Ashley also linked housing and community development so that applicants for community development grants would have to show that they had formulated a program "which includes any activities necessary to provide adequate housing and a suitable living environment for low and moderate income persons. . . ."[18]

Both the Senate and the Barrett-Ashley bills provided some clues as to the prevailing attitudes in Congress. First, New Federalism had taken hold to a considerable extent. The separate urban development programs of old, each with its own array of requirements and regulations, seemed likely to be done away with. In their place would be a single community development grant that could be used for a wide variety of activities at the discretion of the local community. Although a block grant mechanism would still subject community development funds to general federal guidelines, eliminating the separate federal programs would represent a long step in returning decisionmaking authority to local governments as the president had urged.

Second, community development funds would be made available based on a formula, not on the traditional first-come, first-served principle. Community development funds thus would be spread more widely through cities across the country, not concentrated heavily among those most sophisticated in applying for federal grants. Third, there seemed to be a willingness to link subsidized housing and community development activites, possibly requiring the applicant to make a specific commitment to provide housing for the poor as a condition of receiving community development funds. Fourth, traditional subsidized housing programs were in trouble; although the Senate was pushing for their retention, the Barrett-Ashley bill lined up with the administration in virtually abandoning them altogether. The administration's cash assistance idea was gaining adherents.

Finally, a metropolitan approach to housing and community development problems seemed to be absent from everyone's agenda, despite George Romney's identification, only a year before, of "Balkanization" as the key problem to be faced. Testifying about the Barrett-Ashley bill, former HUD Secretary Robert Weaver strongly criticized the bill's failure to adopt metropolitanwide planning. Pointing out that grants would be made to suburban governments only if the suburbs elected to apply for them, Weaver argued that suburbs would not apply. Moreover, he said, the proposed allocation formula for housing funds, based on factors such as population, poverty, and the amount of overcrowding, would result in the bulk of the funds going to central cities. Even suburbs that were interested in providing housing for the poor would not be entitled to much money if their populations were relatively low, if they were relatively affluent, or if they had little overcrowding. The effect of this formula, coupled with the absence of a metropolitan approach, Weaver said, would be to accept "the status quo of racial and economic stratification in metropolitan areas and assure that this pattern is perpetuated and even intensified."[19]

With only a few dissenting votes, the Senate's Housing Subcommittee reported out a consolidated housing and community development bill, which the full Senate passed in March.[20] The block grant approach for community development programs was adopted, while the subsidized housing programs were essentially continued, although with some important changes, such as broadening the range of incomes among families in subsidized housing.[21] However, Weaver's plea for a metropolitan approach was ignored. Instead, the bill authorized HUD, on a demonstration basis, to assist localities that would undertake areawide dispersed housing programs. The committee report "emphasized" that nothing in the section "force[d] any metropolitan area to undertake any program which deals with the location of low- and moderate-income housing," but merely provided HUD with demonstration money to assist areas "which decide on their own to undertake this approach."[22]

The administration had perceived the Senate as unfriendly territory and did not fight strenuously there to obtain a bill more to its liking. (Lynn simply announced he would recommend a veto of anything like the Senate bill.) In the House, the story was different. During the spring, Lynn himself or his undersecretary appeared almost daily at the deliberations of the Housing Subcommittee, where Lynn and Ashley negotiated like parties to a business deal. In the end, Lynn got most of what he wanted on housing—termination of all construction subsidies except the modified section 23 program—while agreeing to accept block grants instead of revenue sharing for community development funds. On the last day of April, the housing subcommittee unanimously reported out a modified Barrett-Ashley bill, which, after action by the full committee, passed the House on June 20, 1974.[23]

Of the many significant differences between the House and Senate bills, the biggest was the Senate's insistence on continuing the construction subsidy programs. Through July and the beginning of

August, as the conference committee met without reaching agreement, it seemed possible that disagreement on that issue would sink the legislation, for by now it appeared that both the House and Senate would soon be caught up in impeachment proceedings. Then in early August, after what a Senate subcommittee staff member called one of the longest and most difficult conferences in housing legislation history, a compromise was finally reached—mostly it was the Senate conferees who did the compromising—and an agreed bill was reported out of committee. It quickly passed both the House and Senate in the middle of August, and on August 22, 1974, less than two weeks after the resignation of Richard Nixon, President Gerald Ford affixed his signature. The Housing and Community Development Act of 1974, as the new law was called,[24] comprised 108 pages of small type that radically restructured the nation's housing and urban development programs.

NEARLY COMPLETE VICTORY

The new legislation represented a nearly complete victory in the administration's long battle to end the traditional subsidized housing programs. Theoretically, the section 235 and 236 programs were kept alive, a concession extracted by the Senate conferees, but the law did not require HUD to use them at all, and Lynn made it clear that he did not intend to do so. Conventional public housing was also kept alive technically, but appropriations for it were miniscule.

The new and virtually exclusive housing subsidy was basically what the administration had wanted: a modified section 23 leasing program that eliminated construction subsidies and essentially relied on families to find their own housing in the private market. Under the new program, now lodged in section 8 of the housing law,[25] an eligible family was supposed to locate an available apartment, that is, to find a private landlord willing to rent to it under the section 8 program (including, if the family and landlord were agreeable, the apartment in which the family was then living). The landlord was then to enter into a lease directly with the tenant, not with the local housing authority as under the old section 23 program. Rental charges could not exceed the "fair market rents" to be established by HUD for a range of apartment sizes for each metropolitan area. The assisted family would pay between 15 and 25 percent of the family income toward the rent, the exact amount to be determined by HUD regulations, and the balance—called "housing assistance payments"—would be paid to the landlord directly by the local housing authority administering the program. Landlords were free to participate in the program or not as they chose, and those who chose to do so were also free to select or reject tenants; only racial, not economic, discrimination was prohibited.

Newly constructed or rehabilitated apartments could also be rented under the section 8 program, but a clear preference was expressed for leasing in existing buildings. Building new apartments for leasing would be permitted only in areas where HUD determined there was a shortage of existing housing. Morevoer, construction or rehabilitation costs could not be subsidized by HUD (although with HUD's approval the contract to make assistance payments could be pledged as security for a construction loan and the mortgage could be insured by FHA).

"[P]romoting economically mixed housing" was one of the stated purposes of the section 8 program, the first time Congress had addressed economic as well as racial segregation. Families whose incomes reached as high as 80 percent of the median income in the area were to be eligible for section 8 housing (although 30 percent of the units had to go to those whose incomes were less than 50 percent of the median). Since 80 percent of the median income figure in large cities ranged up to around $12,000 for a family of four, compared to median incomes of less than half that amount for families in public and section 236 housing, under the new law housing subsidies would go to a much wider income spectrum than in the past.[26]

In addition, local veto powers of the sort that had hamstrung the public housing and rent supplement programs—cooperation agreements for the former and approval resolutions for the latter—were eliminated. Although local land use powers such as zoning were unaffected, section 8 housing would not be subject to the specific local approval requirements that had plagued those earlier programs.

The community development part of the law was more of a compromise. As the administration had wanted, the old individual urban development programs (urban renewal, Model Cities, neighborhood facilities, open space, historic preservation, urban beautification, and water and sewer facilities) were eliminated. Now all were consolidated into a single federal grant for community development that could be used for a wide variety of "eligible" activities at the discretion of the local government.[27] Most community development grant amounts would be computed under a statutory formula based on population, poverty, and housing overcrowding.[28] Thus, local communities would be "entitled" to community development funds, as under revenue sharing.

However, the new law adopted the "block grant" approach rather than the revenue-sharing mechanism the administration had wanted.

Local governments would be required to apply for funds under an application procedure intended to assure that the money would be used consistently with community development objectives stated in the law. Still, the procedure was much simpler than under the former, individual programs. HUD was required to approve the community development plan included with the application unless the plan was "plainly inconsistent" with generally available facts or the activities proposed were "plainly inappropriate" to meet the stated needs and objectives. Moreover, the community merely had to certify its compliance with certain additional federal requirements, such as civil rights laws and other federal regulations.[29]

A significant feature of the community development grant application process was the totally new requirement of a "housing assistance" plan. This plan was to include an assessment of the housing needs of poor persons "residing in or expected to reside in the community," an annual goal for the number of dwelling units or families to be assisted to meet the estimated need, and a specification of "general locations" for any proposed new or rehabilitated housing.[30] Through its housing assistance plan, the local government was supposed to relate its proposed community development activities to an overall plan for housing poor families who already lived in the community or who might be expected to reside there in the future. The plan was to govern HUD's approval of proposals from private developers or local housing authorities for subsidized housing. Thus, for the first time in the history of federal urban development and housing programs, the two activities were to be formally and specifically linked as part of a rational, overall plan. One of the new law's stated objectives was said to be to foster the undertaking of housing and community development activities "in a coordinated and mutually supportive manner."[31]

DISPERSAL—THE MISSING LINK

Several features of the new law made its impact on housing dispersal doubtful. First, the extent to which section 8 could actually stimulate new construction was uncertain, since the law only provided for subsidizing rents, not building costs. Second, Robert Weaver's concern about the formula for distributing housing funds between the central cities and the suburbs was not dealt with. Although HUD was given some discretion in allocating section 8 funds among communities, it was nonetheless directed to take account of data on population, poverty, housing overcrowding, vacancy rates, and the amount of substandard housing.[32] As Weaver pointed out, collectively those factors would tend to support far heavier allocations to central cities than to suburbs. Obviously, the concentration of the poor in central cities was not going to be relieved if those selfsame cities received the bulk of housing subsidy funds.

Third, the link between community development and housing appeared to be largely illusory; it did not assure that any subsidized housing would actually be provided in communities that received community development funds. Although the act required an applicant for community development money to prepare a housing assistance plan, it did not require the plan to be carried out. Nothing required that section 8 housing assistance payments actually be made in the amounts and places called for by a local community's housing plan. In fact, given the structure of the law, it was difficult to conceive how any such assurance could be provided in the normal situation. Applicants for the two sources of funds—community development and housing assistance—would ordinarily be different entities. The typical community development applicant would be the local city government (states and so-called urban counties could also apply), while local housing authorities or private owners and developers would generally be the applicants for housing assistance funds. (Occasionally, a local city government might itself engage in housing development.) Once a local government prepared a satisfactory housing plan, its housing "obligation" would presumably be satisfied. The local government appeared to have no duty, or power for that matter, to see to it that housing authorities or private owners and developers applied for and used any housing assistance funds whatever. Even the vague reference, in the early Senate and Barrett-Ashley bills, to "actions" or "activities" to be undertaken to meet housing needs was missing from the final version of the new law; the 1974 act spoke not of housing "activities" but of a housing "plan."

Perhaps Congress expected that the mere existence of an official local housing plan, coupled with elimination of the local veto power, would remove many of the obstacles to dispersal of low income housing. If a local government wanted community development money, it would now have to prepare a housing assistance plan, and to be realistic the plan would presumably have to include some subsidized housing. Under the new law, the local government could then object to proposals by a housing authority or private developer only on the ground that it was inconsistent with its plan, and even that objection could be overridden if HUD found no inconsistency.[33]

But the fact remained that the housing plan was drawn by a body that, under the law, appeared to have no obligation to execute it. Implementation would depend heavily on the ability of poor families to find private landlords willing to rent existing homes and apartments to them. One could well be skeptical about how many landlords of existing housing in nonghetto areas would be willing to rent to ghetto dwellers, or about how many inner city families would even be motivated to search for apartments outside ghetto and ghetto-fringe neighborhoods.[34] As for new construction (where authorized by HUD), that depended on the voluntary decision of public and private housing developers. And since the city was not required to cooperate with a proposed new section 8 development by rezoning or relaxing other land use controls (just as the 1974 act did not call on the city to lift a corporate finger to achieve the housing goal it had specified in its housing plan, neither did it require the city to assist housing developers who were trying to achieve that same goal), the old land use control games could apparently by played just as effectively under the new law as under the old.

Finally, the new law virtually ignored any metropolitan approaches to housing problems. Neither metropolitan housing agencies nor metropolitan planning was mandated. The closest the new law came to recognizing the "real city" nature of the housing problem was to provide a monetary incentive for purely voluntary areawide housing plans. Indeed, because of its requirement that housing plans be prepared separately by each local jurisdiction applying for community development funds, it could be said that the new law actually moved away from, not toward, a metropolitan approach.

Abandoning a metropolitan thrust was not accidental. In mid-1973, as the administration's housing policy began to crystalize, some of the staff of the House of Representatives' Housing Subcommittee held a strategy session at Hilton Head in South Carolina to consider some key questions about new housing legislation. A consensus developed that the time was ripe to try to link community development with subsidized housing. But the staff also agreed that one such controversial matter was enough freight to pile into a new legislative vessel; a second, Ashley's old metropolitan housing agency proposal, should therefore be left ashore, at least temporarily. Ashley's acquiescence in the views of the staff thus led directly to the result that the major new thrust of the housing law as eventually enacted was the linkage between community development and housing, not metropolitan arrangements.[35]

Early experience under the new act was not encouraging. Because of the time consumed in grinding out new regulations, the section 8 program did not really get underway until the spring of 1975. A year and a half later, by September 30, 1976, about 60,000 existing housing units had been leased, and work had begun on about 15,000 units to be newly constructed or substantially rehabilitated. However, the absence of metropolitan arrangements made it difficult for the participants in the existing housing program to move to another local jurisdiction; about half remained in their own apartments, and there were virtually no moves by minority families to nonminority communities. And many of the "newly" leased units were merely paper "conversions" of leases under the old section 23 program, now shifted to come under section 8. As for new construction, indications were that, without construction subsidies, inflated building costs had outstripped the ability of the private housing industry to produce any significant amount of new subsidized housing. In a break with the administration, the president of the Federal National Mortgage Association criticized the section 8 program as lacking in the incentives needed to create new subsidized housing units.[36]

Nevertheless, Carla Hills, who succeeded James Lynn as HUD secretary after Lynn had been in office less than two years, held to the view that existing housing should be the primary source of shelter for poor families. While continuing to express optimism about the ability of the section 8 program to produce large numbers of subsidized units, she acknowledged that her information on reported vacancy rates was inadequate. It was "appalling," she said, that "we are making tough policy calls [presumably the continued emphasis on existing housing] without the kind of data we need."[37]

Equally troubling were the indications that HUD was paying very little attention to the administration of the housing assistance plans. During the first year of the new community development program, HUD routinely approved housing plans that failed to live up to the requirements of the new law. Plans that used grossly inadequate data to describe lower income housing needs, adopted low income housing goals only (or primarily) for the elderly rather than for poor families, made no provision at all for subsidized housing, and ignored altogether the directive to avoid concentrating subsidized housing in low income or minority areas still received HUD approval.[38] In addition, HUD ignored negative comments on housing assistance plans made by regional planning agencies.[39] (Some communities, Warren, Michigan, among them, chose not to apply for community development funds to which they were "entitled" on a formula basis because they feared that getting involved with federal community development plans would somehow leave them less free to resist subsidized housing.[40]) Although there were indications that HUD would be stricter in the second year,[41] the early experience gave little encouragement that the section 8 program could provide significant amounts of subsidized housing or, even if that were accomplished, that it could do so in ways that would tend to reduce metropolitan apartheid.

In some respects, notably the creation of even a weak link between housing and community development, the new law reached toward higher ground. In addition, its findings and stated purposes could not be faulted. The act strongly emphasized helping the poor—community development and housing activities had to be primarily for their benefit. Moreover, the act expressed both dispersal and economic integration objectives through its finding that the problems of urban areas arose in significant measure from "the concentration of persons of lower income in central cities," and its objective of reducing the "isolation of income groups within communities."[42]

But the essential thrust of the new law was to utilize the existing housing stock and to do so in accordance with local, not metropolitan, plans. It was extremely unlikely that any significant amount of dispersal could be achieved with that approach. As George Romney had said a few years earlier, it was impossible to effect any substantial change in the pattern of residential segregation without an increase in overall housing supply, and that meant construction subsidies.[43] In addition, housing and community development problems could not be effectively confronted without metropolitanwide plans for housing dispersal. For all of its innovations and high-sounding language, a law that failed to assure a significant amount of new construction and that lacked a metropolitan approach was not likely to change residential segregation patterns.

Chapter Four

Even to Avoid Disaster

As the promise of the 1968 housing law began to fade, so also did the hope that the courts might overcome local hostility and require some housing dispersal. Despite a few early victories, it soon became apparent that the courts were incapable of dealing effectively with racial and economic residential segregation. The rock of metropolitan apartheid remained solidly implanted on the nation's landscape.

"FAVORABLE" DECISIONS

Courts played virtually no role in combating residential segregation before 1968. The discriminatory practices of public agencies and private individuals that helped produce segregated housing patterns were largely insulated from judicial attack by the local approval provisions of the federal housing subsidy laws, by the absence of any significant legal tradition against racial or economic discrimination in housing, and by the accepted practice in state courts of supporting local land use powers.

In 1968, the situation changed dramatically. The Fair Housing Act and the case of *Jones v. Mayer** suddenly created a strong legal impetus against racial discrimination in housing. In addition, the 1968 housing law vastly enlarged traditional subsidized housing programs and eliminated requirements for local approval in the new section 235 and 236 programs. Private developers, responding to profit incentives in the new programs, had good reason to look to the suburbs, where land was often more plentiful and cheaper than in the

*See Chapter One, p. 27, for fuller discussion of this case.

inner cities. Suburban communities that did not wish to participate in the new programs would now have to expose themselves to judicial attack by employing their local land use powers. Finally, the urban riots, the Kerner, Kaiser, and Douglas reports, and the cumulative effect of the long civil rights struggle of the 1960s all helped to heighten judicial awareness of residential apartheid.

Early litigation took two forms. One approach was to attack a community's use of land control or local approval powers to block a specific proposed housing development. Most such cases were brought in federal court and charged that the purpose or effect of the local action (or inaction) was racially discriminatory and therefore violated federal constitutional or statutory rights. The second approach was broader. Cases of this sort did not focus on any specific development proposals, but sought to recast a community's entire land use shceme or to change the location pattern of all of its future subsidized housing. In federal courts, it was charged that historical patterns proved that local powers had been used in a racially discriminatory manner. In state courts, the argument was that land controls were valid only when used to enhance the welfare of *all* the people of the community, whereas in fact they were being employed to benefit the rich and disadvantage the poor.

Some early cases met with success. In Lawton, Oklahoma, for example, the local Catholic church proposed a rent supplement project on land no longer needed for its parochial school. Rezoning for multifamily development was required and presumably would have been routinely granted—the surrounding property was already zoned for multifamily use—were it not for the fact that the neighborhood was white and the church's expressed intention was to open the proposed project to black families. After hearing protests by residents, the Lawton City Council denied the rezoning request on the ground that a multifamily project would increase the burden on public services. In 1969, a suit charging racial discrimination was filed in federal court. Calling Lawton a racially segregated city, the district judge said the evidence persuaded him that the real reason for the city council's refusal to rezone was to accommodate the desires of the local residents to keep blacks from a white section of town. The equal protection clause of the Constitution, he said, precluded the city from thus implementing the discriminatory views of its white residents. In 1970, a U.S. court of appeals affirmed the decision. Although race had not been discussed publicly at the city council meetings, the court added, proof of racial discrimination did not have to depend on open statements of an intention to discriminate.[1]

Similar decisions followed. In Lackawanna, New York, when the Catholic Diocese of Buffalo proposed to build section 235 homes in a white area of the city, the land was rezoned for open space, and building permits for the project were then denied. In 1970, a lower federal court ruled that the city officials' real purpose was to exclude blacks from the white area of the racially divided city and ordered the building permits issued. Again a court of appeals affirmed.[2] In suburban Atlanta in 1971, a federal court ordered building permits to be issued for two proposed public housing projects (county officials had tried to halt construction after they learned, belatedly, that public housing was involved); and in Cleveland in 1972, a federal court similarly required building permits to be issued for two proposed public housing projects in the predominantly white section of the city. Both decisions were upheld by courts of appeal.[3] In 1974, in the St. Louis suburb of Black Jack, Missouri, and in 1975, in the Chicago suburb of Arlington Heights, Illinois, federal appeal courts ordered rezoning for section 236 projects intended for integrated occupancy in all-white communities.[4]

In all of these cases, the courts ruled that, in order to block proposed housing developments, local land control powers had been used in a racially discriminatory manner. In addition, each opinion took note of the pattern of residential segregation in the community, and most commented on the broad significance of the pattern.[5]

A few federal court suits not limited to specific projects also produced favorable results. *Gautreaux v. Chicago Housing Authority** involved a decades-old practice of placing Chicago public housing exclusively in black neighborhoods. In 1969, a lower federal court decision in the case invalidated the long-standing practice of "clearing" all proposed CHA sites with Chicago aldermen (which in effect provided them with a means to exclude blacks from the neighborhoods they represented) and directed that the majority of future public housing in the city be placed in white neighborhoods.[6] In another aspect of the Cleveland building permit case that dealt with the historical segregation patterns in that city's public housing, a federal court ordered that future public housing be located in white sections of the city for an indefinite period.[7] In 1973, again in Cleveland, another federal court judge rendered a decision with possibly the greatest potential of all. He held unconstitutional the refusal of five nearly all-white Cleveland suburbs to sign cooperation agreements with the Cuyahoga Metropolitan Housing Authority, whose jurisdiction included Cleveland and its suburbs. The judge pointed

---

*For a detailed discussion of the *Gautreaux* case, see Appendix.

out that in view of the nearly all-white character of the Cuyahoga County suburbs, the high percentage of blacks in Cleveland public housing, and the need for low income housing throughout Cuyahoga County, the suburbs' refusal to permit the development of public housing was intended to and had the effect of excluding blacks and perpetuating racial segregation.[8]

In the state courts, the broader attacks on local powers finally succeeded in New Jersey. In March 1975, after long deliberation, the New Jersey Supreme Court rendered a landmark decision in a case involving Mount Laurel, a township located near the major industrial center of Camden. Mount Laurel's zoning had essentially restricted its residential areas to single family, detached dwellings. Townhouses, apartments (with minor exceptions), and mobile homes were not allowed at all. In addition, large lot sizes, floor area minimums, and other requirements in effect limited construction to homes for families with middle incomes and above. The entire land regulation system was attacked on the ground that low and moderate income families were thus unlawfully excluded from Mount Laurel. The plaintiffs included Mount Laurel residents living in dilapidated housing, former residents who said they had been forced to move elsewhere because of the absence of suitable moderately priced housing, and nonresidents living in Camden slums who said they wished to secure decent housing outside the city.

In considering the case, the New Jersey court said that it would assume that the Mount Laurel land use plan had not been adopted to exclude prospective residents on the illegal basis of race; the court would accept Mount Laurel's candid concession that its land regulations were intended to exclude lower income people and to attract upper income residents for the fiscal purpose of keeping property taxes low. With the issue thus clearly defined, the court ruled against Mount Laurel. A community could not, it held, keep out low and moderate income families by failing to provide, through its zoning ordinances, for any realistic opportunities for the construction of low and moderate income housing. The zoning power had to be used to promote the welfare of *all* the people; it could not be employed to discriminate against the poor and favor middle and upper income residents. Mount Laurel was directed to amend its land use laws to "make realistically possible the opportunity for an appropriate variety and choice of housing for all categories of people who may desire to live there, of course including those of low and moderate income."[9] Because the ruling dealt with the zoning plan for an entire municipality and was based on economic discrimination (rather than on racial discrimination, which was more difficult to prove), the

Mount Laurel decision greatly pleased those who had been struggling against exclusionary housing practices.

FEDERAL COURT OBSTACLES

In spite of these significant victories, it soon became clear that the potential of litigation for effecting major changes in residential segregation patterns was limited. Lawsuits tended to be costly, time-consuming, and restricted in their impact even when they succeeded.[10] But soon the prospect of success itself diminished, at least in the federal courts.

In 1970, a lower federal court struck down a provision of the California constitution requiring proposed public housing projects to be submitted to local referendums. The court ruled that poor persons were thus deprived of the equal protection of the laws, because the referendum requirement applied only to publicly assisted housing for the poor and not to other assisted housing, such as for veterans, state employees, or moderate income families. The court also ruled that because minorities were disproportionately represented among the poor, the referendum requirement likewise denied equal protection to minorities. In 1971, however, in a 5–3 decision reversing the lower court, the Supreme Court held that referendum requirements showed a "devotion to democracy" and could not be upset on equal protection grounds unless it could be demonstrated that they were "aimed" at a racial minority. Implicity, it rejected the lower court's view that showing an adverse impact on the poor—rather than on a racial minority—sufficed to establish a violation of the equal protection amendment. (Because of the financial burdens that might result from public housing construction, the Court maintained, it was not unreasonable to give the local citizenry a voice in deciding whether any such projects should be built.)[11]

The decision spurred the adoption of local referendum provisions by many municipalities. Some applied only to low income housing projects, some to all multifamily developments, some to all zoning changes of any kind. Regardless of the form, the effect was generally to block subsidized housing.

Litigation over referendum provisions again reached the U.S. Supreme Court in 1976. The case involved the Cleveland suburb of Eastlake, which in 1971 had adopted a referendum requirement for all proposed zoning changes. The supreme court of Ohio had invalidated the Eastlake requirement, ruling that it was an unconstitutional delegation of legislative power because it contained no standards to guide the voters' decision. Four Ohio justices wrote a concurring opinion condemning the provision as exclusionary as well (its "restrictive purpose ... is crudely apparent on its face") and noted that the amendment was specifically adopted to prevent multi-family housing. The opinion said that "[t]he inevitable effect of such provision is to perpetuate the de facto division in our society between black and white, rich and poor. . . ."[12]

In June 1976, the Supreme Court reversed the Ohio decision. Since the referendum privilege had been reserved for the people by the Ohio Constitution, the Court held that it was not to be viewed as a delegation of legislative power, and the requirement of standards to guide voters was therefore inapplicable. As for the "broader issues" discussed by some of the Ohio judges, the Court simply declared that if the "substantive result" of a referendum were arbitrary, bearing no relation to the public health, safety, morals, or general welfare, it could be set aside.[13] Given the difficulty of meeting that burden of proof, coupled with the need to show that a referendum was "aimed" at a racial minority, the Court clearly had placed a formidable obstacle in the path of those seeking dispersed housing for the poor.

Plaintiffs in housing cases soon also encountered difficulties in proving racial discrimination. In 1974, a U.S. court of appeals reversed the judgment that the Cuyahoga Metropolitan Housing Authority had obtained against five Cleveland suburbs. It ruled that in declining to sign cooperation agreements with the authority, the suburbs had done nothing more than exercise an option given them by federal law. On that account, there was no basis, the court said, to find that their conduct constituted racial discrimination. The opinion ignored the argument that, based on the heavy preponderance of black families among those applying to the authority for housing, the action of the suburbs affected blacks much more than whites and therefore had a racially discriminatory effect.[14]

Another adverse decision involved the New York City Housing Authority. As early as 1966, New York Mayor John Lindsay had announced a scattersite public housing program for vacant land in outlying areas of New York City. One of the purposes, he said, was to "open housing opportunities in sound, predominantly white, middle-income neighborhoods for those now confined to the city's ghettos."[15] In 1967, under this new policy, the housing authority proposed a public housing project and a federally aided moderate income project for a site in the North Riverdale area of the city known as Faraday Wood. Several years later, in the face of intense and continuing opposition from the neighborhood, the city first eliminated the public housing component, then abandoned the entire project. In early 1971, a lawsuit was brought to try to resurrect the proposal, but a lower federal court upheld the city administration's right to drop the project. It reasoned that the political response of public officials to local opposition did not constitute racial discrimination. The fact that some community residents may have opposed the project on racial grounds did not persuade the court that other legitimate concerns, such as too rapid population growth and the overtaxing of community facilities, were not the overriding reasons for community opposition.

In December 1974, a U.S. court of appeals affirmed the lower court ruling, concluding that the community opposition that had led to the abandonment of Faraday Wood was, for the most part, not racially motivated but sprang rather from racially neutral concerns, such as objections to high rise apartment buildings. Moreover, since the project had evolved into a predominantly middle, not lower, income development, its abandonment would not disproportionately affect minorities in any event.

A dissenting opinion pointed out that, although the community attempted to disguise its racial motivations with legitimate concerns, when the Russians ultimately acquired the same site to construct a high rise apartment building for their United Nations personnel, community opposition evaporated. True, the project had acquired a predominantly middle income complexion, but that was done in large part to make the development more palatable to the local community; in fact, the purpose of the Faraday Wood project had been to provide decent affordable housing for the poor outside the ghetto. We have a wall, the dissenting opinion stated, between affluence and poverty that some were attempting to breach by litigation aimed at land use controls or by the promotion of subsidized housing in outlying city neighborhoods and suburbs. The defeat of Faraday Wood seriously blunted those efforts.

A third court of appeals decision seemed light years away from the *Lawton* and *Lackawanna* opinions of a few years earlier. In 1974, a lower court had ordered Toledo's planning commission to grant rezoning for three proposed scattersite public housing developments, holding that the commission's refusal to do so was racially discriminatory because, in effect, it denied housing opportunities to blacks. All the usual, racially neutral, grounds for the commission's action were rejected. However, in 1975, a court of appeals ruled that the lower court had erred in inferring that racial discrimination was the reason for the commission's refusal to approve the public housing sites. In reversing the lower court, the appeals court declared that the concentration of blacks in a certain area of the city did not prove racial discrimination, adding:

We live in a free society. The time has not yet arrived for the courts to strike down state zoning laws which are neutral on their face and valid when passed, in order to permit the construction at public expense of large numbers of low cost public housing units in a neighborhood where they do not belong, and where the property owners, relying on the zoning laws, have spent large sums of money to build fine homes for the enjoyment of their families.[16]

Finally, three cases decided by the Supreme Court in 1975 and 1976 substantially increased the difficulties facing plaintiffs trying to prove racial discrimination in housing and land use cases in federal courts.

In 1975, the Court denied "standing" (the right to make claims that would be entertained by a federal court) to a group of plaintiffs seeking to attack the allegedly exclusionary zoning laws of Penfield, New York, a suburb of Rochester. Because no specific proposed housing project was involved, the Court held that no plaintiff could show "concrete facts demonstrating that the challenged practices harm *him*, and that he personally would benefit in a tangible way from the court's intervention." The decision seemed to mean that, unless unusually intrepid developers could be found who were willing to incur the delay and expense of lengthy litigation, those seeking to attack exclusionary zoning would find the doors of the federal courts closed to them.[17]

Then in 1976, rejecting the contrary statements in some earlier lower court opinions, the Supreme Court ruled that a claim of racial discrimination under the Constitution could not be sustained solely by showing that the challenged action had a racially disproportionate impact—rather, it was necessary to prove an "invidious discriminatory purpose"[18] Although the decision was rendered in a case that did not involve housing, the Court soon employed the principle to reverse the 1975 decision of the court of appeals in the Arlington Heights zoning case.[19]

Thus, seven years after the initial victory in Lawton, the prospect for changing resdiential segregation patterns through litigation in the federal courts was discouraging. The precedents set by the California, Eastlake, Cuyahoga, New York, Toledo, Penfield, and Arlington Heights decisions would make it extremely difficult to develop subsidized housing over local opposition wherever community groups and city administrations had good legal advice.

STATE COURT OBSTACLES

As the losses in the federal courts mounted, proponents of housing dispersal counseled that housing litigation should be brought in the state courts. With its emphasis on the economic discrimination inherent in the exclusion of lower income housing, the *Mount Laurel* ruling did not require proof of racial discrimination. Moreover, contrasting sharply with the philosophy of the Toledo opinion, it called for municipalities to provide realistic opportunities for low income housing through their zoning laws. Nor did the federal standing rules apply in state courts.

However, the prospects for success in the state courts were not entirely bright. First, unlike federal court precedents that tended to be useful, if not binding, in other federal judicial districts, state court opinions were more likely to be limited in their ultimate effect to the state of origin. Although *Mount Laurel* was a significant victory, New Jersey was acknowledged to be among the very few states whose courts had indicated much receptivity to the arguments that had succeeded in *Mount Laurel*. The extent to which *Mount Laurel* would be followed in the courts of other states was uncertain.

Second, *Mount Laurel* was itself a limited decision because the case involved a growing community whose zoning ordinances precluded all future multiple family construction, and which had admitted that its motivation was purely fiscal. Thus, courts in other jurisdictions, and in fact, lower courts in New Jersey, had considerable leeway to distinguish the *Mount Laurel* case from less extreme situations.

Third, the impact of *Mount Laurel* could be blunted by *Ramapo* type timed development controls.* The *Mount Laurel* opinion did state that growth control arrangements, even where permissible, could not be utilized as exclusionary devices or to stop all further development, but had to include provision for low income housing.[20] Nonetheless, even where a *Mount Laurel* type of case succeeded, the extent of the opportunity it would provide for building low income housing might thus be severely limited.[21]

Beyond these considerations, however, loomed one seemingly insurmountable problem: the removal of zoning barriers in no way substituted for an affirmative housing delivery system; it gave no assurance that any low income housing would actually be built. On that issue, one of the *Mount Laurel* judges filed a separate, partly dissenting, opinion, whose contrast with the majority opinion illuminated the critical issue of remedial action.

Housing construction costs had long since escalated to a level that made it impossible for low income housing to be provided without government subsidies. As long ago as 1968, the National Commission

---

*See Chapter Two, p. 53, for fuller discussion.

on Urban Problems (the Douglas Commission) had reported that there was "no way" then or at any foreseeable time that the poor or near poor could buy or rent standard housing at private market rates: "There is no magic way by which the poor can be decently housed without subsidy."[22] Thus, declared the *Mount Laurel* dissenting opinion, there was little hope that the private housing construction industry could satisfy housing needs even if all exclusionary barriers were removed. As the costs of housing continued to slip farther beyond the reach of the poor, "the practical value of zoning reform diminishes and becomes increasingly contingent on the establishment of new State and federal housing subsidy programs." For that reason, the dissenting judge wanted to impose affirmative obligations on Mount Laurel to plan for and provide housing opportunities for the poor.[23]

The majority opinion declined to go that far. "Courts do not build housing, nor do municipalities," it said. That function was performed by private builders or public housing authorities. The municipality's function was "to provide the opportunity through appropriate land use regulations." The most the majority opinion would acknowledge in that regard was that Mount Laurel had "at least a moral obligation" to establish a public housing authority.[24] (It has not since done so.)

The majority opinion was probably correct—experience indicated that courts were not very effective in requiring the construction of housing. Court orders against housing authorities had not produced much subsidized housing, regardless of whether the authorities were reluctant or eager to carry out a dispersal program. The *Gautreaux* case illustrates the former situation. The Chicago Housing Authority had been ordered to build additional housing in white neighborhoods "as rapidly as possible," but after years of delay and numerous legal battles, very little had actually been accomplished. Ten years after the lawsuit had been filed, and although most of the legal battles, including one in the U.S. Supreme Court, had been won, by mid-1976 CHA still had only built a grand total of sixty-three new apartments in white neighborhoods in Chicago.[25]

Unlike the CHA, the Atlanta and Cuyahoga County housing authorities had seriously tried to disperse their public housing, but the results were indistinguishable from those in Chicago. A year and a half after the 1971 decision in the Atlanta case, the director of the housing authority submitted a report to the judge to explain why no new public housing had been built. Zoning and the cost of construction were problems. Public resistance to dispersal of federally assisted low income housing remained high. There was little or no commitment on the part of HUD to face the expense and other problems of dispersal. In frustration, the judge admitted: "There is nothing I can do. The court, by the nature of the institution, cannot go out and execute the laws. I can't build public housing or have it built. . . ."[26] In Cleveland, too, partly because of the housing moratorium that dried up subsidy funds, partly because available land in white areas of the central cities was now quite scarce, the Cuyahoga Housing Authority was able to provide only nominal amounts of new housing in white neighborhoods of the city.

Thus, as the *Mount Laurel* dissenting opinion pointed out, not even the existence of subsidy programs, the presence of developers willing to use them, and the elimination of zoning barriers would assure the construction of low income housing. Notwithstanding the presence of these three favorable factors, municipalities could still prevent construction of low income housing. Something *more* was needed, the dissenting opinion stated. That something was "active municipal cooperation," the absence of which could thwart the housing process as effectively as outright exclusion.[27]

Yet the subsequent history of *Mount Laurel* itself showed that active municipal cooperation was not likely to be forthcoming. In the months following the decision, a number of lower court judges declined to apply the *Mount Laurel* ruling to the cases before them on various grounds—for example, that the municipality in question was too small or already too highly developed.[28] In a public speech, now retired Justice Hall, who had written the majority *Mount Laurel* opinion, blamed municipal officials and lower court judges for ignoring the "essential spirit" of the decision.[29] Mount Laurel itself submitted a revised land use plan that appeared to be an evasion of the court order, not an effort in good faith to comply with it, and two years after the decision was rendered, continuing litigation seemed to be the prospect. The bleak outlook was captured in a colloquy in another zoning case argued before the New Jersey Supreme Court, this one involving Old Bridge Township. The same judge who had dissented from *Mount Laurel*'s refusal to require affirmative action declared, "Born in controversy and reared in criticism . . . I have not yet found a municipality to embrace" the concepts of *Mount Laurel*. He advised the attorney for Old Bridge that without creative action, the *Mount Laurel* case would "remain a dead letter as it is today." Replied the attorney, "You can't attempt to do the impossible."[30]

Thus, whether cases were brought in federal or state courts, whether developers were anxious to build subsidized housing or were ordered to do so, it appeared that resourceful local officials and residents would generally be able to frustrate even the will of the courts to provide low income dispersed housing.

THE METROPOLITAN
PERSPECTIVE AGAIN

A final, pessimistic observation concerning the role of the courts remains—even "active municipal cooperation" by some municipalities will not suffice to deal with a metropolitanwide problem. In the long run, it would not benefit Atlanta to cooperate actively with the Atlanta Housing Authority if nearby Fulton County and its suburbs did not also cooperate. (As the trial judge in the Atlanta case said, "[U]nless drastic changes occur, it is not merely possible but certain that Atlanta will become, in essence, a black city with a solid white perimeter."[31]) Even if individual suburbs were themselves inclined to cooperate, they would almost certainly insist on the simultaneous collaboration of neighboring communities before taking action, for otherwise a single, isolated community would risk being considered as the sole suburban outpost for the poor. Yet areawide cooperation on any meaningful scale would probably be at least as rare as "active municipal cooperation." The *Mount Laurel* opinion said that authorization for regional zoning would be a logical and desirable legislative step,[32] but few states in the nation seemed likely to take that step within the foreseeable future.[33]

Two *successful* court actions highlighted the ultimate inability of the judiciary to deal with residential apartheid on a metropolitan basis. In the first, Hartford, Connecticut, sued HUD to cut off community development funds to seven of its suburbs. Hartford contended that the suburbs had failed to include reasonable housing goals in their housing assistance plans, particularly for prospective workers who might be expected to live in the area in the future. Reading the 1974 Housing and Community Development Act broadly, the federal judge agreed, and in early 1976 enjoined payment of the funds, an apparently significant victory for metropolitanwide housing dispersal. But cutting off community development funds did not produce "active municipal cooperation," let alone housing. Instead of changing their housing plans, some of the suburbs appealed. Even if they were eventually to lose, low income housing would not necessarily result. Like Warren, some or all of the suburbs might simply choose to forego federal funds and thus avoid entangling federal alliances. And if the housing assistance plans were ultimately changed to the judge's satisfaction, implementation would still be questionable. Hartford's "brave" effort, although valuable in highlighting a metropolitan dispersal theme in the 1974 act, only emphasized how far short of a metropolitan housing delivery system the 1974 act had stopped.[34]

The other metropolitan judicial effort arose out of the *Gautreaux* case. After HUD, as well as the Chicago Housing Authority, had been held liable for racial discrimination in site selection, HUD had been directed to cooperate with the CHA to provide remedial public housing predominantly in white neighborhoods. However, the trial judge refused to direct HUD and CHA to undertake development in suburban areas as well as in Chicago. But in August 1974, over HUD's vigorous objection, the U.S. court of appeals held that a metropolitanwide plan was called for and directed that the case be returned to the lower court for the development of such a plan.[35]

On appeal to the U.S. Supreme Court, HUD argued that a metropolitan plan would infringe on local prerogatives, which Congress had carefully preserved in the 1974 Housing and Community Development Act: the law only required community development fund recipients to file housing plans addressed to the needs of lower income persons residing or expected to reside in the community, not to the needs of an entire metropolitan area.

Moreover, the argument continued, a metropolitan order in *Gautreaux* would conflict with the Court's own 1974 decision in *Milliken v. Bradley*, a major school desegregation case in Detroit. In *Milliken*, the Court had rejected a metropolitanwide approach to remedy the problem because it had not been shown that segregation in Detroit schools had affected suburban schools or that the suburban districts had been guilty of any wrongdoing. The nature of the wrong should determine the scope of the remedy, the Court said, and a wrong confined to the city of Detroit should not be remedied by requiring "innocent" outlying areas to consolidate their school districts with the guilty Detroit district.[36]

Nevertheless, in April 1976, in a unanimous (8-0) decision in the *Gautreaux* case, the Court approved the concept of a metropolitan remedial order against HUD, while at the same time adhering to its *Milliken* views about the sanctity of local prerogatives.[37] Because HUD had already determined that the entire metropolitan area was the appropriate geography for administering its programs, the Court said that the *Milliken* principle—the scope of the remedy should be determined by the nature of the violation—would not be breached by an order directing HUD to exercise its funding and administrative powers on a metropolitan scale to provide relief in *Gautreaux*. However, the decision carefully preserved intact all local prerogatives. No innocent suburban housing authority could be compelled to apply for housing subsidy funds. No innocent suburban community could be compelled to apply for community development funds and thereby be forced to prepare a housing assistance plan. Even if a community chose to apply and did prepare such a plan, nothing in the decision mandated its implementaion. No rights granted to local communities under the Housing and Community Development Act of 1974 were invaded in any way. No land use powers were even touched by the decision. As with the *Hartford* case, the effect was therefore more likely to emphasize, in a general way, that housing problems were metropolitan problems, rather than actually to produce suburban housing for inner city residents.[38] Thus, although *Gautreaux* was a helpful decision, its net effect was to emphasize the limitations that both the structure of the 1974 act and legal theory had placed upon the courts as an instrumentality for dealing with residential segregation.[39]

* * *

This brief review of eight years of housing litigation suggests that for the most part local officials will continue to reject low income housing for their communities and will not embrace the "essential spirit" of *Mount Laurel*. Even in those rare instances when municipal officials want to break the pattern of segregation, they may, as in *Faraday Wood*, succumb to local pressure. More often they will fight, with timed development controls, referendum requirements, and lawsuits. Occasionally they may lose in court, as in Lawton and Lackawanna. More often, as later cases such as Toledo and Eastlake suggest, they will win. Sometimes they will lose in court but win anyway, as in Black Jack and Atlanta. Trying to entice local governments with community development funds is unlikely to make much difference. Some will spit out the bait, as in Warren. Some, having taken it (but being careful not to swallow the hook), may have it snatched back, as in Hartford's suburbs. Perhaps some few may be "caught." And in a few states, such as New Jersey, an enlightened judiciary may be able to prod local officials into effective action. But in general, active municipal cooperation and metropolitanwide planning are the essential ingredients in combating metropolitan apartheid, and those are the very elements courts are almost certainly unable to supply.

The Supreme Court's *Gautreaux* decision, said a U.S. court of appeals judge, had pointed toward the feasibility of desegregating housing in segregated suburban areas. But when it came to planning for solutions, "the judicial branch of government is almost powerless. . . ." Those who knew the history of housing over the last forty years, the judge added, knew the role federal housing agencies had played in bringing about our present problem of increasing apartheid. The same agencies, he said, could undo the damage they had done, but for that we would have to look to the executive and legislative branches, not to the courts. "[C] ourts are called upon to pass judgment on what has happened rather than to plan improvement or even to avoid disaster."[40]

Part II

Chapter Five

Is Heroism Necessary?

Frustration and futility have characterized past efforts to forge a housing policy to counteract metropolitan apartheid. The question now is: What should we do?

The threshold issue is whether to "do" anything at all. So far as affirmative government action goes, metropolitan apartheid may be a condition best left alone. More than one respected student of urban affairs holds that the scope and severity of the problem have been exaggerated. There is also considerable skepticism that a dispersal policy would produce the benefits—either for individual relocated families or for society at large—that its proponents claim. Thus, the "heroism" such a policy would require may be both unnecessary and unwise.[1]

HOW BIG A PROBLEM?

To establish the scope and severity of the apartheid problem—and the need for government to do something about it—thoughtful observers, such as Anthony Downs, generally describe the American urban condition this way: (1) the proportion of the population of central cities that is black and poor is steadily increasing, particularly in large metropolitan areas; (2) simultaneously, the major growth in metropolitan areas—new buildings, job expansion, investments in new schools and other public facilities—is taking place in the suburbs; and (3) the concentration of the black and poor in central cities, excluded from the opportunities provided by new growth suburban areas, gives rise to a spreading "contagion" of social problems in overburdened central cities and accelerates the trend toward the "two nations"—black and white, separate and unequal—described by the Kerner Report.[2]

Critics of a dispersal policy, such as Nathan Glazer, frequently question the accuracy of this description.[3] They argue that statistics showing blacks and whites separating into central cities and suburbs give only a "large and general picture." Metropolitan areas present remarkable variety. For example, some central cities include large tracts of land that are developing in "suburban" fashion, while some older suburbs have evolved into mini–central cities, complete with minighettos. Thus, an increase in black central city populations does not necessarily mean an increase in black ghettos, and increasing black suburban populations do not necessarily mean that the ghettos are shrinking.[4]

Moreover, according to the critics, there is not enough evidence to indicate whether existing concentrations of blacks have resulted from choice, poverty, or discrimination. If the explanation is choice, that presumably would be the end of the matter in a democratic society. If the explanation is poverty, we may expect that urban concentrations of blacks will decline as economic conditions improve; rising incomes should enable blacks to live in more and more residential areas. (In a widely discussed article published in the spring of 1973, black economic gains were called "nothing short of revolutionary," so impressive that a majority of blacks could actually be said to have reached the middle class—defined, somewhat subjectively it is true, as having enough to eat, adequate clothing, and safe and sanitary housing.[5])

As for discrimination, the argument runs, barriers are falling at an increasing rate for middle and working class blacks—some suburbs already have sizeable black populations. In fact, segregation indexes for 1960-1970 give a clear indication of a reversal of the trend toward growing black segregation, even as opinion polls show increasing numbers of persons who view themselves as living in integrated neighborhoods.[6] In sum, Nathan Glazer concludes, "[W]e are talking about a problem that undoubtedly exists, but that also is much less of a problem than most observers assume."[7]

The view that residential apartheid is a grave enough problem to call for serious, affirmative government action begins with evidence that points in the direction of discrimination—not poverty or choice—as the dominant cause of the metropolitan apartheid condition. Economist John Kain has observed that "without exception" studies show that only a fraction of the pattern of black residential segregation can be explained by low income or other measurable socioeconomic differences.[8] Systematic evidence to support the hypothesis of self-segregation is lacking; in fact, surveys of black attitudes indicate a preference for living in integrated neighborhoods.[9] After examining the evidence, urbanologist Karl E. Taeuber concluded flatly that (1) the assertion that racial residential segregation is caused largely by economic factors is unsubstantiated; (2) the assertion that it is a reflection of black choice runs counter to nationwide public opinion polls; and (3) "the prime cause of residential segregation by race has been discrimination both public and private."[10]

The hope that improved economic conditions will erode residential segregation of blacks now seems tenuous. Black economic gains of the 1960s came to a halt even before the recession years in the 1970s and in some respects are being rolled back. In 1972 black median income, a traditional gauge of black progress, was down to 59 percent of white, just where it had been in 1967 and a 2 percent drop from its high in 1969 and 1970. From 1971 to 1972, the number of blacks with incomes below the poverty line grew by several hundred thousand, while over a million whites escaped from the poverty classification. Unemployment among blacks grew slightly while dropping among whites (up to 10 percent for blacks, down to 5 percent for whites), pushing the black-white jobless ratio to two to one.[11]

Figures for 1973 showed no reversion to the gains of the 1960s. On the contrary, black median income was down another percentage point to 58 percent of white, back to where it had been in 1966. The 1973 rise in median income of whites (9.1 percent) was enough to offset inflation, while the rise for blacks (5.7 percent) was not. Blacks therefore not only dropped further behind whites but lost real income as well.[12]

These negative trends grew more pronounced as the nation moved into major recession in 1974. The familiar adage, "last hired, first fired," began to assert its grim reality; in many areas, black unemployment moved well into double digit figures and in some central city ghettos reached over 30 percent.[13] A Congressional Budget Office study, released at the end of 1975, declared that a moderate recovery strategy that reduced unemployment overall to 6.6 percent by the end of 1978 would not necessarily close *any* of the gap between black and white unemployment rates.[14] The case for an improvement in black economic circumstances seems highly doubtful.[15]

Optimism about the rate at which discriminatory barriers are falling seems similarly unjustified. Assertions that substantial desegregation occurs as blacks move into areas whites leave almost carries its

own refutation unless "temporary" is inserted before "desegregation." By far the greatest part of black residential movement into
white neighborhoods has been at the fringes of the expanding central
city ghettos, the very areas from which whites tend to flee most
rapidly. In such neighborhoods, "desegregation" may be extremely
transitory.

Racial residential segregation remains intense, despite a drop in the
Taeuber segregation index from 86 in 1960 to 82 in 1970.[16] A
recent analysis of urbanized areas helps to put the segregation index
figures in geographic perspective. (Urbanized areas—a central city or
cities and "surrounding closely settled territory," according to the
Census Bureau definition—exclude exurban areas and therefore include only those parts of metropolitan areas outside the central city
into which blacks are most likely to move.) The analysis covered
twenty-nine of the largest urbanized areas in 1950, 1960, or 1970,
including thirty-nine central cities—all those having a population of a
million or more in 1970—and almost 40 percent of the total U.S.
population in that year. The examination showed that in the twenty
years from 1950 to 1970 the percentage of blacks in the central city
population of the twenty-nine areas more than doubled, from 12.7
percent to 25.9 percent. In the same period, the percentage of blacks
in the suburban population of the same areas rose only from 4.1
percent to 4.6 percent. City after major city whose black population
rose dramatically to 30 and 40 and 50 percent was surrounded by
"closely settled territory" having a black population of 3 and 4 and 5
percent.[17]

Where black suburbanization is occurring, it appears to be following patterns of the past. A survey of forty-four northern metropolitan areas disclosed that in 1970, forty had segregation indexes that
were higher for the urbanized areas than for the central city alone;
this was also true in twenty-seven of forty-four southern metropolitan areas. Chicago metropolitan area figures help to provide an
explanation—over 90 percent of the increase in black suburban population from 1950 to 1970 occurred either in nine old industrial
suburbs whose racial segregation patterns were like those of Chicago
itself or in five virtually all-black suburbs. Aside from those fourteen
communities, the black population of the Chicago suburban area,
which comprised over three million whites in 1970, increased by
fewer than 10,000 persons over a twenty year period.[18]

It is true, as Nathan Glazer says, that there is great variety in the
national pattern of racial concentration, both within central cities
and outside them. Houston is a special case in several ways; Seattle
and Portland and Minneapolis have few blacks; in Denver and some

other cities in the Southwest, Spanish-speaking persons are the largest minority group. But massive concentrations of blacks constitute the essential pattern in the majority of our largest metropolitan areas.

Moreover, ghetto expansion seems likely to continue, not to be confined at the periphery by neighborhoods that remain stable. Although black migration into cental cities dropped considerably during the 1960s, over 80 percent of black population growth during the decade took place in the cities.[19] The age structure of the central city population and the high minority birthrate are the reasons. In the central cities of the Northeast, for example, one-third of the black population is under the age of fifteen, compared with only one-fifth of the white population, while the proportion of whites of retirement age is more than double that of blacks.[20] These demographic factors indicate that the present trend toward the concentration of blacks in central cities will continue.[21]

Discriminatory barriers against the black middle-class are falling, and white neighborhoods are more tolerant of middle class blacks— sometimes dramatically so.[22] More and more blacks can also be expected to move into the middle class (though the number who do so is likely to be far less than the increase in the population of the black poor ghetto). But the cards remain impossibly stacked against the vast majority of blacks who are poor. Metropolitan apartheid endures and is likely to intensify as the trend toward massive central city concentrations of those who are both black and poor persists. The assertion that we have much less of an apartheid problem than most observers assume is ultimately unpersuasive.

BENEFITS FOR FAMILIES

The next issue concerns the benefits supposed to be derived from a housing dispersal policy by families who choose to relocate: (1) better access to expanding suburban job opportunities; (2) higher quality public schooling; and (3) increased opportunity to "upgrade" by escaping from crisis ghetto conditions.

Between 1960 and 1970, the number of employed persons in the central cities of the nation's fifteen largest metropolitan areas declined by nearly 850,000 (7 percent), while the number of persons working in the suburbs of those cities rose by over 3,000,000 (44 percent). From such figures many observers conclude that most new jobs are now to be found in the suburbs. They also contend that this suburban job location trend is likely to persist.[23]

Although some critics disagree with this "job mismatch" thesis, pointing to statistics which seem to show an upsurge in central city employment in the mid-1960s,[24] census figures nonetheless reveal an absolute job loss in the largest central cities over the full decade. By 1970, suburbs equaled or exceeded central cities as the principal location of jobs in nine of the fifteen largest metropolitan areas.[25] From 1969 to 1973, of fourteen selected central cities, only Houston had a substantial gain in jobs, and only one other city, Los Angeles, showed a slight gain. (Houston was one of the few big cities able to expand through annexation of outlying districts, and Los Angeles' boundaries included large areas that would be considered suburbs in older cities.) All the other central cities in the list held about even or sustained job losses. Most, including four of the five largest, were in the latter category, and several of the losses were very large for just a four year period—6-7 percent for New York, Chicago, Philadelphia, and San Francisco; 9-11 percent for St. Louis, Baltimore, and Milwaukee; nearly 20 percent for Detroit.[26] Any middecade upsurge in central city employment seemed not to have lasted.

In addition, most of the lost employment was in manufacturing, precisely the sector where jobs were needed for growing central city populations of minority poor who were least able to take on white collar jobs or to follow the blue collar ones to the suburbs. New employment opportunities in the central cities consisted largely of service jobs held by suburbanites.[27]

John Kain and others have explained that changing transportation patterns, particularly the great increase in truck over rail and barge traffic made possible by post–World War II highway construction, encouraged the decentralization of industry.[28] Two of the obvious consequences appear in the contrast between new industrial parks and shopping complexes strung in ever-increasing numbers along suburban thruways and the for-sale signs on older inner city factory buildings, as well as in the reverse commuting phenomenon that may be observed during rush hours on almost any expressway connecting the central city with its suburban ring.[29] Most commentators agree that the economic role of the central city—at least of the older central city—is shifting from that of a manufacturing and trading center to a service center. Whether, as some have argued, large areas of the city are simply losing their economic value or, as others contend, the economy of the city is being transformed by the shift, there is no doubt that the nature of the jobs available in central cities has been changing dramatically. As one writer has observed, "The concentration of low skilled entry jobs, which once characterized the cities' economic base, is substantially a thing of the past."[30]

For the low-skilled central city laborer who is both black and poor, the transformation spells economic disaster.

Opponents of a housing dispersal policy are also skeptical about the assumed educational benefits for children of poor families who relocate to suburbia. There is little evidence, they say, that improvement in educational achievement would follow from integration or from the larger per pupil expenditures that generally characterize suburban school systems.[31] But chaotic classrooms, shortages of books and supplies, high absenteeism, large numbers of psychologically disturbed students, violent behavior, and other negative conditions in crisis ghetto schools do suggest that many potentially able students are deprived of learning opportunities that they would receive and profit from in most suburban schools.[32] In a newspaper interview, the young black principal of a Chicago ghetto school made this point with some poignance:

I want to make them assimilate the middle-class ethic. . . . I'm not talking about a white ethic—I'm talking about a white-and-black middle-class ethic. I'm talking about wanting to be excellent in school, appreciating education. That's what I want to give them. And that's hard.[33]

Finally, critics believe that suburban relocation would only marginally improve the quality of life for central city blacks. "Upgrading" or "betterment" may occur among members of the same class, they acknowledge, but it is unlikely to take place across class lines. Good relations among blacks and whites in integrated areas appear to depend upon similarity of class; yet the ghetto is poor as well as black.[34] The most probable consequence of an attempt to mix classes as well as races would be to produce a good deal of "stress."[35] Moreover, class mixing and the upgrading that is supposed to ensue require that the middle class stay, not flee, and accept the lower class newcomers, not fight them—unrealistic requirements not likely to be met.

In addition, there is a view of the ghetto as "home" for many blacks. It is a misunderstanding, says one author, to assume that blacks want to break out of Harlem.

They want to transform the Harlems of their country. These places are precious to them. These places are where they have dreamed, where they have lived, where they have loved, where they have worked out life as they could . . . a slum like Harlem isn't just a place of decay. It is also a form of historical and social memory.[36]

Edward Banfield says that typically the lower class black feels "very much at home" in his slum; to a greater or lesser extent, his environment is "an expression of his tastes and style of life." The very qualities that make the slum repellent to others make it "serviceable" to him, as a place of excitement, of specialized (particularly criminal) opportunities, of concealment.[37]

Although the possibilities for upgrading across class as well as race lines must be considered speculative, there seems to be little doubt that ghetto families have only marginal opportunities to improve themselves significantly so long as they remain trapped in crisis ghettos. They would benefit from leaving both because of their escape from the adverse environment of the crisis ghetto and because of the increased job, education, and housing opportunities to be found outside the ghetto.[38] It is true, Downs acknowledges, that what he calls "positive uplift" effects are uncertain. The residents and institutions of the middle class community might not respond to the needs of the new, lower income neighbors. If too small a number of the poor moved into the new community, they might feel isolated. Some of the poor might have so adapted their behavior patterns to ghetto conditions that they could not readapt to a middle class environment. But notwithstanding the uncertainties of "positive uplift," Downs' view is that escape from the overwhelmingly detrimental environment of concentrated poverty areas is in itself likely to be beneficial.[39] The frequently pathological ghetto environment makes it almost a miracle when a young black successfully negotiates the chaotic inner city school, the violent streets, the other familiar aspects of crisis ghetto existence, and emerges as a functional adult. However great the obstacles to "making it" in an alien, inadequately "prepared," perhaps hostile, middle class community, the odds against the miracle happening there are bound to be somewhat less. Crime and drugs *are* less prevalent; schools *are* better; job opportunities *are* likely to be improved. The institutional structure upon which "betterment" or "upgrading" frequently rests—recreational facilities, community programs, health institutions, and the like—is already in place, or in new growth communities will soon be provided. The structure is designed to serve the resident middle class, not—as in the case of ghetto supermarts—to gouge the poor. Even without programs or services specifically designed to meet the special needs of the low income residents, these facilities, programs, and institutions will be found in virtually every middle class community in far greater abundance than in the crisis ghetto. It is difficult to fault the view that in the aggregate these advantages would compensate for a good deal of "stress," a quality, after all, not lacking in ghetto life.[40]

The problem of isolation might be dealt with by "clustered" developments. "Integration" can be used in a salt and pepper sense— physical distribution of middle and lower income, or black and white, populations so that in a spatial, residential sense the metaphor would be apt; each neighborhood within a community and even each block within a neighborhood would have a small share of the total minority population. But there is another sense in which "integration" may be used. Philip Hauser has defined it as "an opportunity for social interaction, for participation in a common life process."[41] It is consistent with providing such an opportunity for a minority to cluster itself within a community if both the cluster and the community are small enough so that the minority will use many of the community's basic white middle class institutions. Integration, in this sense, would undoubtedly be preferable to some, perhaps most, of the minority population willing to consider abandoning their traditional neighborhoods because it would help to avoid the isolation that the salt and pepper variety of integration might entail while still providing the opportunities of which Hauser writes. Now, Hauser says, we have produced such vast black urban enclaves that, just in terms of the physical measurement of the ghettos, the average ghetto black is at a considerable remove from any social interaction with whites. "[W]e may have transplanted the sub-cultural isolation of the rural south into such mass enclaves in the north as to negate the theoretical opportunity for social interaction."[42]

In addition, there may be some question about how many ghetto residents are psychologically rooted to the "serviceable" ghetto environment because it satisfies their tastes and lifestyle, and how many have acquired certain tastes and styles because they live in the ghetto and would acquire different ones if they were elsewhere (in the next generation if not in this).

It may be acknowledged that to some unknown, but undoubtedly considerable, degree the ghetto dweller lives where he does because there he is close to his friends and relatives, to institutions that are important to him, perhaps to work—because he "belongs" and for all of its flaws the ghetto is "his." Many ghetto dwellers would not for a moment consider giving up those benefits for the sociologists' abstraction of the "betterment" supposedly to be found in an alien community.

But many might—if afforded the option. The concept of a persistent lower class lifestyle or culture that remains impregnable to middle class influences is not rigidly held even among those, such as sociologist Lee Rainwater and Edward Banfield, who have examined that style or culture most thoughtfully.[43] Rainwater says that lower

class people "know what they would like if only they had the resources of the average working-class man—they would want a quiet,
rather 'square' life in a quiet neighborhood far from the dangers,
seductions, and insults of the world in which they live."[44] Banfield
acknowledges that Rainwater's view may be true of many poor
people, especially women, though he adds that for others "the dangers and seductions (if not the insults) of the lower-class world are
life itself."[45] But Banfield goes further. Notwithstanding his controversial thesis that the lower class frequently behaves in antisocial
ways not so much because of blocked opportunities but because it is
a distinct and persistent type, and his pessimism about the possibilities of class upgrading *in the large,* Banfield says: "That most
people—including the disadvantaged poor—eventually respond to
situational inducements ('opportunities') in ways that, although they
may not conspicuously affect their own life styles, profoundly affect
those of their children or grandchildren appears very likely."[46] He
also seems to suggest that upgrading can occur *only* through cross-
class influences.

> It would seem that, even on the most optimistic view, the individual will
> not develop his full intellectual and emotional capacities except as, sooner
> or later, he comes under normal (as opposed to lower-class) influences.
> Apparently he will suffer some permanent damage if he passes his first
> two or three years in an extremely deprived environment, but much, per-
> haps most, of his initial disadvantage may be overcome if by early adoles-
> cence he gets support and stimulation from peers, teachers, or fellow
> workers.[47]

The opportunity for such stimulation to occur may well be increased
to the extent that ghetto dwellers are enabled to change their residences to middle or even working class communities.[48]

The phenomenon of middle class flight is not necessarily an insuperable problem. The middle class community is essentially interested in maintaining the dominance of its values and behavior
patterns in the life of the community. If it were made clear that the
scale of lower income "move-ins" would be small enough to leave
that dominance unthreatened, it need not be assumed that middle
class families would either fight or flee.[49] Moreover, because of the
increasing constraints of the availability of land and rising land
prices, much of the new housing construction over the next few
decades will inevitably take place in new suburbs that still have large
undeveloped land areas, not in the central city or in the already
densely developed inner ring of suburbs. In such cases, whole communities are being created for large numbers of incoming residents

who enter the new developments more or less simultaneously. The disruptive potential of planned class mixing is obviously minimized under those circumstances.

Apart from theorizing, there is some evidence—admittedly fragmentary—that class mixing can work, even from the point of view of the middle class. In 1969, the Massachusetts Housing Finance Agency actively began to promote the financing of privately developed low, moderate, and middle income housing throughout the state.[50] A minimum of 25 percent of the units in each MHFA-aided development were required by law to go to low income families.[51] By 1974, MHFA had provided financing for nearly 25,000 units of housing in over 150 developments having an average income mix of about 30 percent low income, 45 percent moderate income, and 25 percent full market tenants, with approximate income levels of under $6,000 and $12,000, and up to $30,000, respectively. In that year, the agency released a study, covering sixteen of its early projects, which had been designed to determine whether housing developments with a mixture of income levels "worked" in terms of tenant satisfaction.[52] The projects, which housed 3,200 families, were mostly garden type apartments located in suburbs and smaller cities and towns across the state. All had low and moderate income tenants with appropriate subsidies, and the majority had unsubsidized, higher income level tenants as well who paid full market rents. The study included interviews with tenants (including tenants in similar developments without income mix), developers, managers, architects, and towns officials, as well as demographic studies of the communities involved, evaluations of the individual developments, and information from each of the 3,200 households in the projects.

The study's key conclusion was that the factor of income mix was related to tenant satisfaction only secondarily, and that such matters as the location, design, construction, and management of the projects were far more significant.[53] "Broad income mix 'works' in these MHFA developments," the report stated, "producing higher levels of satisfaction at all levels—market, moderate-income and low-income—principally because these developments are superior in design, construction and management."[54]

Congress itself moved sharply in the direction of income mixing in the Housing and Community Development Act of 1974. The very first finding in the act was that the nation's urban communities were facing critical problems because of the growth of population in urban areas "and the concentration of persons of lower income in central cities."[55] One of the specific "objectives" of the act was "the reduction of the isolation of income groups within communities and geographical areas"; another was "spatial deconcentration of housing opportunities for persons of lower income."[56] It would obviously be difficult to achieve those objectives without opening up middle class communities to the poor. To remove any doubt, Congress said explicitly that the new section 8 housing program not only had the purpose of aiding lower income families to obtain decent housing— the traditional objective—but also of "promoting economically mixed housing."[57] In principle at least, Congress was thus willing to try what Massachusetts was trying.

BENEFITS FOR SOCIETY

Beyond betterment of the lives of those who choose to relocate, it is also intended that a housing dispersal policy may have a positive impact on American society as a whole—by bringing about a fairer distribution of the fiscal and social costs of dealing with metropolitan area poverty; by increasing the possibility of improving conditions in crisis ghetto areas without displacing urban decay to adjacent neighborhoods; and by reducing the likelihood of major confrontations between two spatially separate and unequal societies.

As to the first of these claimed benefits, it is indisputable that the burdens attributable to the poverty-stricken portion of the metropolitan area population are at present unfairly distributed among metropolitan communities, with the central city bearing far more than its fair share. The causes for the serious fiscal difficulties in which central cities find themselves are many, and it would be a gross oversimplification to attribute them solely to concentrated poverty areas or to suggest that a housing dispersal policy alone would eliminate them. But some amelioration would undoubtedly flow from a dispersal policy. It is a legitimate "benefit" to be weighed in the public policy balance.

The second hoped-for benefit—the belief that housing dispersal would increase the possibilities for improving crisis ghetto conditions—is admittedly speculative. Such improvement is "an extremely complex process that no one fully understands how to accomplish."[58] Yet some dispersal, though not itself a remedy, is almost certainly a necessary ingredient.[59] Indeed, Downs argues that ghetto "enrichment" without housing dispersal is a contradiction in terms, because it is not possible to renovate crisis ghettos without generating major outward movements of people who now live there.[60]

It is certainly true that the performance record of neighborhood rehabilitation efforts that have not involved dispersal is unencouraging. Probably the only known examples that were really successful are to be found in the old urban renewal program, where the low income neighborhood was cleared of most or all of its poor population and the refurbished area turned over to commercial interests and the middle or upper class.[61]

Similarly, ghetto rehabilitation by indigenous community development corporations has not been particularly successful. A few such entities—corporations owned and controlled by community residents—have managed to stimulate some degree of economic development and neighborhood improvement in particular ghetto areas. But the obstacles to their widespread success, including the difficulties of obtaining sufficient capital and adequately skilled personnel, finding markets, and generating broad enough community support, are very great. Even an optimistic examination of their potential rejects the view that community development corporations can generate sufficient profits to finance significant social and community services. Internal ghetto development and dispersal must be considered to be complementary, it says; "efforts at opening up housing and employment opportunities in the suburbs must be pressed vigorously," in addition to developing stronger support for community development corporations.[62]

Another study, by the Brookings Institution, suggests that for the federal government to have an impact on the quality of neighborhoods it must improve public services at the local level, adding that revenue sharing is one way to provide the necessary resources. The study notes, however, that resources alone are not sufficient and that some mechanism is needed to assure that funds are targeted for poor neighborhoods.[63] Putting aside the view that without some dispersal even targeted resources would not suffice, the fact is that no such mechanism exists; in any event, it would run counter to the priciple of nearly complete local discretion in the use of revenue-sharing funds. Yet the revenue-sharing record affords little hope that such targeting will otherwise occur. Preliminary findings in a nation wide study of the uses of revenue-sharing funds indicated that in 1972 and 1973, the first two years of the general revenue-sharing program, their principle effects were (1) to support or balance general budgets, frequently by paying for salary increases; (2) to reduce projected capital investment backlogs; and (3) to reduce property taxes. Public safety was by far the largest single expenditure; only minor amounts were devoted to the needs of the poor.[64] By mid-1974, only 1 percent of revenue-sharing funds had been used for housing and community development activities.[65] These findings indicate that urban ghettos will not be major recipients of revenue-sharing funds.

The Brookings Institution study also suggests that community development block grants of the sort provided by the Housing and Community Development Act of 1974 could be the vehicle for a ghetto rehabilitation effort. Not surprisingly, however, community development funds appear to be going the way of Model Cities funds—spread throughout a city for a variety of purposes to "give" something to the greatest number of voters. One criterion for Chicago's community development plan, for example, was the location of community development projects throughout the city.[66]

There are, of course, a variety of proposals for aiding the revitalization of the inner city, ranging from new forms of taxes and tax incentives to metropolitan government.[67] Some, perhaps all, are useful; it is beyond the scope of this book to attempt to evaluate them. However, one ingredient in any successful inner city revitalization formula will be a significant amount of housing dispersal. Both experience and common sense compel the conclusion that it will be impossible to improve crisis ghetto conditions significantly without some reduction of the ghetto's overwhelmingly dense concentration of black poor.

It is sometimes argued, however, that far from improving ghetto conditions, dispersal efforts may actually worsen them. For example, some urbanologists contend that attempts to provide integrated housing for blacks fail because of fierce opposition by white communities and result in little new housing for blacks at all. Abandoning the integration objective, they say, would enhance the prospects for much-needed massive housing subsidies; striving for both objectives only denies blacks housing altogether.[68] Three approaches are urged: (1) build new subsidized housing in outlying ghetto enclaves or in marginal and underused areas where it is possible to enlarge ghetto boundaries without excessive neighborhood friction; (2) upgrade existing ghetto housing through rehabilitation; and (3) establish city run receivership programs to take over deteriorated buildings.

All three approaches have in fact been tried on an extensive scale. A major receivership effort in Chicago ultimately went out of business even though the city's receivership agency had a large professional staff and the cooperation of local judges, and even though Mayor Daley—in the city that above all others was supposed to "work"—badly wanted the program to work. The failures of rehabilitation have already been noted. And improved housing—not new, but significantly better than that in the core ghetto—has been provided in large amounts by white families fleeing from the ghetto fringes. But the results have been little more than an expansion of the ghetto's perimeter and deterioration at its core. Better physical shelter has not changed the ghetto into a decent neighborhood. As one writer observed, "If a neighborhood is no longer regarded as a good place to live, the condition and quality of its housing become almost irrelevant to its survival."[69]

Others contend that housing dispersal would erode growing black political power. At the time of HUD's open communities policy, Anthony Henry of the National Tenants Organization, whose members are overwhelmingly poor and nonwhite, argued in this fashion: "[C]enter cities are the heart of U.S. economic life. . . . [T]here is an effort to disperse those centers at exactly the time when the black and the poor are coming to power there."[70] An article in the *Yale Law Journal* criticized the *Gautreaux* decree's dispersal thrust on the same grounds: "[T]he development of the ghetto," it said, "provides for the political representation of a group with particular goals and concerns and provides the basis for the equality necessary for a free choice of residence."[71] Some even suggest that we should avoid "discriminating" against those who need housing, yet prefer to remain in areas of minority concentration.[72]

It would of course be ironic—and indefensible—for government to continue to deny housing choice to the black poor on the ground that, after a generation of denial, blacks had decided they did not want the opportunity to choose after all. (The evidence that the black community is not of one mind and that many blacks, perhaps a majority, would prefer to live in integrated communities has already been referred to.) However, it is likely that in many metropolitan areas, enclaves of blacks are already so large that no foreseeable degree of housing dispersal would affect black accession to political power.

Finally, if central cities are not revitalized, black political power over them may be worth very little. One commentator made the point this way:

> The growing number of black mayors often find that the cities they speak for no longer command great economic and political power in state capitals and Washington. They now lead financially troubled cities, largely abandoned both by business and the middle class, and increasingly seen as dumping grounds for the poor, chronically dependent on outside aid. Too often black leaders win control of empty shells.[73]

Responding to Anthony Henry, NAACP General Counsel Nathaniel Jones agreed:

> We are concerned that the urban and ghetto problem cannot be successfully attacked until those confined in the inner city have the opportunity to go where the jobs and housing are. . . . What good does it do to have

political power over a decayed corpse? That's why I'm against the Tony Henry argument.[74]

Downs has expressed his understanding of the attraction of "black power" and the necessity that black leadership must espouse some form of it for a people long deprived of any realistic opportunity for political and economic development. But he also believes that the argument is deeply flawed, because blacks are so inextricably enmeshed in a society dominated by whites that their problems can never be solved in isolation.

Downs concludes that it is not really possible to create two separate societies truly equal in opportunity. Even if a ghetto enrichment strategy were successful far beyond any reasonable expectation, it would still leave a significant gap in opportunity and achievement between the separate white and black societies that would remain a source of major tension. "[E]xperience proves that men seeking equality are not placated by even very great absolute progress when they perceive that a significant gap remains between themselves and others in society who are no more deserving of success than they."[75]

Like improvement in ghetto conditions, the hope that housing dispersal would reduce the risk of confrontation between two spacially separate and unequal societies is also speculative. Yet the risk is of such a serious nature that it argues strongly for any policy that, however speculative, offers any prospect of alleviation. The National Commission on Violence, headed by Milton Eisenhower, has expressed grave concern that, unless effective measures are taken, we may eventually see central city business districts deserted after working hours, high rise buildings guarded as fortified cells for upper income populations, urban residents buying guns, and the middle class retreating in even greater numbers to racially and economically segregated suburbs. Between the unsafe, deteriorating central city on the one hand, and the relatively safe and more prosperous suburbs on the other, hatred and division would deepen.[76]

Judge George Edwards of the U.S. Court of Appeals has said that reading hundreds of case histories of conflict and crime makes him feel like a pathologist in the basement of a hospital examining frozen section slides from a patient upstairs. "Let me tell you what I see," he went on:

I see an increasingly segregated America. I see a strange and dangerous kind of apartheid developing. . . . How could we, if we wanted to, create a more dangerous condition that this—the downtown district owned by whites and occupied by them by the thousands upon thousands in daytime hours—all the rest of the central city occupied by black residents—the central city surrounded by a white suburban ring in a state dominated by whites. If you add a majority of white policemen, firemen and school teachers dealing with crime and fires and children in black neighborhoods while black youth has the biggest percentage of unemployment in America, such a picture presents a certainty of race conflict.[77]

It is true that the destructive riots of the 1960s have not been repeated in the 1970s. But can we be confident that we will continue to avoid them?[78] Many metropolitan areas have probably arrived at the point foreseen by the Eisenhower Commission; some ghetto neighborhoods are unsafe even during daylight hours and are almost entirely out of police control during the nighttime. A *Time* cover story on crime reported that large sections of Chicago's ghetto areas are "canyons of fear" at night and that criminals themselves are frightened to work the streets in big city areas.[79]

The rapid and continuing increase in crime is a general phenomenon affecting white middle class suburbs and rural areas as well as central cities. The causes are undoubtedly complex, and few profess to know the cures. Yet, as Norval Morris, a noted criminologist, argues, "It is trite but it remains true that the main causes of crime are social and economic."[80] This observation about Houston in the *Time* article supports that view:

Houston ... sprawls over 503 square miles, and its population of blacks and Mexican Americans is spread throughout the city rather than concentrated in a ghetto. The unemployment rate is relatively low. Apparently for these reasons, Houston, the fifth largest city in the U.S., has a crime rate that ranks 34th among the nation's biggest cities; and no one hesitates to go downtown at night.[81]

Even those who believe that it is easy to exaggerate the "urban crisis" admit that the huge enclaves of minority poor in our larger cities pose an extremely serious problem for society.

[I]t is clear that the existence of a large enclave of persons who perceive themselves, and are perceived by others, as having a separate identity, not sharing, or not sharing fully, the attachment that others feel to the "city," constitutes a potential hazard not only to present peace and order but—what is more important—to the well-being of the society over the long run.[82]

A policy that promises, however uncertainly, to alleviate that condition in some degree merits serious consideration on that ground alone.

* * *

Glazer sums up by saying: "To my mind, the suburbanization of blacks proceeds at a pace related to their economic and occupational rise, and the benefits to be gained from attempting a massive hastening of this pace seem doubtful."[83] The "suburbanization of blacks" (by which Glazer apparently means the outward movement of blacks who "make it" to the middle class) is not the same as ghetto dispersal. The "normal" pace of black economic and occupational advancement is likely to have little if any effect upon the mass ghetto enclaves of central cities. If they could be achieved, the benefits to be derived from encouraging ghetto dispersal, or at least from arresting further ghetto expansion, seem less doubtful than critics believe. The detriment—the hazard to the well-being of society—from failing to do so is potentially formidable.

✳ *Chapter Six*

Houser of Last Resort

It is one thing to declare that housing dispersal is desirable; it is quite another matter to demonstrate that it is technically feasible. Apart from the questions of costs and politics, which will be discussed later, there are three issues to consider in determining whether a broad-based housing dispersal program could be carried out: the required amount of physical shelter must be constructed, it must be dispersed in a rational way, and an appropriate portion of it must be made available to minority, ghetto families. This chapter considers each issue separately.

NO INSUPERABLE PROBLEMS

Experience with the section 235 and 236 programs showed that it was possible for the federal government to stimulate the private construction industry to build large numbers of housing units for the poor and near poor. In the years 1970 and 1971, federally subsidized housing production exceeded 465,000 units annually, nearly double the amount produced during the preceding thirty-five years, that is, since the entry of the federal government into the housing business in 1934.[1] However, the serious problems that plagued the section 235 and 236 programs ultimately led to their virtual demise. The question, then, is whether it is possible to stimulate private industry to construct the new housing needed for an adequate housing dispersal program without creating the problems that the section 235 and 236 programs encountered.

Housing in the Seventies, HUD's housing policy study, analyzed the section 235 and 236 programs in detail. Despite the scandals and the shoddily constructed homes and apartments that beset those programs, HUD's study concluded that the "housing quality" of recipients had improved by one third in the section 235 program and by one half in the section 236 program. The major problem was not poor construction; it was the high default and foreclosure rates that had led to so many deteriorating, and eventually abandoned, buildings.[2]

There is reason to believe those high rates were the consequence not of improper program design, but of poor administration. Widescale mismanagement was documented in a number of congressional hearings and admitted by HUD and was further dramatically evidenced by indictments of HUD employees. In early 1973, Senator William Proxmire's Subcommittee on Priorities and Economy in Government concluded that "the primary problem with housing subsidies has been HUD mismanagement."[3] In mid-1974, Representative Edward Koch, whose Committee on Banking and Currency had spent considerable time exploring scandals in the housing programs, concluded that "the most glaring weaknesses in the existing program operations can be attributed to inept HUD program management, rather than to the defects in the programs themselves."[4] President Nixon himself said that one "persistent misconception" was that foreclosures on homes subsidized under the section 235 and 236 programs were prime contributors to the inner city housing problem. Most inner city foreclosures, he pointed out, involved housing financed under *unsubsidized* FHA mortgage insurance programs that dated back to the 1930s.[5] That being so, it was obviously necessary to look beyond the structure of the subsidy programs for the cause— for example, to the complete abandonment of traditional insuring criteria by HUD when ordered by Congress to make FHA financing available to inner city neighborhoods.[6] Reviews of the section 235 and 236 programs by the General Accounting Office and HUD's own Office of Audit also pointed to program mismanagement by HUD as a basic problem.[7]

However, valid criticisms could be made about the design of the programs. For example, as a HUD official pointed out, since the structure of the section 235 and 236 programs provided no incentive to economize on construction costs, widespread fraud, or at least inflated construction costs, were almost certain to result.[8] Under the section 235 program, the more expensive the house, the higher the subsidy. Since higher priced units brought higher profits, the builder was happy to oblige.[9] In the section 236 program, under which ownership was restricted to nonprofit and limited profit sponsors, the principle incentives to investors were favorable depreciation rates and reduced or deferred capital gains taxes on disposition of the property. The depreciation deduction increased in direct ratio to costs and therefore constituted an incentive for higher, not lower, development costs, while favorable tax treatment on disposition attracted in and out investors who were interested mainly in a quick turnover of their capital rather than in good management over the long term.[10]

Mismanagement and structural flaws undoubtedly both contributed to the section 235 and 236 problems. The relevant point, however, is that there is no reason why both defects could not be corrected in any new construction subsidy program. The mismanagement can be understood as, in part at least, the result of special circumstances such as the abandonment of traditional FHA insuring criteria and the desire to provide housing assistance quickly in inner city areas. A housing dispersal program concentrating on new developments in suburban areas would obviously not repeat those mistakes. Structural flaws could be corrected by redesigning the programs. For example, the subsidy arrangements could be modified to discourage unnecessarily costly construction and provide incentives for good continuous management by making the depreciation deductions or other tax benefits contingent on the property being held for a minimum period of time.

Such changes would, of course, reduce the appeal of the programs to builders and investors and make it relatively more difficult to achieve desired production levels. However, the construction industry is currently in a depressed state. Apart from the general downturn in economic conditions, inflation in construction costs has been so pronounced that the market for unsubsidized new housing is severely limited. A subsidized housing program that provided jobs and profits, even with certain restrictions, would probably still attract a substantial number of developers in an activity-hungry housing industry.

Undoubtedly there would be some localities where even a soundly designed construction subsidy program would fail to attract a sufficient number of private developers to produce the desired level of new housing construction. For such situations, two alternatives remain. The first would be for the federal government itself to be given the power to engage in direct construction—to be the "houser of last resort"—just as the federal government has long possessed the power to build or to arrange for the building of airplanes and dams. In fact the government did just that when it built housing for defense workers during World War II.[11] Federal houser of last resort powers have been recommended by many housing analysts for years. "The real answer," one observer proposed back in 1966, "is for the federal government to build directly wherever there is racial exclusion and housing needs for minorities are demonstrated."[12] Both the Douglas and Kaiser reports recommended that if state and local governments failed to respond adequately to national goals for providing housing for the poor, the federal government, equipped with the power of eminent domain, should itself assume the responsibility.[13] Last resort powers, another veteran housing policy analyst declared, offer "a policy for democratic urban growth."[14]

Such a proposal may appear revolutionary to those long accustomed to the decentralized nature of government subsidized housing. What is called "upsidedown federalism"—the federal government regulating such minutiae as the height of doorknobs while leaving to local officials the vastly more significant decisions as to whether and where housing is to be built—appears to us as the norm. But federal housing policy began quite differently. In the beginning, under the National Industrial Recovery Act of the early 1930s, the federal government was itself the condemnor of land and the builder of housing for the poor, a pattern that was halted by a lower federal court decision in the mid-1930s.[15] Subsequent rulings have made it virtually certain that the courts would not bar a return to that course today. In fact, a last resort power of sorts, little noticed and infrequently used, already exists. A 1971 law, providing federal financial assistance for families uprooted by highway construction and other federal projects, authorizes federal program administrators to construct replacement housing wherever they find such direct intervention to be necessary.[16]

However, as "last resort" implies, direct federal construction would probably not be the norm. To assure that the desired housing would be built, Congress would not have to abandon but merely rationalize our familiar decentralized system. Suitably empowered metropolitanwide development agencies would be the appropriate instrumentalities, as several commentators have suggested.[17] Such agencies would be economical because of their size and would be more easily administered than the approximately 2,500 individual housing authorities HUD presently must deal with. They would thus constitute a vehicle for the volume production of subsidized housing far beyond the capability of the present local housing authority system. A federal law authorizing HUD to provide housing through such entities instead of through local housing authorities might well lead to their creation by state law, just as local housing authorities were established in response to the Housing Act of 1937. Providing new housing through such metropolitan agencies would most likely be seen by state and local officials as preferable to having it provided by the federal government. Wherever states failed to act, the federal last resort powers would be used.[18]

The second aspect of a housing dispersal program must be a means of assuring that the housing units to be constructed would be rationally distributed over an appropriate geographic area. A two step approach is required: devising the geographic distribution plan and providing the means to implement it in the face of local land use controls. Both steps are necessary if we are to avoid the sham of "dispersing" new subsidized housing largely or exclusively into fringe areas in the path of likely ghetto expansion or into newly created suburban ghettos.

The techniques for creating a geographic distribution plan are fairly well developed. In the Dayton, Ohio, area the regional planning agency prepared a voluntary, metropolitanwide allocation plan that in 1970, in an unusual spirit of cooperation, was accepted in principle by most of the political jurisdictions in the Dayton metropolitan area.[19] Since the adoption of the Dayton plan, several other, more sophisticated approaches have been developed, notably in the Twin Cities area and in San Bernardino County, California. The various allocation plans generally use certain objective criteria to prescribe the amounts and general location of new housing. The most frequently employed criteria can be grouped into three categories: those that measure some aspect of the need for low income housing in a defined planning area, such as the number of substandard or overcrowded homes and apartments and the size of the low income population; those that identify distributional factors, for example, the lowest number of existing subsidized or low income homes and apartments and the highest mean value of homes; and those that relate to the suitability of the planning area for new residential construction, such as the amount of vacant land and the availability of water and sanitary facilities.[20]

There is, of course, no single correct way. Some allocation plans call for averaging all crtieria, while others weigh them in order of relative importance. Some assign numbers of housing units to planning areas, while other define "priority" areas for new construction.[21] The important point is that dispersal planning techniques are now widely discussed and utilized by professionals. The provide methods for geographically allocating housing in a rational and fair manner that the federal government could use in exercising its last resort powers.[22]

The second step, providing the means to implement a dispersal plan in the face of local land use controls, would require that the federal government's last resort powers include the power to override local zoning so that purchased or condemned land could be used for the intended purpose. No legal difficulties are to be anticipated in this regard, for the Constitution and the laws of the United States are declared to be the "supreme" law of the land. If the federal power to condemn land and build subsidized housing were upheld by the courts, the "supremacy clause" of the Constitution would override any local zoning of land acquired for that purpose.[23] In addition, to insure the federal power's effectiveness, a building code for federally subsidized housing should be included in the housing dispersal program. It too would probably be sustained under the supremacy clause or, alternatively, under the "necessary and proper" clause of the Constitution, which authorizes Congress to enact all laws necessary and proper to the execution of governmental powers.[24]

As in the case of construction, the ultimate employment of federal powers for planning and land use control might well be the exception rather than the rule. If Congress gave the federal government the authority to formulate allocation plans and to override local zoning laws, as well as last resort construction powers, but metropolitan agency officials were given the option of preparing their own dispersal plans consistent with general federal guidelines, the likelihood is that local communities would prefer to do the planning as well as the construction themselves. Local officials are presently unresponsive to housing dispersal needs because they have the option *not* to satisfy them. If it became clear that those needs *would* be satisfied, the only question being whether planning and implementation would take place at the federal or local level, local action would, in most instances, surely be seen as preferable. ("Active municipal cooperation" would then be forthcoming as the only way to preclude federal action.) The ultimate federal power would have to be used rarely, if at all.[25]

In sum, planning for the dispersal of low income housing presents no insuperable legal or technical problems. Rational techniques exist and have already gained considerable acceptance among planners. These could be used by HUD if necessary, but local agencies would almost certainly carry out the planning, as well as the construction, if the federal government were possessed of last resort powers. As a result, all newly constructed federally subsidized housing, whether built privately or by local or federal government agencies, would be required to be located in accordance with a metropolitanwide housing dispersal plan whose implementation could not be frustrated by local land use controls.

The third and final element of a housing dispersal plan is to pro-

vide a means of assuring that an appropriate portion of newly constructed nonghetto housing be made available to ghetto residents. (It
is not the purpose of a dispersal plan to supply subsidized housing
exclusively for the poor who already live in suburbia.) This is a
sensitive matter, for it conjures up notions—however false—of government moving people about the landscape, telling them where to live.
It must be emphasized, therefore, that housing dispersal is voluntary.
Housing *opportunities* are to be provided for those who wish them,
nothing more. To achieve this, two criteria may be employed.

First, the 1974 Housing and Community Development Act states
that one objective of national policy is to reduce the concentration
of poor persons within central cities. Based on that already established policy, one criterion for eligibility for the new housing would
be residence within a central city poverty area—access to new subsidized housing in the suburbs or outside poverty areas of the central
city would be offered on a priority basis to poor persons residing in
central city poverty areas.[26] Second, the 1968 Housing and Urban
Development Act, as interpreted by the Supreme Court, calls for
racially integrated living patterns and the disbandment of ghettos.[27]
This suggests another criterion—that of race. Access to new subsidized housing located in predominantly white areas would be offered
on some priority basis to minorities who lived in central city poverty
areas.

To help minimize resistance to the new housing by the community
in which it is to be located, it would also be desirable to make some
portion of it available to lower income families already living in the
area. Various formulas for determining priority and eligibility suggest
themselves. For example, the *Gautreaux* decree provided that 25
percent of the new housing to be supplied should be made available
to Chicago Housing Authority tenants, 25 percent to people on the
waiting list for CHA apartments, and the remaining 50 percent to
poor people living in or near the neighborhood in which the new
housing is to be located.[28] The precise arrangements in each metropolitan area should be locally adopted as part of the housing allocation plan, subject to general federal guidelines; federal power in this
respect would also be employed only in the event that local authorities refused to act.

It is possible, of course, that few ghetto dwellers would opt to
move to a strange, perhaps hostile, community. To aid in making
such moves, a certain amount of counseling would have to be provided, perhaps by community fair housing groups working with
metropolitan housing agencies or with HUD.[29] In addition, incentives such as moving costs, or perhaps an income supplement for a

limited "get settled" period, might also be required. Special efforts could be made to find jobs for families willing to move, and a priority for the new housing could be given to those for whom jobs were found.[30] As indicated, the legislative justification for such higher subsidy levels for minorities willing to move out of central city ghettos may be found in the provisions of the 1968 and 1974 acts.

Conditioning eligibility for subsidized housing on low income is, of course, no departure from present housing policy. Offering a priority based on poverty area residence would be a policy innovation, however, for we have not heretofore linked access to subsidized housing such a geographic factor. (Access to public housing *has* been limited to those who already reside within the jurisdiciton of the housing authority.) But the innovation does not appear to raise any legal problems and, as indicated, its justification may be found in existing legislation.

The racial priority suggested, on the other hand, raises serious questions for a democratic society. Racial quotas in various contexts—education, employment, housing—have been much discussed. They have received vigorous support as being necessary to redress centuries of racial discrimination, and they have been just as vigorously criticized as being fundamentally inconsistent with individual, humanist values. In the specific context of remedying deliberate segregation by government, the Supreme Court has approved the temporary use of racial targets or guidelines.[31] At least one lower federal court has gone even further and argued that the 1968 Civil Rights Act justifies, and perhaps obligates, HUD and housing authorities to use quota type systems to maintain integrated housing projects and neighborhoods.[32] On the other hand, social scientist Daniel Bell argues that although racial discrimination irrevocably conflicts with humanist values because it denies a justly earned place to a person on the basis of an "unjust" group attribute, quotas demand that one must have a place primarily because one possesses a particular group attribute. "The person himself has disappeared. Only the attributes remain."[33]

Although racial quotas may ultimately be necessary to preserve integrated communities—a Hobson's choice in a democratic society—the evidence so far is insufficient to justify that conclusion, particularly if, as discussed in Chapter Five, the objective is to be integrated communities, not integrated projects. On this basis, relatively small all-black projects or neighborhoods within a larger white community would be acceptable. Thus, after an initial racial priority designed to reduce residential apartheid, access to subsidized housing could be left to the operation of the market, subject of course to effectively enforced antidiscrimination laws and HUD's affirmative action marketing requirements (discussed in Chapter Two).

It is possible that even this initial racial priority could be eliminated. Central city housing authority tenants and applicants constitute an existing pool of predominantly black ghetto residents who are identifiable victims of past discriminatory site selection policies. It might well be possible, at least in many metropolitan areas, to achieve a reduction in residential segregation simply by offering priority access to the new housing (as in the *Gautreaux* case) to persons on housing authority waiting lists and living in central city projects.

Although the specific arrangements might vary from one metropolitan area to another, overall federal guidelines would establish the general framework for metropolitan area planning by local officials. The purpose of those guidelines would be to assure that new subsidized housing in nonghetto areas would be offered to minority ghetto families in substantial numbers, and that those families who indicated an interest in such offers would be given counseling and other assistance to make their moves out of the ghetto realistically possible.

With this, the three part housing dispersal policy would be complete: federal construction subsidies coupled with federal last resort construction powers; federal metropolitan planning powers coupled with federal power to override local zoning and building laws; and a priority system to assure that the new housing would be offered to central city ghetto dwellers. It is, of course, not possible to be certain that a housing dispersal policy would "work," but the available techniques suggest that a reasonable basis exists for undertaking the effort. Such an initiative would at last put the federal government in a position to implement national housing objectives.[34]

BEYOND THE BOUNDS OF POSSIBILITY

Still, account must be taken of the view that the existence of theoretically effective techniques is not determinative when it comes to social problem solving by government In the aftermath of the assassination of John Kennedy, and particularly following his own electoral victory in 1964, Lyndon Johnson was able to mobilize the country in support of social reform legislation on a broad front. Federal aid for education, Medicare and Medicaid, the Economic Opportunity and Civil Rights Acts of 1964, the Housing Act of 1965, Model Cities in 1966—all were spewed out of the congressional hopper in a brief three year span. The spirit of the time was that little was impossible.

With will, and a hefty social budget, we could forge institutional arrangements that would lead to the good, if not the great, society.

By the onset of the Nixon administration, certainly by the end of the 1960s, many hopes had turned to ashes. Instead of model cities we had urban riots. Public education in the inner city remained a disaster; welfare rolls were growing. The failures, as they were seen to be, of Great Society programs lead to considerable skepticism about the federal government's ability to carry out large-scale social engineering. Although it was acknowledged that Vietnam had siphoned away energy and resources that otherwise might have fueled the Great Society effort, many observers now say that the federal government is unable to do much of anything well on the domestic front. Social problems would not be solved by "throwing federal money at them." New Federalism would therefore return power and responsibility to state and local officials, who, being "closer" to the local scene and now freed by revenue sharing of federal red tape, were supposed to be better able than Washington bureaucrats to confront our domestic difficulties effectively.

Neither the early mood of buoyant optimisn nor the later sackcloth and ashes stance seem justified in retrospect. Summing up at the conclusion of a thoughtful symposium in *The Public Interest*, the symposium editors concluded that the record of the Great Society "turned out about as any sensible person should have expected." There were some successes, some failures, some experiments that were partly successful, others whose returns did not justify the effort. The record did not suggest that it was a law of nature that social legislation could not deal effectively with social problems, or that state and local governments would always do better than the federal government. "Our own conclusions are much more modest," the authors said, "and leave much more room for case-by-case judgment."[35]

Yet the view persists that *this* problem is beyond the power of the government to cope with effectively. Edward Banfield asserts that no government, federal, state, or local, can do much of anything about the ghetto problem, because the ghetto problem is essentially insoluble.

> We cannot solve these problems or even make much headway against them by means of government action not because, as many seem to suppose, we are selfish, callous, or stupid, but rather because they are in the main not susceptible to solution. For one reason or another, solving them is beyond the bounds of possibility. In the largest class of cases, solution depends upon knowledge that we do not and perhaps cannot possess.[36]

Banfield contends that as more blacks move into middle and upper class communities, the concentration of the lower class slum will necessarily increase (and the "worsening" will be perceived as further evidence of callousness and neglect by authority, not as a consequence of the improved position of blacks). "The increasing isolation of the lower class is a problem, to be sure, but it is hard to see what can be done about it. The upper classes will continue to want to separate themselves physically from the lower, and in a free country they probably cannot be prevented from doing so."[37]

A somewhat similar view is expressed by Nathan Glazer. In an essay published in 1971 entitled "The Limits of Social Policy," Glazer argued that conservatives as well as liberals had mistakenly come to believe that for every problem there had to be a specific solution. In the conventional view, widely held across the political spectrum, a "sea of misery," scarcely diminished by voluntary charitable efforts, made it appropriate for government to start moving in, "setting up dikes, pushing back the sea and reclaiming the land, so to speak."[38]

Social policy (defined as public policies intended to protect people from the accidents of modern society and to maintain a decent minimum of living conditions) was our effort to provide a substitute for the traditional ways of handling distress—through the family, the ethnic group, the neighborhood, and community institutions such as the church—that seemed to be breaking down. However, in its effort to deal with the breakdown of these traditional agencies social policy tended to encourage their further weakening.

> [E]very piece of social policy substitutes for some traditional arrangement, whether good or bad, a new arrangement in which public authorities take over, at least in part, the role of the family, of the ethnic and neighborhood group, or of the voluntary association. In doing so, social policy weakens the position of these traditional agents. . . .[39]

There was, then, no sea of misery against which we were making steady headway. Our efforts to deal with distress themselves increased distress. For example, the history of our efforts to expand income support policies—"to improve the condition of the poor without further damage to those social motivations and structures which are the essential basis for individual security"—suggested that improvement and damage inevitably went together. The larger question was how we might prevent further erosion of the "traditional constraints that still play the largest role in maintaining a civil society."[40]

Glazer's concern reflects the bedevilment that has attended many social policy initiatives. It is arguable, however, that housing dispersal is different. Traditional constraints break down when the societal environment breaks down. Relatively speaking, they tend to maintain themselves when the societal environment remains intact and traditional working and middle class virtues predominate. To speak of "social motivations and structures which are the essential basis for individual security" within crisis ghettos is to speak of what no longer exists in the degree necessary to the maintenance of decent society and of what may well not be recoverable within the ghetto environment. The persistence of Banfield's lower class is one thing; crowding the members of that class into huge enclaves from which there is no longer much realistic hope of escape is quite another.

It may be, then, that a housing dispersal policy that would induce some families to relocate into relatively more intact social environments (in numbers that would not seriously threaten the stability that exists in the communities to which they move) would, on balance, support rather than erode traditional constraints. Through such a policy, larger numbers of families would be enabled to live in communities in which relatively intact traditional constraints were helping to maintain a decent society, while fewer would be required to remain in areas within which those constraints were largely absent.

Chapter Seven

A Somewhat Higher Priority

Although providing alternative housing opportunities to central city ghetto dwellers may be technically feasible, the question of costs remains. Would the costs, as one critic suggests, be "overwhelming"?[1]

THE QUESTION OF COSTS

The 1970 census disclosed that about half the 25.4 million poor lived in nonmetropolitan areas while slightly over 5 million lived in suburban areas, leaving 7.8 million in the central cities.[2] Anthony Downs suggests that a possible objective would be to reduce the absolute number of poor living in central cities by 50 percent in a decade—surely a substantial goal. If it were achieved, the suburbs would have a larger number and higher percentage of the poor than the central cities.[3] Assuming that this objective is to be accomplished by providing shelter for low income families in suburban areas, the first question is, how many housing units would be required?

To answer that question, Downs first estimates the likely population increase for the remainder of the decade, the likely reduction in the number of poor families as a result of possible economic growth (an estimate now unfortunately out of date as a result of the severe recession that began in 1974), as well as the percentage of population growth likely to occur in new, rather than existing, suburban areas. Based on these estimates, Downs concludes that achieving the suggested goal would require subsidies for approximately 58,000 new and 68,000 existing low income housing units in suburban areas (the latter group to be subsidized through some form of housing allowance), or a total of about 126,000 units per year. Since in 1971 over 430,000 new units (mostly sections 235 and 236 and public housing) were federally subsidized, of which approximately 108,000 were located in the suburbs, producing the required number of units should pose no great problem for the construction industry.[4]

It is true that these calculations are based on 1970 census figures and that the ghetto population has grown since then. The estimates also assume a decrease in the number of poor families as a result of economic growth, whereas, in fact, there has been a sharp economic decline. Nor do these estimates provide for any moderate income or market rent units to be included in the subsidized developments. On the Massachusetts model,* a 100 unit subsidized project would provide only about twenty-five apartments for low income families, the rest going to moderate income and market rate tenants. Finally, Downs' figures include no ghetto construction, whereas it would be difficult to justify a policy that did not allow for any new subsidized housing within the ghetto.

But the margin between 58,000 projected new units per year and the 430,000 actually subsidized in 1971 is great. Moreover, a 50 percent reduction in the number of poor in central cities in a decade sets the target very high; a somewhat lower percentage and a somewhat longer time span—say, a reduction of one-third over a dozen or fifteen years—would still represent a substantial achievement while diminishing significantly the number of new units required to be subsidized annually. Finally, subsidized housing construction is a fine pump primer in a period of economic decline. It not only creates employment within the housing industry but helps keep numerous supplier industries busy. Some economists have prescribed precisely such antirecession medicine.[5] In short, solely from the point of view of our ability to produce the required number of new dwelling units, Downs' projected figures are not unrealistic.

What about the dollar costs of subsidizing new and existing housing at such a level?[6] First, it should be noted that the 1.25 million figure (126,000 units per year for ten years) is less than a quarter of the 6 million new and rehabilitated subsidized units Congress adopted as a ten year national housing goal in the 1968 Housing Act. Even trebling the Downs figure to 3.75 million to allow for new subsidized housing in the central city and for units to be made available to middle income tenants would still leave the ten year figure well below two-thirds of the congressionally established goal. Referring

*See Chapter Five, p. 107.

to the economic cost of providing the six million subsidized units in his 1970 annual report on housing goals, Nixon said that "the likely claim on the economy involved in reaching the housing goal is certainly modest."[7] Total housing goals, of which subsidized housing was one part, represented a share of the gross national product that was not particularly high by historical standards.[8] Housing would have to be given a "somewhat higher priority in the bidding for national resources," and some resources would have to be shifted from other uses into housing. But, the president said, the extent of the shift need not be large.[9]

If a housing production goal of six million new and rehabilitated subsidized units over ten years was, in the president's view, a reasonable objective in economic terms, the more modest Downs goal should also be considered reasonable. As Downs concluded: "The annual rates of subsidizing additional suburban housing units for low-income households necessary to carry out this strategy are feasible."[10]

However, following the Warren debacle, by 1971 the president's attitude toward the costs of subsidized housing had changed considerably. The 1971 annual housing report estimated that if the six million unit goal were met by 1978, the federal government would, in that year, be paying at least $7.5 billion annually in housing subsidies, a sum that over the life of the mortgages could amount to the "staggering" total of more than $200 billion. "Clearly," Nixon said, "the public interest demands that the Federal Government not stand impassively at the cash register and continue to pay out whatever is necessary to feed runaway inflation of housing costs."[11]

Some statistics, however, will help place the president's figures in perspective. One approach, typically taken by proponents of housing subsidies, is to point out how small a portion of the annual budget or gross national product has been allocated historically to housing subsidies. For example, the 1968 Kaiser Committee report contained a table showing that from fiscal year 1962 through 1967 about $356 billion was spent for national defense, $33 billion for stabilizing farm prices and income, $24 billion for space exploration, and $22 billion for federal highway construction. During the same period, about $8 billion went for all housing and urban renewal programs combined, only $1.25 billion of which was for federal housing subsidies. The report concluded that compared with expenditures for other programs, the cost of meeting the congressional goal of subsidizing six million new or rehabilitated units in ten years was not high.[12]

Beginning in 1969, the enactment of the section 235 and 236 programs, as well as increased public housing authorizations, led to a substantial rise in housing subsidy expenditures. Compared with the rest of the budget, however, HUD's annual housing subsidy expenditures remained quite small, never reaching even 1 percent of total federal expenditures. In fiscal year 1970, when total federal expenditures exceeded $196 billion, HUD's housing subsidy payments amounted to less than $1.3 billion. In fiscal 1971, housing subsidies dropped slightly, while total expenditures increased to $211 billion; and in fiscal year 1972, the last full fiscal year before the housing moratorium, HUD housing subsidy payments still hovered around $1.5 billion, while total expenditures increased to $231 billion.[13]

Nixon's projected $7.5 billion annual figure by 1978,[14] while large in relation to the historic trend of housing subsidy expenditures, is not that large in relation to other social welfare budget items even at current expenditure levels. For example, the Ford administration's 1976 budget proposed that $14.6 billion be spent for education, manpower, and social services; $28 billion for health services; $15.6 billion for veterans' benefits and services; and nearly $119 billion for social security, unemployment insurance, and other social insurance programs. Proposed "community and regional development" expenditures, of which housing was only one part, were $5.9 billion. Total proposed federal outlays were $349.3 billion.[15] It may also help to provide perspective on the $7.5 billion figure to note that the cost in 1972 of allowing homeowner deductions for mortgage interest and property taxes was estimated to be $6.75 billion.[16]

Annual expenditures are not the whole story; consideration must also be given to the commitment to make future annual payments over the life of the mortgages. In public housing, for example, the federal subsidy contract covers debt service on the total capital costs of a project; generally, the agreement calls for the costs to be paid back over forty years. Annual subsidy expenditures for new housing construction in a given year thus represent contractually binding commitments to annually increasing expenditures as more units are built in the future. They can quickly mount to Nixon's $200 billion figure.

Despite the apparent distinction, there may not be much difference between contractually promised future payments and those we are "free" to discontinue. Probably overstating the issue somewhat, Downs claims that it is unrealistic to regard contractual commitments for future spending as more binding than noncontractual commitments that political considerations would render difficult to eliminate.[17] Yet it remains true that as more subsidized housing units are produced, the total commitment grows rapidly and "mortgages" future budgets.

Computing long-range costs based on HUD's probable share of the six million units targeted in the 1968 act, Downs estimates that over a forty year period from 1969 the discounted present value of the total subsidy costs would be $67 billion using a 5 percent discount rate and $39.2 billion using a 10 percent rate.[18] In 1973, HUD computed the run-out costs of all subsidized housing commitments made through fiscal year 1973 using discount rates of 5 percent and 7.5 percent as $40.6 billion and $30.6 billion, respectively.[19] Although inflation has now outdated these estimates, the total budget has grown to reflect inflationary costs, and the figures are still of interest relative to the costs of other federal budget items, which, when similarly treated, run much higher.

Nixon's *undiscounted* $200 billion figure should of course be compared with the undiscounted cost of other programs. (The tactic of projecting annual housing subsidy costs over a forty year mortgage period and producing "staggering" totals was often employed in the debate over housing policy triggered by the moratorium.) On this basis, Medicare and Medicaid, debt interest, and defense expenditures would produce forty year totals of $496 billion, $576 billion, and over $3,000 billion, respectively.[20]

Figures such as these do not lend themselves to precise analysis, and it is hard to draw much of a qualitative judgment from them. But they do show that historically only a very small fraction of federal expenditures has been devoted to subsidized housing. If Downs' dispersal goal were to be adopted, the fraction would increase but would continue to be a small portion of total federal expenditures. It is difficult, therefore, to view Downs' goal as unfeasible on economic grounds. Trebling his projection of subsidized units (to allow for inner city and mixed income developments) would still leave us at an expenditure level that could hardly be deemed excessive in relation to the seriousness of the residential segregation problem and to the level of expenditures for other budgetary items. Those who are convinced of the benefits to be derived from a successful dispersal policy would probably not shrink from paying the projected dollar cost of it—if they thought that dispersal could be made to work.

HOUSING ALLOWANCES

Another cost-related consideration, apart from absolute dollar costs, remains. In the 1973–1974 debate over housing policy, it was vigorously contended that, compared to a system that used the existing housing stock, the cost of a construction subsidy system was too high. Again and again the point was stressed that building new housing was the most expensive way to cope with the problem and that a cash payment or housing allowance system to increase the effective purchasing power of the poor and to enable them to find decent shelter in existing housing would be cheaper and more effective.[21]

The cost of a housing allowance program depends on the level of benefits to be provided, the proportion of income that recipients would be required to pay, and the percentage of eligible families that would receive the benefits. The midpoint of a cost range developed by the Urban Institute, as of 1972, was $7.1 billion annually.[22] President Nixon's September 1973 housing policy statement estimated that full implementation of a housing allowance program would cost $8 billion to $11 billion annually.[23] These estimates are in the same range as the estimated costs of the new construction program just discussed. However, the comparison is based on the assumption that allowances would be made available to all who were eligible, whereas a new construction program produces a limited number of housing units and therefore serves only a fraction of the income-eligible population. If allowances were confined to that same fraction, the cost of a housing allowance program would be considerably less than the cost of a new construction program.[24]

When the supply of low cost housing is slim, however, it is doubtful that housing allowances will really satisfy the shelter needs of the poor more cheaply than construction subsidies. The Douglas Commission report stated that an increase in housing purchasing power that did not, at the same time, materially increase the supply of available housing could only result in higher prices for the existing supply.[25] Others have made the same point.[26]

Apart from these uncertainties, the unfortunate reality appears to be that housing allowances will not relieve metropolitan apartheid. For example, in two modest housing allowance experiments conducted by Model Cities officials in Kansas City and Wilmington, the comptroller general reported that in the former city, although about 8 percent of the black participants moved into white areas, most black families moved into black neighborhoods and most white families into white neighborhoods. In Wilmington, "almost as a rule," Spanish-American families moved to or remained in Spanish-American neighborhoods, blacks stayed in predominantly black neighborhoods, and whites in white neighborhoods. "Not one black family attempted to integrate a white neighborhood."[27] The program director of the Kansas City experiment said: "While the program was demonstrating its ability to help poor families, it was simultaneously reinforcing the pattern of segregation and racial turnover. . . ."[28] In its 1976 report on the continuing, overall housing allowance experiments,

HUD stated that preliminary evidence "indicates few fundamental changes in mobility rates or location patterns." In particular, little movement had been observed between central cities and suburbs.[29]

Quite apart from the matter of costs, Anthony Downs points out a major drawback of relying solely on housing allowances:

> Over two-thirds of our population growth will occur in new-growth suburbs during the next two decades. Low- and moderate-income households cannot live in older housing in these areas because all the housing is, by definition, brand new. Unless we want to exclude people in the lower half of the nation's income distribution from these new areas we must use some type of subsidies applicable to brand new units.[30]

Indeed, even those who argued most effectively against construction subsidies, and urged on cost-efficiency grounds that some form of housing allowance was to be preferred, did not claim that allowances were likely to be effective in reducing metropolitan apartheid. Typical of the view that federal housing policy should concern itself only with providing physical shelter is this statement made in the course of advocating a particular housing allowance type of approach: "No attempt is made to engage in social restructuring by altering the locational decisions of target households. These are decisions better made at the state and local levels."[31]

Housing allowances should undoubtedly be employed wherever vacancy rates in nonghetto areas are sufficient to justify their use— provided they are accompanied by adequate counseling and related services to make housing opportunities in outlying city and suburban areas realistically available to ghetto dwellers.[32] But it seems clear that if dispersal is the objective, housing allowances must be viewed as an adjunct to, not a substitute for, a new construction program.

THE MOST DIRECT SOLUTION

Another argument bears indirectly on costs, or at least on how, from a cost-effectiveness point of view, we should spend available social welfare dollars. It is a widely held view that persistent gross disparities between the affluent and the poor, as well as the large absolute number of households in poverty, are a basic cause of many social problems. (The wealthiest 20 percent of families in the United States receive about 42 percent of all family income, while the poorest 20 percent receive less than 6 percent, percentages that have not changed significantly since World War II.[33]) If poverty is at the root of the ghetto problem, then it should follow that the most direct solution would be to raise the incomes of ghetto residents. Poverty, after all, is the lack of adequate income; the straightforward response to an inadequate income would be to increase it by the delivery of cash.[34]

If we are to commit billions to a policy designed to relieve metropolitan apartheid and the poverty conditions existing in central city ghettos that are a part of it, possibly the money might be better spent directly on increasing the incomes of the poor rather than indirectly on providing them with housing opportunities outside the ghetto. Perhaps a strategy of reducing income disparities by income supplements should have the highest priority.

Notwithstanding the logic of this view, on balance the claims made for the "income strategy," which is the generally accepted term for government programs supplying cash rather than goods or services, do not seem to justify making it the *exclusive* strategy against metropolitan apartheid. The government first began income maintenance with early New Deal legislation in the 1930s, which attempted a three-pronged approach: jobs for those who could work; social insurance for those too old to work or deprived of their normal breadwinner; and public charity for those lacking both breadwinner and insurance, a group expected eventually to disappear. Thereafter, as a comprehensive congressional report states, the evolution of income maintenance programs rested on three related assumptions:

> First, the assumption that all employable people can obtain adequate incomes from work. It was assumed that general public education would prepare workers for jobs, for which adequate pay would be assured by the minimum wage law. . . .
> Second, the assumption that workers and their families should be publicly (socially) insured against identifiable risks to the steady flow of earned income—risks such as involuntary unemployment, old age, death, and disability of the breadwinner.
> Third, the assumption that until social insurance coverage became effective for all workers, those who lacked such coverage should receive cash based on need. This residual program of public assistance, it was agreed, would provide income to those who could not or should not work—the aged, the blind, the disabled, and women raising children alone.[35]

Despite huge increases in income maintenance payments, these assumptions were not borne out. By fiscal 1973, federal, state, and local governments provided a grand total of about $91 billion in cash payments for income maintenance programs, $56 billion of it in federal social security, unemployment, and other social insurance programs; $22 billion in state and federal "deferred compensation" programs for veterans, civil service employees, and others; and $13 billion in state and federal welfare or public assistance programs for the poor.[36] Much of this vast expenditure has relatively little to do with poverty, but some of it, particularly in the category of cash assistance to the poor, does. Yet it is difficult to see how such "anti-poverty" payments affect conditions in central city ghettos, or poverty itself for that matter.

Whether because of favorable economic conditions, President Johnson's war on poverty, or the cumulative effect of income maintenance programs, the number of poor persons declined dramatically from 39.9 million in 1960 to 23.1 million in 1969.[37] During the same period, federal government expenditures on income for the poor grew by leaps and bounds. For example, payments for the AFDC (aid to families with dependent children) program alone grew from $1.149 billion in 1961 to $3.546 billion in 1969.[38] Yet it was precisely in the latter half of the 1960s that central city deterioration began to fester into urban riots. At about the same time, housing abandonment grew more widespread, signaling a further stage in the decay of crisis ghetto areas.[39] Then, as if to compound the irony, while cash income maintenance payments to the poor continued to increase dramatically (federal, state, and local payments nearly doubled from about $7.5 billion to nearly $14 billion between 1968 and 1973), the number of poor dropped only slightly, and the condition of inner city ghettos worsened appreciably to the point where, it may be recalled, George Romney suggested "writing off" some of them as beyond redemption. The conclusion seems evident that there are limits to the effectiveness of the income strategy as the exclusive antidote for central city deterioration and the problems of poverty.

Of course, one may argue that the public assistance system we have evolved needs to be "rationalized" (hardly anyone now defends it as logical), that more of the available assistance dollars should be targeted on the poor, and that if this were done the income strategy would be far more effective. Perhaps. But "rationalizing" is no mean feat. One thoughtful study, distinguishing between the effort to reform the present welfare system and the attempt to substantially reduce poverty, lists six major issues in the reform area alone.[40] The difficulties are compounded when the focus is broadened to include the problem of alleviating poverty. For example, nearly two-thirds of the poor are not eligible for public assistance. Since most are from families in which at least one adult member works, the difficult issue of how to supplement income without eroding the incentive to work immediately arises.[41]

The work-incentive problem is particularly troublesome and probably requires imposing a relatively low ceiling on direct cash assistance to the poor. Thus, as payment levels to the unemployed are increased, the working poor must also be compensated, for otherwise public assistance payments will provide higher incomes than lower paid jobs. But as the working poor are covered, the number of persons entitled to benefits, and hence total program costs, rise very rapidly, particularly if benefit levels are increased. After what Senator William Proxmire called "the most thorough and thoughtful analysis of our welfare program which has ever been undertaken," a congressional committee proposed a benefit level of $3,600 for a penniless, two adult family of four. (This compared with a poverty level figure for an urban family of four of $4,550 for 1974.)

It is contended by some analysts that "if lower class people are to be enabled to participate successfully in conventional society, the social and ecological situation to which lower class people adapt must be changed."[42] It is not likely that merely increasing assistance payments to ghetto dwellers incrementally, which, for the reasons given, is all we can expect as a practical matter, would significantly affect the pathological environment of the ghetto. It is doubtful that the vast social needs of crisis ghetto residents—decent schooling, satisfactory health care, adequate police protection, reasonable employment opportunities, etc.—could be met without massive improvements in income.[43] On the other hand, for those who desire to do so, moving from a crisis ghetto into a middle class culture and environment *is* a way to bring about such a change.

Income maintenance payments are obviously necessary. Efforts to rationalize the welfare system, and to target a larger percentage of income maintenance dollars on the needy, will and should continue. But neither the history nor the present course of income maintenance programs provides sufficient assurance that, in addressing metropolitan apartheid, a hugely expanded income strategy would be preferable to an approach we have yet to try—a housing dispersal policy.

Chapter Eight

Tolerance for the Intolerable

This book has attempted to provide a brief overview of the scope and nature of racial and economic residential apartheid in the United States—how it came about and how past efforts to deal with it have failed. It has suggested that housing dispersal is an essential ingredient in any solution. This final chapter does not assert that an effective housing dispersal policy—even if viewed as socially desirable and technically and economically feasible —is politically possible; it does suggest that we cannot know for sure that it is not.

OUTSIDE THE REALM OF DISCUSSION

In the late 1960s, political scientist Harold Wolman addressed a series of questions about housing policy to people in the housing field whom he called the "decisionmaking elite." Their answers led Wolman to conclude that "the possibility that the federal government might take the initiative, select sites, and build housing itself is simply outside the realm of discussion in the United States at the present time." No decisionmaker and only one group outside the official decision-making process (the NAACP) suggested moving toward a "federal approach" to housing. There seemed to be an unspoken consensus, Wolman wrote, that whatever changes might be made in housing matters would be made within the framework of local initiative, local site selection, and private construction.[1]

The rhetoric of the 1972 presidential election clearly indicated that these attitudes had not changed. Shortly before election day,

George McGovern, surely the most reform-minded presidential candidate in a long time, announced:

> I believe fervently that while new housing opportunities out of the ghetto are both needed and desirable for America's urban poor, that the residents of all communities where such federally backed communities are being considered should be consulted fully at every step of the planning. A government which makes arbitrary decisions and then thrusts these decisions on the citizenry is no government at all.[2]

Four years later, the candidates of both parties could easily have reused the McGovern speech. Campaigning for the Democratic nomination, Jimmy Carter let slip his view that ethnically "pure" neighborhoods should be preserved against the "intrusion" of "alien" groups. Although he hastened to explain that he strongly opposed housing discrimination, Carter carefully drew a line between using governmental power to combat discrimination and using it affirmatively to promote housing dispersal. As clearly as he was for the former, he was against the latter.[3] Carter's Democratic opponents, as well as President Ford, campaigning for the Republican nomination, promptly made what capital they could out of Carter's "ethnic purity" phrase. However, they also made it clear that they shared Carter's view of the proper governmental role.[4]

It appeared that an effective housing dispersal policy remained, as Wolman had put it, simply outside the realm of discussion.

WITHIN THE DOMAIN
OF POLITICAL POSSIBILITY

Perhaps one may find an interesting parallel in Daniel Moynihan's book on the Nixon administration's proposed Family Assistance Plan (FAP). In his discussion Moynihan quoted from a 1969 paper, "The Political Feasibility of Income by Right," by political scientists William Cavala and Aaron Wildavsky: "Income by right is not politically feasible in the near future. The President will not support it and Congress would not pass it if he did. The populace is hugely opposed." Moynihan went on to note that Cavala and Wildavsky interviewed some fifty congressmen, most of whom were also "hugely opposed," and that even the liberals who supported the idea did not expect anything to come of it. When asked about the possibility that an income-by-right measure would pass the House of Representatives, their reply was, "None, zero, absolutely no chance." According to Cavala and Wildavsky, three considerations militated particularly against the possibility of passage. First, a policy to provide unearned income ran counter to widely held, deeply felt American values about work and achievement; second, the amount of money that would have to be raised by taxation to support a guaranteed income would be very large; and third, both labor unions and militant black leaders would be opposed for fear that a guaranteed income would undermine their respective positions.[5]

Yet, as Moynihan was quick to point out, at the very moment in March of 1969 when Cavala and Wildavsky were interviewing congressmen, a plan for a guaranteed income was being presented to the president. Five months later, Nixon proposed the plan to Congress, and nine months after that, the House of Representatives passed the measure.[6] In the end, of course, Cavala and Wildavsky were right; the Family Assistance Plan was not finally enacted, and the opposition of labor unions and militant black leaders did contribute importantly to its demise. But FAP did come close. It *was* proposed by the president and it *was* passed by one house of Congress. Those events, Moynihan felt, placed income-by-right on the national agenda of pending legislation. Although by no means certain of passage, FAP was nonetheless "now within the domain of normal politics, and likely to remain so until either enacted, or discredited by information and events."[7]

These more than mildly surprising events, Moynihan argued, call for some modification of traditional political theory concerning what is feasible. Political science has always contended that collective attitudes and values do not change very much or very rapidly. Yet the experience of FAP suggested that on rare occasions the general rule did not apply. An "extraordinary, discontinuous forward movement in social policy *did* occur, and in the very least promising of circumstances." Moynihan thought that those who demanded fundamental social change could point to the events leading up to the proposal and near enactment of FAP as evidence that "fundamental" rather than merely "incremental" social change was a realistic option for American society.[8] It would therefore be useful to inquire into the circumstances under which such unusual events may occur. Attempting to examine why Cavala and Wildavsky were somewhat off the mark, Moynihan proposed two tentative notions of his own.

First, he noted that Cavala and Wildavsky did say that standard assumptions about gradual and minimal change in the political system ignored the role domestic crises had come to play in our policymaking. Nixon's decision to propose FAP, Moynihan said, was "based on a conviction that the great growth in welfare dependency, and the anticipated continued growth . . . did indeed reflect a domestic crisis of much wider implications than those normally associated with the issue."[9] In this context, Moynihan quoted political scientist John F. Manley: "What the family assistance plan reveals is that national policymaking institutions have a high but limited tolerance for the intolerable. If needs are pressing enough and if existing programs are inadequate enough, the politically unfeasible may become feasible."[10]

Second, Moynihan suggested that presidential leadership was of great importance. If the president were to move first, congressmen who might otherwise have felt they had to be strongly opposed would find it easier to support a measure. Presidential rhetoric was also significant. In the FAP situation, the president declared that the Family Assistance Plan was not a guaranteed income plan—a phrase so charged with negative connotations that the label itself would have rendered the proposal politically impossible. Nothing required, Moynihan said, that a guaranteed income be called a guaranteed income, and when the president chose to call it something different— chose indeed to say that it was not guaranteed income—a number of political assumptions had suddenly to be modified.[11]

THE GHETTO WAY STATION— A DEAD END

If political feasibility depends on how pressing needs are and how inadequate existing measures are perceived to be, surely the twin aspects of metropolitan apartheid—the degradation of the black ghetto and the divisiveness of two separate and unequal societies— satisfy both criteria.

Conditions in the inner cities, where most of the black poor now live, steadily worsen. Abandonment of structurally solid housing persists and spreads.[12] Inner city schools continue to deteriorate and education becomes a mockery. Inexorably rising crime rates make life intolerable for those who remain in or near the expanding ghetto and accelerate the outflow of the city's industrial and middle class lifeblood. Most central city economic indicators—bank deposits, jobs, payrolls, tax bases—continue their steady decline.[13]

Although the immigration of poor minorities to central cities has virtually ceased in many places, natural increase among the minority poor already in the cities, the continuing exodus of middle class whites, and the persistent exclusion of the minority poor from most suburban areas steadily intensify our racial and economic division. A 1974 presidential report on national growth and development pointed out that while the white population of the suburbs increased by fifteen million during the decade between 1960 and 1970, the white population of central cities decreased by 1 percent. Then, in the four years between 1970 and 1974, the rate of decrease in central city white population accelerated to over 8 percent. The report concluded:

> [B]lacks continue to represent an increasing proportion of the central city population and a decreasing proportion of the suburban population. . . . Despite rising incomes and more open housing, in percentage terms and absolute numbers minorities remain heavily concentrated in well-defined neighborhoods.[14]

Thus, the racial and economic gap between the city and the suburbs progressively widens. Without major changes in public policies, these trends are likely to persist, for they have developed despite an impressive array of antidiscrimination laws, a substantial drop in the number of poor, a major improvement in the quality of the housing stock, and an enormous increase in spending for social welfare purposes.[15]

Over the years, a succession of poor, unskilled minority groups—Irish, Jewish, Italian, Eastern European, and others—have lived in the ghettos of major American cities. Whether or not life in those ghettos was harsher than in the black inner city ghettos of today,[16] the former occupants could look forward to making their way into the mainstream of American life in the course of a generation or two. The ghetto was a temporary stopping place, a "way station." The city slum, with its cheap housing close to factories and other sources of low-skilled employment, was the logical and accepted place for an immigrant family to learn the language and acquire the skills that would enable it, or its children, to move on. "Living in the slums," according to a government pamphlet, "was a temporary discomfort, cheerfully endured, because of an animating faith that prosperity and comfort were just ahead."[17]

It now seems clear that the same process is not working for ghetto blacks. The reasons are complex and perhaps not fully understood. The rules of the job market have changed; access for low-skilled workers is now more difficult.[18] The nature of available jobs has changed; more skills are now generally required. Job locations have shifted; ghetto dwellers are now confronted with the job mismatch condition. The changing economic circumstances of central cities, their worsening fiscal problems,[19] the special historical experience of the American black—whatever the full explanation in all its complexity may be—now, for too many ghetto residents, the animating faith in prosperity has been replaced by a depressing certainty that little will be different a few years or a generation hence. They, and their children, and *their* children, are born and live out their lives in the way station, and no train comes through. The black ghetto of today has become a permanent, dead-end way of life.[20]

This swiftly drawn picture of American apartheid of course oversimplifies. Population trends in the 1970s are not clearly defined. Some cities depart from the general pattern, and the picture is, in any event, truer of the older metropolitan areas of the Northeast and northern Midwest regions than of the newer ones of the Southwest. (In fact, among urbanologists it is considered inexcusably naive to speak of *the* central city and *the* suburbs.[21]) In general, however, it is an accurate picture of the larger metropolitan areas where the great majority of the black population lives. Karl Taeuber calls racial residential segregation the "persisting dilemma,"[22] while the *New York Times* observes that the term "big cities" may be becoming a euphemism for "poor and black."[23] Even the Banfields, who do not share the fear of a "two nation" confrontation, concede that the "huge enclaves" pose a serious threat.[24]

Many people may have recognized by now that reducing the concentrations of minority poor in central cities is a prerequisite to any significant remedy for the continuing deterioration of the cities. It is not only scholars such as Kain and Downs, or the members of presidential study commissions, who hold that view. The resolution several years ago of the U.S. Conference of Mayors that federal aid be denied communities that failed to provide housing opportunities for the poor, and the city of Hartford's lawsuit against its suburbs (both previously mentioned), indicate that there may be broader acceptance of the proposition that suburban housing opportunities must be provided to the inner city poor. Perhaps, therefore, new and even radical policies designed to deal with metropolitan apartheid may have greater acceptability than conventional political wisdom would indicate.

Some evidence for that suggestion may be found in a 1974 Gallup poll based on personal interviews conducted with 1,509 adults living in more than 300 selected U.S. localities. The subject of the survey was a hypothetical plan to move welfare families (the "worst case" for housing dispersal) on a voluntary basis out of inner city ghettos into others areas (possibly small towns or suburbs), where they would presumably have better living conditions and more job opportunities. The precise question asked was:

A plan has been proposed to invite welfare families now living in ghetto areas of large cities to move to areas of the Nation where living conditions and job opportunities are better. The government would pay the costs of moving as well as living costs until these families found jobs. Would you favor or oppose such a plan?[25]

Group responses were predictable. The rich were opposed; the poor were in favor. The whites were opposed; the blacks were in favor. What was surprising, however, was that in most cases, margins of opposition were slim. In fact, and this result may be considered astounding if the poll is at all representative of national opinion, public opinion *favored* the proposal by a margin of 48 to 44 percent (some 8 percent expressing no opinion). Nationally, nonwhites were in favor by a margin of 70 to 20 percent, while whites opposed the proposal by a margin of only 47 to 45 percent. Among city dwellers, residents of large cities were in favor by 51 to 42 percent, and residents of smaller cities were also in favor, but by slimmer margins, while only the residents of cities with populations of less than 2,500 were opposed (by a margin of 46 to 45 percent).[26] And what, one wonders, would be the poll results if the question were not limited to welfare families? Or if the proposed dispersal plan required that, say, 50 percent of those moving from the ghetto to new neighborhoods were to have jobs assured to them before they left, and only 50 percent were therefore to be unemployed at the time of the move? Perhaps there is more general acceptance than might have been suspected of the view expressed by Felix Rohatyn, financial "overseer" of New York City's fiscal crisis, that the country "cannot continue half suburb and half slum."[27]

If so, the time may be ripe to capitalize on that acceptance. The preponderance of the country's population growth of millions of people over the next generation will take place outside central cities. Additional job growth, at least in the sort of jobs for which low-skilled workers can qualify, will also occur most heavily outside central cities. If we so desire, that growth can be shaped in a way that will alleviate rather than exacerbate metropolitan apartheid. As one commentator put it in congressional testimony in the early 1970s:

[N]ow would seem to be the time to choose between a continuation of present patterns and the establishment of more acceptable rationally prescribed patterns which would channel growth through a public interest framework. It would have been far better had we adopted such a policy prior to the establishment of the interstate highway program and the FHA and VA mortgage guarantee programs. But our failure then has afforded us a chance to witness the mistakes. . . . If we take advantage of the knowledge gained from these mistakes, and choose now to employ the considerable influence of the federal purse in producing the housing which is needed over the next thirty years, and also in asserting some control over the patterns in which it is actually placed on the earth, we can do at least as much good for our metropolitan areas in the remainder of this century as the harm we have already perpetrated in the past quarter century.[28]

Ironically, the course of school desegregation provides another argument in support of the "time may be ripe" thesis. Embedded in the Supreme Court's 1954 opinion outlawing segregated schools was, as the late Alexander Bickel termed it, an "original ambivalence." The *Brown* decision made it unconstitutional for a state to use racial classifications in drawing up school district boundaries (except to remedy past wrongs), yet it also declared that racially separate schools were inherently unequal. Over the course of the following decade, it became clear that merely substituting racially neutral pupil assignment systems, such as allowing students to transfer on request, would not eliminate separate schools. The "inherently unequal" doctrine of the original decision then forced the Court to require positive action to eliminate racially separate schools even though these were no longer being maintained as such by deliberate racial classification. (This obligation rested on the theory that the persisting effects of earlier segregationist actions by the school system had to be eradicated.) Thus, racially conscious steps such as redrawing boundary lines, pairing schools, and busing came into extensive use.

But these developments in school desegregation coincided with the increase in racial residential separation of the late 1950s and 1960s, particularly the physical expansion of the central city black ghetto. The exodus of whites from central cities and the enormous growth in the proportion of black students in large central city school systems led to *increased* racial separation in many school systems, eroding earlier desegregation gains. It became apparent that only massive busing—massive both in terms of numbers of pupils to be transported and distances involved—could eliminate the racially separate schools of the larger central cities. It also became apparent, however, that busing on the required scale might not be politically feasible, and perhaps not legally feasible either.[29] Although busing would remain an available and useful tool in many circumstances, by the mid-1970s it began to appear that in the largest urban centers, where most black school age children lived, racially separate housing patterns would effectively block much school desegregation.

Yet the nation had made a major psychological investment in desegregating its schools. More than twenty years of struggle, not only with legal theory and the practical problems of desegregation, but with the ethic of racially separate schools, have had some impact on the national conscience. Many citizens would be disturbed at the prospect of a de facto return, all these years after *Brown*, to a pattern of racial separation in public schools for most black schoolchildren. Turning back those pages of history will surely be accompanied by some feelings of regret and guilt. And therein may lie a political possibility.

In the early 1970s, more people began to contend that the way to deal with segregated schools was to deal with segregated housing. Senator Ribicoff, in a hearing on housing legislation in 1971, declared: "[T]his bill . . . is more important to the whole problem of integration than the school bill by itself. You will find that if we build housing where the jobs are, we will eventually have a situation where people will be going to their school in a truly integrated community."[30] As efforts to desegregate many large urban school systems founder, as an image emerges of all-black schools in the major central cities, perhaps it may become possible for national political leaders to assert that a federal housing dispersal policy should be the quid pro quo for the abandonment of mass busing.

THE CALL FOR LEADERSHIP

Which brings us to the second Moynihan ingredient for turning the politically unfeasible into the feasible: presidential leadership. Here we have no crystal ball; no one can predict whether or not we shall have the needed leadership. Nearly ninety years ago, Lord Bryce wrote in *The American Commonwealth* that "perhaps no form of government needs great leaders so much as democracy."[31] Surely those words were never truer than they are today. Democratic institutions are on the defensive, not only throughout the world but within the United States as well. Bookstore shelves overflow with trenchantly pessimistic analyses of our national psyche. Typical of this genre of national self-criticism is a recently published book, *The Dying of the Light*, by Arnold Rogow,[32] who perceives our institutions as decaying and points to the dissolution of those shared values that make a free society possible. Throughout his work the theme of race "sounds powerfully, . . . giving it a tone of despair."[33] Our problems are broader and deeper than the metropolitan apartheid that is dividing us along racial and economic lines, but it is unlikely that the president, if he does choose truly to lead, can address the vast problems facing the nation today without also addressing that division.

Should presidential leadership be asserted, the rhetorical possibilities seem clear. It was taken for granted in the nineteenth century, says John B. Oakes of the *New York Times*, that under the Constitution the federal government had a responsibility for the consequences of natural disasters that crossed state lines, such as floods or droughts. Why is it so difficult in the late twentieth century, he asks, for us to accept a federal responsibility for the floods of human beings who crossed state lines into the great cities in search of relief from the drought of poverty, unemployment, and despair?[34] And who, once they reached the cities, he might have added, were kept confined to the ghettos not by the "natural" order of affairs but, in large measure, by the force of law and ill-conceived government policies, while on the other hand, other government policies mightily assisted those who wished to depart. Presidential leadership and presidential rhetoric need not therefore be directed to changing a "natural" condition; they could, instead, be directed to the unfairness of not using government power to redress the continuing effects of both deliberate and inadvertent government misdeeds. A president with moral vision and courage, willing to make that explanation to the American people, might be able to modify some political assumptions about the feasibility of a federal housing dispersal policy.

In the last analysis, the matter of political feasibility reduces to speculation and guesswork—unprofitable enterprises. For those who view metropolitan racial and economic apartheid as this country's "most explosive" domestic problem, there can be only one response —we must try to combat it with an effective program. For those who believe, with Glazer and Banfield, that matters are not really in such a sorry state and that we cannot do anything helpful anyway, trying would be useless or worse. At the close, Gunnar Myrdal's prescient observation comes to mind—that gross inequality in this field is not only a matter for conscience but is expensive in the end. It *has* turned out to be terribly expensive, and only the most deeply pessimistic among us are likely to be absolutely certain that we are unwilling to learn from that experience.

✳ Appendix

Waiting for Gautreaux

Since this book is an outgrowth of the *Gautreaux* case, this appendix supplies a brief description of the course of that litigation for the interested reader.

On August 26, 1965, a Chicago group called the West Side Federation sent a letter to Robert C. Weaver, the federal government's top housing official, asking Weaver not to approve the Chicago Housing Authority's latest group of proposed public housing sites. An amalgam of fifty-three black neighborhood organizations, the federation was one outgrowth of the previous year's massive civil rights rally led by Martin Luther King in Chicago's Soldier Field.

The federation letter was factual and low key. It pointed out the "pervasive pattern" of segregation in CHA projects, most of which were located in the most solidly segregated areas of the city. CHA's newest proposal for nine more ghetto developments, four of them high rises, six next to large existing public housing projects, would surely mean more of the same. "There exists no ascertainable reason," the letter said, "why the [new] sites were selected in the Negro ghetto."[1] It argued that their selection constituted "discrimination" within the meanng of the Title VI of the 1964 Civil Rights Act, the then recently passed civil rights law that prohibited discrimination in any program receiving federal money.

The impetus for the West Side Federation letter had come from Harold Baron, research director of the Chicago Urban League. Baron viewed CHA's latest site proposals as a clear violation of the 1964 law and saw in the situation the potential for changing a federally funded public housing system virtually all of whose nonwhite tenants were given no choice but to live in solidly black neighborhoods.

In mid-October, the West Side Federation received a seven page, single-spaced reply to its August letter. The gist of the government's response, which was signed by the commissioner of the Public Housing Administration, Marie McGuire, was that because most CHA applicants appeared to want to live in ghetto neighborhoods, as shown by the "location preferences" in their applications, CHA's proposed ghetto sites complied with Public Housing Administration site selection regulations. The regulations stated that the aim was to select "from among otherwise available and suitable sites those which will afford the greatest acceptability to eligible applicants."[2]

McGuire's letter also contained this key sentence: "We are also advised that sites other than in the south or west side [Chicago's black ghetto areas], if proposed for regular family housing, invariably encounter sufficient objection in the [City] Council to preclude Council approval."[3] In other words, because Chicago's aldermen refused to approve locations outside the ghetto, nonghetto sites were not "otherwise available" for Chicago public housing, and therefore there was no violation of law.

With legal objections thus disposed of, planning for the new CHA projects proceeded apace; final city council approval came the following summer. The day the approval was announced, the *Chicago Sun-Times* carried an editorial, "Public Housing's No. 1 Mistake," accompanied by a cartoon showing a huge steel beam, labeled "Public Housing," being hoisted into the air by a construction crane of the "New Ghetto Construction Co." Undeterred by the criticism, CHA promptly proposed still another group of projects, 1,300 units on twelve more ghetto sites.

Harold Baron and the West Side Federation were also undeterred. Baron feared that McGuire's reasoning would encourage other state and local governments to require the approval of federal programs by local bodies, such as Chicago's City Council, even though they were not themselves the recipients of federal funds. Under the McGuire theory, the receiving agencies would not have to comply with Title VI because they would be acting under orders from other local bodies who, since they were not receiving federal money, were not subject to the law. Title VI would thus be neutralized, and federal funds would continue to flow to local institutions and agencies whose practices reinforced racial segregation. Baron and the federation sought help from the American Civil Liberties Union in Chicago.

One of the legal issues ACLU lawyers[4] began to wrestle with was particularly troublesome. Would it suffice to show the location pattern of CHA projects—the segregationist *effect* of CHA site selection—to prove discrimination, or was it necessary to prove intent to discriminate against blacks on the part of CHA? To be safe, the lawyers decided to advance both theories separately. They could win hands down on an "effect" theory—CHA's projects were demonstrably located in the black ghetto; they did not know whether or not they could prove intentional discrimination.

Another question was whether to sue Chicago and its city council as well as CHA. The lawyers decided not to do so because suit against fifty individual aldermen (they could not be sued as a group), charging them with discrimination, would have presented enormous practical difficulties.

In early August 1966, soon after the final city council approval of CHA's latest proposed projects, a case was filed as a class action against CHA on behalf of all CHA tenants and everybody on CHA's waiting list. A separate suit against HUD was also filed, alleging that HUD had assisted CHA's discriminatory housing policy by providing financial support. The complaints charged that CHA's placement of virtually all of its projects in black ghettos was a violation of Title VI of the 1964 Civil Rights Act and also of the equal protection clause of the Constitution. The first named plaintiff, the one by whose name a case usually gets to be known, was Dorothy Gautreaux.

The case was assigned to the late Judge Richard B. Austin, a former prosecutor, state court judge, and one-time candidate for governor who had been appointed to the federal district court in 1961 by President John F. Kennedy. Austin had a sarcastic wit and a reputation as a "tough little scrapper." He was five feet four inches tall, with a bristly white crew cut that made him look, as one reporter put it, as if he had an acrylic rug on top of his head. One of his proudest accomplishments was having sentenced Jimmy Hoffa to prison for fraud. He lived in an affluent white suburb and was viewed as a friend of Mayor Richard Daley. On the question of race and on most other matters, he was not considered a "liberal." When the author first told him what the Gautreaux case was about, his immediate response was, "Where do you want them to put 'em [CHA projects]? On Lake Shore Drive?"

Austin immediately stayed the suit against HUD pending resolution of the action against the housing authority. CHA then moved for summary judgment, asking that the complaint be dismissed as a matter of law. Taking a leaf from McGuire, CHA argued that the plaintiffs had chosen the areas in which they wished to live and were therefore barred from complaining about CHA's location policy. To support the argument, CHA produced individual application forms showing undeniably that the plaintiffs had expressed a preference for projects in ghetto areas rather than the few in white neighborhoods.

The facts were that CHA employees were instructed to tell black applicants about the long waiting time for projects in white neighborhoods and in this and other ways to "steer" them to the black projects to which CHA wanted them to go. Proof of the steering was essential if the lawsuit was to survive. To secure it, the author searched for CHA's tenant supervisor of the early 1950s (when most of the plaintiffs had filed their applications) and finally located her at an address in Upper Manhattan. On a stormy night late in 1966 she related the story of the steering, complete with a description of CHA's coding system, referring to blacks as "B" families, on documents that listed which projects were open to blacks and which to whites. Her story was duly filed in affidavit form. Affidavits from some of the individual plaintiffs were also submitted. Dorothy Gautreaux's said that before moving to a CHA project, she and her husband and child had all occupied one bedroom in an uncle's apartment. Odell Jones, his wife, and three children were living in two rooms and cooking in the bathroom. Doreatha Crenchaw and her three children lived in a rat- and roach-infested one and a half room flat. The children slept in the kitchen and shared a bathroom with six other families. And so on. Each of the plaintiffs said that their applications had been filled out by CHA interviewers who had told them to choose the project where, according to the interviewer, they could get apartments most quickly.

The affidavits succeeded. In March 1967, Judge Austin held that the plaintiffs had a right to sue, notwithstanding their expressed "preferences" for ghetto locations.[5] However, the judge ruled against the plaintiffs on the intent issue and held that actual intent to discriminate would have to be proved. Without such proof, Austin said, the mere fact that CHA sites had turned out to be almost exclusively in black neighborhoods would not be sufficient to show a violation of the law.

Faced with the necessity of proving intentional discrimination, the lawyers asked Austin to require CHA to turn over all its files and correspondence having anything to do with site selection. The CHA attorney was outraged and complained that it would take thousands of man hours and tens of thousands of dollars to comply with the request. The ACLU lawyers said they would do the job themselves if the judge would require CHA to make its files available. Austin agreed, and a reluctant CHA was forced to open its file cabinets. Through the good offices of the Urban League half a dozen college students were enlisted, instructed what to look for, and set loose with mimeographed forms to record what they found. All that summer, in basements and storage rooms, they pored through filing cabinets and folders. Most of the documents they examined were useless, but a few were very helpful. The most important find was a copy of an agreement CHA Executive Director General William B. Kean had entered into with Alderman Murphy, chairman of the city council housing committee. Its stated purpose was to "insure close coordination" between the housing committee and CHA "to provide for the selection of the most satisfactory sites." In effect, however, the agreement turned the ultimate decision on sites over to the city council's housing committee; CHA would clear all sites with the committee before proposing them to the council and would propose none of which the committee disapproved. The statistical result of the "close coordination" was that in the thirteen years following the 1954 Kean-Murphy agreement, 99.4 percent of CHA's 10,256 family units—all but sixty-three—were placed in black neighborhoods.

Armed with the documents unearthed by the students, the lawyers began to interrogate CHA officials. Thousands of pages of sworn testimony were produced. Most were as useless as most of the documents. Again, however, a few choice questions produced helpful answers. The executive director of CHA admitted that he had told an alderman in a city council hearing that the reason CHA could not "find" suitable sites outside black neighborhoods was that CHA was hamstrung by the city council's veto power.[6] The director also testified that he and the head of the city's planning department would visit Mayor Daley after CHA had made an initial selection of sites, at which point the mayor would say to the planning department head, "John, talk to the aldermen." Later, CHA would be advised of the outcome of the talks and submit only those sites that the aldermen had told "John" would be approved. The CHA general counsel admitted that suitable land in white areas was unavailable solely because of the city council's veto power. In an affidavit, CHA Chairman Charles Swibel acknowledged that the city council had CHA "over a barrel" and that CHA therefore acquiesced by choosing sites in black neighborhoods.[7]

Toward the end of 1968, the ACLU lawyers announced they were ready for trial. Fearing the publicity a trial would generate, CHA again asked Judge Austin to dismiss the case, now arguing that the materials developed during the pretrial period proved that CHA had no actual discriminatory intent and that if anyone was discriminating it was the aldermen. While waiting for a ruling on CHA's motion, the ACLU lawyers filed a similar motion of their own, arguing that the same materials proved *their* case. In February 1969, Judge Austin decided that the facts were not really in dispute and that CHA's own documents and testimony showed that intentional discrimination on its part had been established. He ruled that both Title VI and the equal protection clause of the Constitution had been violated.[8]

The opinion was strong. Austin found that the statistics alone proved a deliberate intention to discriminate. He said that no criterion other than race could plausibly explain the location of CHA's projects[9] and that the testimony of CHA officials corroborated the fact that there was deliberate intention to segregate. Neither the laudable goal of providing needed housing nor the possibility that the aldermen were not themselves racists but were simply reflecting the sentiments of their constituents could justify a governmental policy of keeping blacks out of white neighborhoods.

Austin also held that CHA could not escape liability because the impetus for the policy against choosing sites in white neighborhoods came from the city council. Incorporating the Kean-Murphy agreement in CHA's site selection procedure resulted in a racial veto before CHA could even formally present its sites to the city council. Thereby, Austin said, CHA made the policies of the aldermen its own and deprived opponents of the opportunity for public debate. But even if CHA had not participated in this informal elimination of white sites, its officials, Austin held, were bound by the Constitution not to build on sites chosen by some other agency on the basis of race.

The closing paragraph of Austin's opinion conveyed the judge's sense of the urgency of the problem:

> [E]xisting patterns of racial separation must be reversed if there is to be a chance of averting the desperately intensifying division of whites and Negroes in Chicago. On the basis of present trends of Negro residential concentration and of Negro migration into and White migration out of the central city, the President's Commission on Civil Disorders estimates that Chicago will become 50 percent Negro by 1984. By 1984 it may be too late to heal racial divisions.[10]

Front page headlines announced Austin's decision in Chicago. Mayor Daley expressed his concern that the ruling could slow up public housing construction.[11] Editorials discussed the "public housing dilemma" at length—"the realities of changing neighborhoods and of whites fleeing to the suburbs are eloquent testimony to the difficulties that still lie ahead."[12]

Chairman Swibel denied that CHA's actions had ever been discriminatory. He emphasized that oppositin to public housing by a community might be based on "economic and cultural factors" as well as on race. He said that CHA's great goal had been to build urgently needed housing for low income families and that CHA had proceeded "where the community welcomed public housing and where the need for slum clearance was the greatest." But because of the importance of its goal, CHA would not appeal; it would do its best to comply with Judge Austin's order. Swibel added that Austin's opinion placed the responsibility for the location of public housing squarely where it belonged—"on the entire community as it is constituted by all of its citizens."[13]

Judge Austin's opinion of February 10, 1969, had merely pronounced a dispersal objective. Still remaining was the task of drafting a specific order to achieve the objective, a task that took almost five months. There were long discussions with the judge in his chambers to which each side brought the views of outsiders, such as civic groups, urban planners, other experts, and the U.S. Commission on Civil Rights. The ACLU lawyers argued for a formula that would require a majority of future CHA units to be built in white neighborhoods, urging that the old pattern would surely continue if a specific formula were not imposed. A letter to Austin from the Civil Rights Commission supported that view. We believe, the commission's letter said, that the "essential element" in a decree would be "the requirement of a ratio of white area to black area units."[14]

On the other hand, CHA wanted an order that merely prohibited it from discriminating, without defining that word or spelling out how the past imbalances were to be redressed. It was fearful about ending public housing. In a memorandum to Mayor Daley in February, Swibel said that a formula proposed by ACLU (four new units in white neighborhoods for every one in a black) might mean the end of public housing and even of Chicago's Model Cities program.

Judge Austin also sought advice from HUD on what the order should comprise, but differences in approach between HUD and the Justice Department led to prolonged negotiations and delayed the federal government's response. The joint HUD–Justice Department memorandum that was finally developed expressed a noncommittal attitude on the key question of a specific formula.

As the decree finally emerged from the long discussions in Austin's chambers, it was far from being as restrictive as CHA had feared. Public housing for the elderly was not affected. The large ghetto area projects for 1965 and 1966 already approved could go forward; only future CHA projects would be affected. Three-quarters of future units were to be located in white areas (after the first 700 units—to "match" the 1965 and 1966 programs—were built in white areas). But half the tenants in new projects could be residents from the local community. In white neighborhoods, these would of course be whites. Other provisions of the decree prohibited large, institutionalized projects or the concentration of public housing in any one neighborhood. The hope was that such small-scale, controlled, "ice breaking" in stable communities would build up some experience with which to counter block-busting fears in neighborhoods threatened with wholesale racial change and help stem white flight. Austin also insisted, however, on avoiding even the appearance of tying CHA to a formula that could not be changed. He included in his decree an express provision for modification not only to provide for changed circumstances but (subject to court approval) for any CHA developments designed to "achieve results consistent with this order."[15]

The decree was finally signed on July 1, 1969. Editorial comment was generally favorable, if somber. The *Daily News* said that whatever happened, "one thing that Judge Austin has done is to put Chicago face to face with its most crucial issue—whether it is to be a city united or a city divided." It added: "The [City] Council, under the leadership of Mayor Richard J. Daley, must act in the full knowledge that if the decision is for a divided city, that can only be a stop gap on the way to a city in social and economic ruin."[16]

The *Sun-Times* editorial said that "whites who would flee the city at the sight of a black face must realize they live in a diverse society and they cannot, after all, run forever." The editorial continued that the Austin ruling opened the way for "some truly imaginative planning for a viable bi-racial city," and urged the city to "work to implement a sound Austin plan."[17]

Other comments were less hopeful. The Chicago *Tribune* editorialized that the dispersal of CHA sites ordered by Austin "is something more easily said than done."[18] *Time* magazine quoted the leader of a white homeowners group as threatening: "If the construction really starts, we'll take action of some sort, and not letters or petitions."[19] Congressman Roman Pucinski said the Austin ruling "probably has dealt the death knell to public housing here." He said that the ruling was a "disaster that could cripple the city's $38 million model cities program."[20]

Two years after the signing of the decree, CHA had not built one unit of new housing, even though it had been directed to do so "as rapidly as possible." First, the authority took a year to select sites. Then it decided that it should try to find some suburbs willing to accept a portion of the proposed housing before it submitted its chosen sites to the city council for approval. When Judge Austin learned that CHA had no realistic prospect of persuading any suburb to do so, he ordered the Chicago sites submitted to the city council immediately. But CHA appealed this order—even trying (unsuccessfully) to persuade the Supreme Court to hear the case—thereby consuming another year in the process. When the appeal was finally lost, the sites were at last submitted to the city council on March 5, 1971.

Front page headlines announced the news, complete with detailed maps and street addresses of the sites. Congressman Pucinski attacked Austin again, now for setting himself up as the "housing czar" of Chicago, and vowed to cut off federal housing money for Chicago to stop him.[21] Mayor Daley, at a city hall press conference, denounced CHA's proposed sites as "detrimental" to all the people of Chicago.[22] "These units should not be built," the mayor declared. Public housing should be built "where this kind of housing is most needed and accepted," presumably, that is, in the ghetto.

Meanwhile HUD, under the direction of its regional administrator for the Chicago area, Frank Fisher, had also been building up pressure on the city. Fisher had taken the position that federal funding for Chicago's huge Model Cities program would be imperiled unless the city came up with a tangible program to deal with Chicago's shortage of low and moderate income housing.

On February 1, 1971, however, George Vavoulis was appointed to replace Fisher as regional administrator of HUD. A former mayor of St. Paul who had spent most of his adult life as a florist, Vavoulis' approach was to smooth over difficulties, whatever the cost, and to placate Richard J. Daley. His method, he was reported as saying, was heart-to-heart talks. "It seems like housing has become a personal challenge to Mayor Daley," Vavoulis observed: "I think we'll be able to sign an agreement with Chicago soon, so all those [Model Cities] funds will be released."[23]

And so they were. On May 12, 1971, a "letter of intent" was signed by Daley, CHA Chairman Charles Swibel, and Vavoulis. Under the agreement, Chicago would receive immediately $12 million of $38 million in Model Cities funds being held for it, and HUD promised to pay over the remaining $26 million subject to the city's compliance with a modest three stage program. The money would actually be released, however, after the first stage. Among other obligations of the city, sites for 500 CHA units were to be approved by the city council by June 15, another 350 by September 15, and a final 850 by December 15.

In May and June, the city council held hearings on CHA sites, but by the June 15 deadline, sites in white neighborhoods for fewer than half of the promised 500 units had been approved. Moreover, the approved sites were concentrated in the white neighborhoods closest to the ghetto, not scattered throughout the city in more politically sensitive neighborhoods. Nonetheless, Vavoulis released Chicago's Model Cities money conditionally—conditional, that is, upon the city council meeting the September and December deadlines.

During the rest of the summer, the Daley-controlled city council made no pretense of trying to meet the September 15 deadline for approval of more public housing sites and did not even "catch up" on the June 15 obligation. Then, on September 10, 1971, five days before the September 15 deadline, an important development occurred: the U.S. Court of Appeals held that HUD as well as CHA was liable for the public housing discrimination in Chicago.[24] Following the 1969 order against CHA, the long-dormant suit against HUD had been revived.[25] After lengthy arguments, Judge Austin had held in essence that HUD had merely supplied CHA with money and was not itself responsible for CHA's wrongs. Now the court of appeals had reversed that decision, concluding that HUD was responsible for more than just supplying money. The judges relied heavily on Marie McGuire's old letter to the West Side Federation to show that HUD was fully aware of the Chicago realities and therefore had approved and funded CHA's program with knowledge of CHA's discriminatory practices. That, the court said, constituted discriminatory conduct by HUD in violation of both the Constitution and the 1964 Civil Rights Act. Therefore, HUD was legally as responsible as CHA for the Chicago situation.

On September 12, two days after the court of appeals' opinion and three days before the next letter of intent performance date, the author went to see Vavoulis. He pointed out that HUD had only released the Model Cities funds conditionally and that if the city did not comply with the requirements it was supposed to meet by September 15, including city council approval of more white neighborhood public housing sites, HUD would have to withhold any of the $26 million in Model Cities money that had been conditionally released but not used. (None of the funds, it turned out, had yet been drawn down by the city.)

Vavoulis refused to give assurances that HUD would enforce its own conditions. September 15 came and went without compliance. On September 17, therefore, the ACLU lawyers asked Judge Austin to enjoin HUD from paying the $26 million of Model Cities funds to the city until the provisions of the letter of intent were complied with. Austin promptly scheduled a hearing.

The hearing disclosed that HUD had made no serious effort even to discuss the city's failure of performance with the mayor or his subordinates. When the city argued that a termination of Model Cities funds would simply harm the poor residents of the inner city who relied on Model Cities social services such as the hot breakfast program, Austin shot back, "You're telling me it's better for a child to have breakfast than to have the opportunity to move out of the ghetto. Let them have cake, but don't let them move to the Northwest side or the Southwest side."[26]

Soon after the end of the hearing, Austin wrote a blistering opinion. He was plainly incensed at the city's frustration of his decree and enraged at HUD's, as he viewed it, abject surrender to the mayor, whom he compared to Alabama Governor George Wallace standing in the schoolhouse door to block the enforcement of school desegregation. He blasted HUD for its failure to insist on performance of the housing requirements it had itself laid down. Distribution of the Model Cities funds was enjoined until there had been minimum compliance with the decree.

The city, CHA, and HUD quickly appealed and in March 1972 secured a 2-1 reversal from the court of appeals over a strong dissenting opinion. Then, by a 4-3 vote, the appeals court denied a petition to have the case reheard by the entire court. Austin's rhetoric had turned out to be fatal. The personal attacks, excessive indignation, and virtual absence of legal analysis in his opinion led the majority of the court of appeals to conclude that the Model Cities program had little to do with housing, that no breach of Model Cities regulations was involved, and that it was beyond the power of the court to terminate funding for socially useful, nonhousing programs to force compliance with a public housing decree. The injunction on the Model Cities funds was lifted.

With the Chicago City Council still persisting in its refusal to approve the suggested sites submitted to it by CHA, the ACLU lawyers tried another tack: the city and all the members of the city council were added as defendants, and Austin was asked to suspend the state law requiring the council's prior approval of CHA project sites on the ground that the law was being used without justification to frustrate a court-ordered remedy for the wrongs done to the *Gautreaux* plaintiffs.

After a hearing in which the council totally failed to justify (or explain) its nonaction, Austin entered such an order. This time the court of appeals quickly affirmed Austin's ruling; and though the city tried to pursue the case in the U.S. Supreme Court, in January 1974, the Court declined to accept an appeal. By then, however, the Nixon-declared housing moratorium was in effect, and no immediate development of new public housing was possible.

Meanwhile, following the September 1971 decision on HUD's liability, the ACLU lawyers had begun a series of carefully structured presentations to Judge Austin to try to persuade him that HUD should be required to be involved actively in the provision of relief (in addition to merely supporting CHA's efforts in the city) and that the relief should not be confined within the Chicago city limits. However, Austin ultimately refused to grant metropolitan relief, and in September 1973 ruled that a remedy encompassing the entire metropolitan area would be improper because it would involve political entities not involved in the lawsuit and against whom no acts of discrimination had been proved. He entered a simple "best efforts" order against HUD, directing it to cooperate with CHA's remedial efforts within Chicago.

That order was then appealed to the court of appeals and argued in July 1974 before a panel that included former Supreme Court Justice Tom Clark. A few days after the oral argument, the U.S. Supreme Court handed down its decision in *Milliken v. Bradley* (see Chapter Four, pp. 91), rejecting the metropolitan area approach in a Detroit school desegregation case. The decision necessitated the prompt filing of a supplemental brief distinguishing *Gautreaux* and housing from *Milliken* and schools. The following month the court of appeals, by a 2-1 decision, with Justice Clark writing for the majority, reversed Judge Austin, held that a metropolitanwide remedy was proper, and remanded the case back to the district court to work out a comprehensive metropolitan area plan.

In May 1975, the Supreme Court agreed to review the case. After both sides had filed written briefs, the Court heard oral arguments in January 1976 and on April 20, 1976, handed down its 8-0 decision affirming the court of appeals. Justice Stewart, speaking for the Court, ruled that the *Milliken* decision rejecting a metropolitan approach did not impose a general ban on federal courts to order corrective action beyond a municipal boundary, but proscribed relief extending to the suburbs in that case because there had been no showing that the constitutional violations within Detroit had had any effect beyond the city limits. In *Gautreaux*, on the other hand, the relevant "housing market area" was found to extend beyond the city limits, and HUD had the authority to operate throughout the area. Thus, it would not be inappropriate for HUD to attempt to provide housing alternatives for the *Gautreaux* families in the suburban areas, without, however, undercutting the role of local governments. Subject to that limitation, the nature and scope of the remedial action was to be left to the district court.

With the principle of metropolitan area relief thus finally established, it was back to the drawing board. In June 1976, the ACLU lawyers agreed with HUD not to go back before the trial court to seek a formal metropolitan remedial order for one year if, during that time, HUD would take certain initiatives. Among other activities, HUD was to establish and fund a metropolitanwide demonstration program for up to 400 plaintiff families to provide housing opportunities mostly in suburban areas, with a maximum of 25 percent of the families to be housed in minority areas. Through such a program both sides hoped to learn something about the mechanics of providing suburban housing to inner city families before asking the trial court to deal with that question. Because of time-consuming but necessary administrative steps, the program did not get underway until near the end of 1976. (At the present writing, it is still too early to draw any conclusions from the demonstration program.)

Progress in new construction within the city has similarly been painfully slow. Even after the housing moratorium was terminated, the shortage of available land in the white areas of the city and the length of time needed to carry out HUD's recently developed environmental review procedures conspired to limit new CHA construction to less than 150 units built in compliance with Judge Austin's order. Prospects for large amounts of additional construction in the city are further dimmed by escalating construction costs.

The entire process has been protracted and tortuous. Though the *Gautreaux* case has been quite effective in helping to bring to an end the old pattern of concentrating public housing exclusively in black ghettos, it has been far less effective in promoting new housing patterns. Perhaps the case serves well to illustrate the limitations of the courts in bringing about a housing dispersal program and why that task must in the last analysis be the responsibility of the executive and legislative branches of government.

* * *

POSTSCRIPT

As this book goes to press (a number of months after the writing of the text was completed) approximately 175 Gautreaux families have been placed under the demonstration program, all but a few in white suburbs.[27] In July 1977, a new agreement between HUD and the plaintiffs continued the demonstration program for an additional eighteen months and expanded it beyond the Section 8 existing housing program by including new construction subsidy programs as well.[28]

Notes

NOTES FOR INTRODUCTION

1. The Housing and Community Development Act of 1974, 42 U.S.C. §5301(a)(1) (Supp. IV. 1975).

2. Report of the National Commission on Urban Problems, *Building the American City* (Washington, D.C.: Government Printing Office, 1968), p. 5.

3. These figures come from Bureau of the Census, *Current Population Reports*, Series P-60, no. 102 (Washington, D.C.: Government Printing Office, 1974). Poverty areas are those in which 20 percent or more of the population have incomes below the poverty level.

The federal government's statistical poverty definition is based upon a food plan designed by the Department of Agriculture for "emergency or temporary use when funds are low" and is said to be nutritionally adequate. Bureau of the Census, *Census of Population: 1970*, vol. 1, *Characteristics of the Population*, pt. 2 app. B, p. 32. There was no official poverty measure until the mid-1960s. Following commencement of the "War on Poverty" with Lyndon Johnson's State of the Union Message to Congress on January 8, 1964, several government agencies began to indicate the number and types of families that might be classified as "poor," based largely on earlier studies by Mollie Orshansky, an economist with the Social Security Administration, who developed income criteria of need by family size. In 1969, the Budget Bureau designated modified Orshansky poverty measures as the official delineation of the poverty population to be published regularly by the Census Bureau. For a discussion, see U.S. Department of Health, Education and Welfare, *The Measure of Poverty* (Washington, D.C.: Department of Health, Education and Welfare, April 1976).

4. Charles E. Silverman, "The City and the Negro," *Fortune Magazine*, March 1962, pp. 88, 89.

5. Jack Meltzer and Joyce Whitley, "Social and Physical Planning for the Urban Slum," in Brian J.L. Berry and Jack Meltzer, eds., *Goals for Urban America* (Englewood Cliffs, N.J.:Prentice-Hall, 1967), p. 134.

6. Charles L. Leven et al., *Urban Decay in St. Louis* (St. Louis: Institute of Urban and Regional Studies, Washington University, 1972), p. 3.

7. John F. Kain, "Effect of Housing Market Segregation on Urban Development," reprinted in Jon Pynoos, Robert Schafer and Chester W. Hartman, eds., *Housing Urban America* (Chicago: Aldine Pub. Co. 1973), p. 266.

Most central cities do not have large black ghettos and most are not likely to turn all black or to have black majorities. In 1970, whites outnumbered blacks by more than two to one in 211 of the 243 central cities, and demographic patterns were not all alike even in the remaining 32 whose 1970 black populations were at least one-third of their total population. Karl E. Taeuber, "Racial Segregation: The Persisting Dilemma," *Annals of the American Academy of Political and Social Sciences*, vol. 422 (November 1975): 89.

Black concentration in large cities is nonetheless a fact, particularly in the North and West. In 1970, two-thirds of northern blacks lived in seven metropolitan areas containing more than 300,000 blacks each, and two-thirds of western blacks lived in Los Angeles or San Francisco. *Id.* at 92. Although one cannot speak of a typical central city or metropolitan area, the larger cities in which most blacks live exhibit the same racial residential pattern. It is these cities which must be understood to be "the city" to which Kain refers.

8. *Report of the National Advisory Commission on Civil Disorders* (New York: Bantam Books Inc., 1968), p. 1.

9. For some analytical purposes it is essential to separate the issues of racial discrimination and poverty. Here, however, the focus is upon the synergistic amalgam of race and poverty in the black central city ghetto. We are here less interested in the relative weight to be given to factors of race and class in the creation and maintenance of the black ghetto than we are in recognizing that the central city ghetto is now largely black and that the black poor are heavily concentrated there, not scattered throughout the metropolitan area.

10. Thus a monograph on housing problems says that its proposals do not essay "social restructuring" by altering the "locational decisions" of subsidized households. These decisions, it is said, are "better made at the state and local level." Irving W. Welfeld, *America's Housing Problem*, Washington, D.C.: American Enterprise Institute for Public Housing Research, 1973), p. 33. As this book shows, decisions at that level will be decisions to maintain the status quo, which is to say metropolitan apartheid.

A comprehensive examination of land use and urban development questions sponsored by the Rockefeller Brothers Fund and extravagantly praised as a thoughtful statement includes an extensive index, which, however, lacks entries for "blacks," "ghetto," "inner cities," "minority," "poverty," "race," or "segregation." Neither does the report contain any significant discussion of the issues to which those terms relate. William K. Reilly, ed., *The Use of Land: A Citizens: Policy Guide to Urban Growth*, A Task Force Report sponsored by the Rockefeller Brothers Fund (New York: Thomas Y. Crowell Company, 1973).

11. National Commission on the Causes and Prevention of Violence, *To Establish Justice, To Insure Domestic Tranquility* (Washington, D.C.: Government Printing Office, 1969), p. 49.

12. To some the essential problem is the poverty of ghetto dwellers and the cure is therefore income maintenance. To others the problem is racial discrimination or lack of jobs or inadequate public education or bad housing or crime or

the fragmentation of local governments or the erosion of the city's tax base, or combinations of some or all of these or related factors. To still others we lack an adequate understanding of the mix of forces at work and therefore have no basis for evaluating the relative importance of one factor as against others. Meltzer and Whitley, *supra* note 5 at 140.

13. Edward C. Banfield, *The Unheavenly City Revisited* (Boston: Little Brown, 1974).

14. *See,* "The Great Society: Lessons for the Future," a symposium issue of *The Public Interest,* no. 34 (Winter 1974).

15. Banfield, *supra* note 13 at 90–91.

16. Bureau of the Census, *Statistical Abstract of the United States, 1975,* (96th ed. Washington, D.C.: Government Printing Office, 1975), p. 883. For a discussion see Patricia L. Hodge and Philip M. Hauser, *The Challenge of America's Metropolitan Population Outlook, 1960 to 1985* (New York: Praeger, 1968), p. 74.

17. *Statistical Abstract, supra* note 16 at 884–85.

NOTES FOR CHAPTER I

1. Gunnar Myrdal, *An American Dilemma: The Negro Problem and Modern Democracy* (New York: Harper and Brothers, 1944), p. 627.

2. Patricia L. Hodge and Philip M. Hauser, *The Challenge Of America's Metropolitan Population Outlook, 1960 to 1985* (New York: Praeger, 1968), p. 1.

3. Brian J.L. Berry and Jack Meltzer, eds., *Goals for Urban American* (Englewood Cliffs, N.J.: Prentice-Hall, 1967), p. 1.

4. Bureau of the Census, *U.S. Census of Population: 1960,* vol. 1, *Characteristics of the Population,* pt. 1, U.S. Summary (Washington, D.C.: Government Printing Office, 1964).

5. Bureau of the Census, *U.S. Census of Population: 1970,* vol. 1, *Characteristics of the Population,* pt. 1, U.S. Summary (Washington, D.C.: Government Printing Office, 1973).

6. Karl E. Taeuber, and Alma F. Taeuber, *Negroes in Cities: Residential Segregation and Neighborhood Change* (Chicago: Aldine Publishing Co., 1965), p. 1.

7. Morton Grodzins, "Metropolitan Segregation," *Scientific American* CXCVII, no. 4 (October 1957): 33.

8. *Report of the National Advisory Commission on Civil Disorders* (New York: Bantam Books Inc., 1968), p. 250.

9. Ibid.

10. Hodge and Hauser, *supra* note 2 at 53. See also note 7 to the Introduction, *supra.*

11. In 1920 no Chicago blacks lived in census tracts that were more than 90 percent black. In 1950 two-thirds did and the proportion was rising. Brian J.L. Berry, "A Closer Look; Chicago," *City* (January/February 1971), p. 38. The

human reality behind the figures was the "black belt," the worst part of Chicago's slum. Its population density was 75,000 to the square mile, several times that of the rest of the city. There was vacant land outside, where white children played in the "prairies," but little in the black belt. "In this black manheap there is no such thing as a vacancy, though outside there are twenty square miles of vacant land labelled white," complained a black writer in 1949. George A. Nesbitt, "Break up the Black Ghetto," *Crisis*, January 1949, p. 49.

12. U.S. Department of Health, Education and Welfare, *Toward a Social Report* (Washington, D.C.: Government Printing Office, 1969), p. 37.

13. U.S. Commission on Civil Rights, *Twenty Years After Brown: Equal Opportunity in Housing* (Washington, D.C.: Government Printing Office, 1975), p. 4.

14. United States v. City of Black Jack, Civil Action No. 71 C 372(1), District Court, Missouri, Pretrial Brief of the United States, pp. 8–9.

15. *Twenty Years After Brown*, supra note 13 at 3. The Supreme Court decision was Shelley v. Kraemer, 334 U.S. 1 (1948).

16. Anthony Downs, *Federal Housing Subsidies: How Are They Working?* (Lexington, Mass.: D.C. Heath and Company, 1973), p. 3. Although there is much low quality housing in rural and small town areas, not just in the core of the central city, the problem of rural poverty is generally not exacerbated by the massive concentration of poverty so often found in central city ghettos. Rural communities are usually marked by declining population, relatively weak legal controls over the quality and location of housing and less densely concentrated pockets of poverty.

17. Euclid v. Ambler Realty Co., 272 U.S. 365 (1926).

18. Report of the National Commission on Urban Problems, *Building the American City* (Washington, D.C.: Government Printing Office, 1968), hereafter cited as *Building the American City*, p. 208.

19. One technique, large lot zoning, has a direct effect on the supply—and hence the price—of developable land. Land costs rose much more rapidly than total housing costs in the postwar years. *President's Second Annual Report on National Housing Goals*, House Doc. No. 91-292, 91st Cong., 2d sess. (1970), p. 40.

20. R.B. Const. Co. v. Jackson, 137 A.278, 286 (1927).

21. Marion Clawson, *Suburban Land Conversion in the U.S.: An Economic and Governmental Process* (Baltimore: John Hopkins Press, 1971), p. 196.

22. *Building the American City* at 19.

23. *Hearings Before the Senate Select Committee on Equal Educational Opportunity*, 92d Cong., 2d sess. pt. 5, (1971), pp. 2966–88.

24. Josephine C. Brown, *Public Relief 1929–1939* (New York: Henry Holt, 1940), pp. 145–46.

25. 48 Stat. 201.

26. Lawrence M. Friedman, *Government and Slum Housing: A Century of Frustration* (Chicago: Rand McNally, 1968), p. 103.

27. Martin Meyerson and Edward C. Banfield, *Politics, Planning and the Public Interest* (New York: Macmillan, 1964), pp. 121–22.

28. U.S. v. Certain Lands in Louisville, 9. F.Supp. 137 (Ky. 1935), affirmed 78 F.2d 684 (1935), *appeal dismissed*, 297 U.S. 726 (1936), On the eve of the

Supreme Court argument the administration backed off from presenting the case because it feared that a hostile Court might render a broad and unfavorable opinion that could be prejudicial to a number of New Deal programs. Charles Abrams, "The Legal Basis for Reorganizing Metropolitan Areas in a Free Society," 106 *Proceedings of the American Philosophical Society* 177, (1962).

29. 50 Stat. 888.

30. Friedman, *supra* note 26 at 116.

31. 95 *Cong. Rec.* at 8644, 8667. As finally passed, the 1949 Act declared that the general welfare of the nation required housing production and community development to remedy a serious housing shortage, to clear slums and blighted areas, and to realize "as soon as feasible the goal of a decent home and a suitable living environment for every American family. . . ." 63 Stat. 413.

32. McDougal and Mueller, "Public Purpose in Public Housing; An Anachronism Reburied," 52 *Yale Law Journal* 48 (1942).

33. John P. Dean, "The Myths of Housing Reform," 14 *American Sociological Review* 281, 286 (1949).

34. U.S. Housing Authority, "What Housing Can Do For Your City," (Washington, D.C.: Government Printing Office, 1938).

35. *Building the American City* at 110.

36. Abner D. Silverman, "User Needs and Social Services," in *Papers Submitted to Subcommittee on Housing Panels, Committee on Banking and Currency,* House of Representatives, pt. 2, 92d Cong., 1st sess. (June 1971), pp. 579-606.

37. Dean, *supra* note 33 at 284.

38. For a general discussion see Comment, "The Housing Act of 1949, A Federal Program for Housing and Slum Clearance," 44 *Illinois Law Review* 684 (1950).

39. Friedman, *supra* note 26 at 123-34.

40. Gilbert Y. Steiner, *The State of Welfare* (Washington, D.C.: The Brookings Institution, 1971), p. 140.

41. Chester W. Hartman and Gregg Carr, "Housing the Poor," *Transaction* 7 (December 1969): 49.

42. Of the approximately 250,000 public housing units built by central city housing authorities in large metropolitan areas by 1967, a grand total of 76 units had been built by a single city authority in the suburbs. U.S. Commission on Civil Rights, *Racial Isolation In the Schools* (Washington, D.C.: Government Printing Office, 1965), p. 23.

43. Friedman, *supra* note 26 at 123.

44. *New York Times,* October 20, 1960, p. 26, col. 1.

45. *Building the American City* at 112, 130. By 1968 the public housing program had produced fewer than 750,000 units, about half the number private industry was producing in a single year for those who could afford market prices. Martin E. Sloane, "Changing Shape of Land Use Litigation: Federal Court Challenges To Exclusionary Land Use Practices," 51 *Notre Dame Lawyer* 48, 51 (1975).

46. Leonard Freedman, *Public Housing: The Politics of Poverty* (New York: Holt, Rinehart, 1969), p. 140.

47. Friedman, *supra* note 35 at 124.

48. *Id.* at 122.

49. Steiner, *supra* note 40 at 151–52.

50. *New York Times,* October 20, 1960, p. 58, col. 2.

51. Report of the U.S. Commission on Civil Rights, vol. 4, *Housing,* (Washington, D.C.: Government Printing Office, 1961) p. 113.

52. Harrison E. Salisbury, *The Shook-up Generation* (New York: Harper & Row, 1958), p. 75.

53. *Building the American City* at 152.

54. During the same period only a little over 500,000 dwelling units had been constructed for low and moderate income families under all HUD programs. Since the urban renewal demolition figure does not include the thousands of demolitions resulting from other HUD programs and the programs of other federal agencies (e.g., building highways), there is no doubt that in the two decades following World War II the federal government destroyed more homes and apartments of the poor than it built for them.

55. *Building the American City* at 163.

56. Relocation help—services and later some money—was supposed to be provided. But until the end of the 1960s, when the relocation law was beefed up, relocation was handled, as one commentator in the mid-1960s put it, "impatiently, if not ruthlessly." Herbert J. Gans, "The Failure of Urban Renewal," *Commentary* 39 (April 1965): 29, 30.

57. *Id.* In one case decided in the early seventies a federal judge in Michigan employed this precise phrase in concluding that the urban renewal plan of the city of Hamtramck (an enclave within Detroit) had been deliberately used by local officials, with HUD's acquiescence, to force blacks out of the city. Garrett v. City of Hamtramck, 335 F.Supp. 16 (1971).

In the words of a presedential commission report, urban renewal became "a federally financed gimmick to provide relatively cheap land for a miscellany of profitable or prestigious enterprises." *Building the American City* at 153. Candidly acknowledging its impact on the poor, George Romney, secretary of the Department of Housing and Urban Development in the first Nixon administration, later said, "Urban renewal became a program of bulldozing poor people out of their homes." *Hearings on HUD-Space-Science-Veterans Appropriations for 1973 Before a Subcommittee of the House Committee on Appropriations,* 92d Cong., 2d sess., pt. 3, (April 10, 1972), p. 92.

58. *Building the American City* at 164.

59. Nathan Glazer, "Housing Problems and Housing Policies," *The Public Interest,* Spring 1967, p. 30; Joseph P. Fried, *Housing Crisis U.S.A.* (Baltimore: Penguin Books, 1971), p. 68. A similar Veterans Administration program begun after World War II provided loan guarantees for additional millions of homebuyers who were veterans. Fried, pp. 84–85.

60. FHA Underwriting Manual (1938), ¶935; quoted in Gunnar Myrdal, *An American Dilemma,* 20th Anniversary Edition (New York: Harper & Row, 1962), p. 31.

61. In 1968 it was calculated that the relatively poor 40 percent of the population, whose housing needs were of course the greatest, had received only 11 percent of FHA mortgages. *Building the American City* at 100.

62. *Id.* at 101.

63. Gary Orfield, "Federal Policy, Local Power, and Metropolitan Segregation," *Political Science Quarterly* 89, no. 4 (Winter 1974-75): 786 (cited hereafter as "Federal Policy, Local Power").

64. FHA Underwriting Manual, §§935, 937, 951.

65. *Id.*

66. *Hearings Before the Senate Select Committee on Equal Educational Opportunity*, 92d Cong., 2d sess., pt. 5 (1971), p. 2755. Even fire insurance companies refused to insure against fires in integrated sections of the inner city. Under the 1968 Housing Act, fire insurance was made available under the "FAIR" plan (fair access to insurance requirements). *Id.* at 2755-56. For a discussion of the operation of a FAIR plan, see Richard F. Syron, "The Hard Economics of Ghetto Fire Insurance," in *Housing*, George Sternlieb and Virginia Paulus, eds. (New York: AMS Press 1974), pp. 181-92.

67. "Federal Policy, Local Power," *supra* note 63 at 788.

68. *Hearings, supra* note 66 at 2755.

69. Personal interview with John McKnight, associate director, Center for Urban Affairs, Northwestern University, Evanston, Illinois, 1974.

The statements in the Underwriting Manual warning against inharmonious racial groups and recommending restrictive covenants were eliminated in 1947. This placed the federal government in a formal position of "neutrality" on racial discrimination, leaving to private brokers, builders, and lenders with whom the government dealt the decision whether federal housing programs would be carried out in a discriminatory manner. Testimony of Martin E. Sloane, assistant staff director for civil rights program and policy, *Hearings Before the United States Commission on Civil Rights*, Washington, D.C. (June 14-17, 1971), pp. 736-738. However, FHA's previous policies and practices and its posture on restrictive covenants following the Supreme Court's decision in 1948 left little doubt about its inclinations and preferences in racial matters.

In its loan guaranty program, established at the end of World War II, the Veterans Administration's formal policy from the outset was one of neutrality. Like FHA, however, it took no steps to prohibit discrimination by the institutions whose loans it guaranteed, and its administrative policies with respect to segregation paralleled those of FHA. *Twenty Years After, supra* note 13 at 40. As with FHA, the poor were "largely left out" of the VA program. *Building the American City* at 104.

70. Charles Abrams, *Forbidden Neighbors: A Study of Prejudices in Housing* (New York: Harper & Row, 1955), p. 237.

71. Report of the U.S. Commission on Civil Rights, *A Time To Listen . . . A Time to Act* (Washington, D.C.: Government Printing Office, 1967), p. 126. FHA policies also had a self-sustaining, regenerative effect. FHA helped young, white child-bearing families move to the suburbs, and a high natural increase factor was thus built into the increasing white suburban population. Since the fertility of blacks in the cities was also high (not, contrary to some popular opinion, higher than in a number of new white suburbs), the racial separation FHA helped to bring about was reinforced by natural increase.

72. Testimony of George Romney, *Hearings, supra* note 66 at 2754.

73. "Federal Policy, Local Power," *supra* note 63 at 789-90.

74. Testimony of Martin E. Sloane, *Hearings, supra* note 69 at 735. In June 1961, the board passed a resolution opposing racial discrimination in mortgage lending by the financial institutions over which it had regulatory authority. The other regulatory agencies refused to adopt similar policy statements. *Id.* at 738-39.

75. See *Housing, supra* note 51 at 31-53.

76. Executive Order No. 11063, 3 C.F.R. 261 (Supp. 1962).

77. Until 1970, the U.S. Highway Trust Fund paid 90 percent of the cost of highways in the interstate system and 50 percent of the costs of numerous other highways, such as the primary, secondary, and urban systems. 23 U.S.C. § 120 (1970). Under a 1970 revision of the act the latter figure was increased to 70 percent. 23 U.S.C. § 120 (Supp. 1975). See generally, John F. Kain, "Postwar Changes In Land Use in the American City," in Daniel P. Moynihan, ed., *Toward a National Urban Policy* (New York: Basic Books, 1970). Kain notes that during the first decade following World War II (1948-1958) in the central cities of the forty largest metropolitan areas retailing employment dropped three-quarters, manufacturing employment a half, and wholesaling employment a third.

78, Yale Rabin, "Highways As A Barrier to Equal Access," *Annals of the American Academy of Political and Social Science* 407 (May 1973): 63-77; *Building the American City* at 48, 231.

79. *Hearings, supra* note 66 at 66-67.

80. Charles Schultze et al., *Setting National Priorities: The 1974 Budget* (Washington, D.C.: Brookings Institution, 1973), p. 133. It is difficult for some people to view a tax exemption or deduction as the equivalent of a subsidy payment. Stanley S. Surrey, Harvard professor, tax authority and former Assistant Treasury Secretary for tax policy, writes:

> Few realize . . . that while collecting . . . taxes from individuals and corporations, the Government is simultaneously paying between $80- and $90-billion to some of them. It does this by simply not collecting any or all the taxes it might on certain types of activities—those that, because of their claimed value to society, are permitted special tax benefits. If the Government were first to collect this $80- to $90-billion in the regular income tax sweep and then to disburse it again for those benefited activities, we would refer to the process as a subsidy.

Stanley S. Surrey, "The Sheltered Life," *New York Times Magazine*, April 13, 1975, p. 50.

For another discussion of tax exemptions as subsidies, see "Tax Exemptions—The Artful Dodge," *Society* (formerly Transaction) 6 (March 1969): 4-6.

81. *Building the American City* at 57.

82. Edward Banfield, *The Unheavenly City Revisited*, (Boston: Little Brown, 1974), p. 25.

83. *Id.* at 31.

84. *Id.* at 32.

85. *President's Fourth Annual Report on National Housing Goals*, House

Doc. No. 92-319, 92d Cong., 2d sess., (1972), p. 32.

86. Brown v. Board of Education, 347 U.S. 483 (1954).

87. 75 Stat. 50–51.

88. Executive Order, *supra* note 76.

89. 78 Stat. 252.

90. The rent supplement program, 79 Stat. 451–53, is codified at 12 U.S.C. § 1701s (1970); the leasing program, 79 Stat. 455, is codified at 42 U.S.C. § 1421(b) (1970).

91. 80 Stat. 1255.

92. *Building the American City* at 13.

93. *Twenty Years After, supra* note 13 at 34–35.

94. Henry J. Aaron, *Shelter and Subsidies: Who Benefits From Federal Housing Policies?* (Washington, D.C.: Brookings Institution, 1972), p. 135. The rent supplement program, under which the federal government would pay nonprofit or limited dividend housing developers the difference between a fair market rent and the lower rent paid by the tenant (who was required to pay at least 25 percent of income), escaped the local approval requirement in the authorizing legislation, but appropriation acts regularly imposed it. The leasing program, which authorized public housing authorities to lease private apartments at market rents and then sublease them at public housing rentals, had the local approval requirement attached to it from the beginning.

95. National Commission Against Discrimination in Housing, *A Housing Program for All Americans* (New York: National Committee Against Discrimination in Housing, 1964).

96. *Chicago Sun-Times*, July 11, 1966, p. 3.

97. *Id.* at 5.

98. *Chicago Tribune*, August 6, 1966.

99. Summit agreement, reported in *Chicago Sun-Times*, August 27, 1966.

100. *Chicago Tribune*, April 7, 1967.

101. *Chicago American*, May 29, 1967.

102. National Committee Against Discrimination in Housing, *How The Federal Government Builds Ghettos* (New York: National Committee Against Discrimination in Housing, 1967). p. 3.

103. *Report of the National Advisory Commission on Civil Disorders, supra* note 8 at 474.

104. For a list of exceptions to the coverage of the act, see Sloane, *supra* note 45 at 52.

105. Judge Wright, concurring in Mayers v. Ridley, 465 F.2d 630, at 635 (*per curiam*) (1972).

106. Jones v. Mayer, 392 U.S. 409 (1968).

107. Five of the six million subsidized units were to be newly constructed, one million to be rehabilitated. Charles Schultze et al., *Setting National Priorities: The 1972 Budget* (Washington, D.C.: The Brookings Institution, 1971), pp. 276–77. Some idea of the magnitude of the six million, ten year goal may be obtained from this comparison: subsidizing 600,000 units a year would put the rate of subsidized housing starts at more than twelve times the average rate achieved since passage of the Housing Act of 1949.

108. 82 Stat. 477, 498. For codification of the section 235 and 236 programs, see 42 U.S.C. §1715z, §1715z-1 (1970).

109. 82 Stat. 486. For a discussion see Report of the U.S. Commission on Civil Rights, *Home Ownership for Lower Income Families* (June 1971), pp. 81–82.

110. The Report of the President's Committee on Urban Housing, *A Decent Home* (Washington, D.C.: Government Printing Office, 1969), p. 5.

111. *Id.* at 48.

112. *Id.* at 25.

113. *Building the American City* at 4.

114. *Id.* at 5.

115. *Id.* at 30–31.

116. Tom Wicker, "Introduction," *Report of the National Advisory Commission on Civil Disorder, supra* at v, xi.

NOTES FOR CHAPTER 2

1. Remarks by George Romney, *HUD News*, March 26, 1969, pp. 1-2.

2. Remarks by George Romney, *HUD News*, January 8, 1970, p. 1.

3. *President's Second Annual Report on National Housing Goals*, House Doc. 91-292, 91st Cong., 2d sess. (1970), pp. (iii), 16. During the first four years of the Nixon administration nearly 300,000 units of public housing were completed or begun, a striking result when compared to the more than thirty years it had taken to build 800,000 units from the beginning of public housing in the 1930s to the end of the Johnson administration. *President's Fourth Annual Report on National Housing Goals*, House Doc. 92-319, 92nd Cong., 2d sess. (1972), p. 46. In addition, under the section 235 and 236 programs created by the 1968 Housing Act, HUD subsidized the construction of nearly 900,000 homes and apartments for "moderate income" families whose incomes, slightly higher than those of the very poor who were eligible for public housing, left them still poor enough to be fairly called "neglected Americans."

4. *National Journal*, January 17, 1970, p. 118.

5. *National Journal*, January 24, 1970, p. 167.

6. *New York Times*, April 28, 1970, p. 17, col. 1; *Chicago Tribune*, April 28, 1970.

7. *President's Second Annual Report, supra* note 3.

8. *Id.* at 10, 20-21, 42.

9. *Id.* at 10, 15.

10. *New York Times*, June 3, 1970, p. 1, col. 5.

11. "Workable Program for Community Improvement,"*A HUD Handbook*, no. 7100.1 (Washington, D.C. HUD, October 1968).

12. Memorandum from Edward Levin, special assistant, to Francis Fisher, regional administrator, April 16, 1970.

13. Memorandum from Edward Levin to Francis Fisher, February 16, 1970.

14. Letter from Francis Fisher to Ted Bates, mayor of Warren, March 9, 1970.

15. Memorandum from Edward Levin to Francis Fisher, February 16, 1970.

16. Memorandum from Sam Jackson, HUD assistant secretary, to all regional administrators, April 3, 1970.

17. The following account of the May 7 meeting is taken from *The Detroit News*, July 24, 1970, pp. 1, 6A.

18. Memorandum from Edward Levin to Francis Fisher, July 1, 1970, p. 14.

19. *Id.* at 1.

20. Plaintiffs' Post Trial Brief, p. 15, in NAACP v. Warren, Civil Action No. 35843, United States District Court, Eastern District of Michigan, Southern Division.

21. *The Detroit News*, July 21, 1970, p. 1.

22. *The Detroit News*, July 22, 1970, p. 1.

23. *The Detroit News*, July 23, 1970, p. 1; July 24, 1970, p. 1.

24. *The Detroit Free Press*, July 28, 1970.

25. Excerpts from statement of George Romney, *HUD News*, July 27, 1970.

26. *The Detroit Free Press*, July 28, 1970.

27. Memorandum from Edward Levin to Richard C. Van Dusen, undersecretary, July 1, 1970, pp. 7-8.

28. *The Detroit News*, July 28, 1970, p. 16A.

29. *The Detroit Free Press*, July 28, 1970.

30. *Hearings Before the Senate Select Committee on Equal Educational Opportunity*, 92d Cong., 2d sess., pt. 5 (1971), p. 2786.

31. *National Journal*, October 17, 1970, p. 2251.

32. *Id.* at 2251, 2252. (The italics were said to be HUD's.)

33. *Id.* at 2251.

34. *National Journal*, December 11, 1971, p. 2434; *New York Times*, November 22, 1970, p. 1, col. 5. The columnists, Evans and Novak, later reported that Nixon really wanted to purge Romney but was reluctant to do so so soon after his recent dismissal of Walter Hickel from the cabinet. Rowland Evans and Robert Novak, *Nixon in the White House: The Frustration of Power* (New York: Random House, 1971), pp. 358-60.

35. *Public Papers of the Presidents*, December 10, 1970, p. 1106.

36. *Wall Street Journal*, December 16, 1970, p. 14, col. 3. Former Nixon speech writer William Safire says that in outlining what he wanted Safire to put into a forthcoming statement (this was in 1972) on school segregation Nixon said, "I've always been against busing—don't say 'forced busing' by the way, that's too obvious a code word." William Safire, *Before the Fall* (Garden City, New York, Doubleday and Co., 1975), p. 481.

37. *Hearing before the United States Commission on Civil Rights*, Washington, D.C. (June 14-17, 1971), pp. 769, 798, 799, 806.

38. "Statement by the President on Federal Policies Relative to Equal Housing Opportunity," *Id.* at 573-87.

39. *President's Second Annual Report, supra* note 3 at 42.

40. "Statement by the President," *supra* note 38 at 583.

41. *Id.* at 585.

42. *Hearings, supra* note 30 at 2757, 2782.

43. *National Journal,* October 17, 1970, p. 2251.

44. *Weekly Compilation of Presidential Documents,* col. 6, no. 13, March 30, 1970, p. 242.

45. *Hearing, supra* note 37 at 432.

46. *National Journal,* June 19, 1971, p. 1328. The previous year a presidential task force on urban renewal had made the same recommendation. The President's Task Force on Urban Renewal, *Urban Renewal: One Tool Among Many* (Washington, D.C.: Government Printing Office, 1970). The task force also said it felt "strongly" that urban renewal should be used "to help in exorcising the spectre of economic and ethnic apartheid." *Id.* at 4.

47. "Statement by the President," *supra* note 38 at 583.

48. Statement of George Romney, *Hearing, supra* note 37 at 803.

49. Statement of David M. Trubek, *Hearing, supra* note 37 at 828.

50. *Id.* at 851.

51. *Id.* at 853.

52. National Land and Investment Co. v. Easttown Township Board, 215 A.2d 597 (1965).

53. Appeal of Girsh, 263 A.2d 395 (1970).

54. Statement of David Trubek, *supra* note 47 at 855–57.

55. *Id.* at 859–83.

56. Report of the National Commission on Urban Problems, *Building the American City* (Washington, D.C.: Government Printing Office, 1968).

57. *Public Papers of the Presidents,* April 14, 1969, p. 284.

58. *Public Papers of the Presidents,* September 8, 1969, p. 637.

59. *National Journal,* June 2, 1973, p. 801.

60. *New York Times,* January 3, 1974, p. 30, col. 3.

61. Response by Public Interest Groups to Administration Pronouncement on Equal Housing Opportunity, June 1971, p. 12 (unpublished).

62. 42 U.S.C. §3610(d) (1970); 42 U.S.C. §3610(a) (1970).

63. Kennedy Park Homes Association v. City of Lackawanna, 318 F.Supp. 669 (N.Y. 1970), *aff'd.* 436 F.2d 108 (1970).

64. U.S. v. City of Black Jack, Missouri, 508 F.2d 1179 (1974). Until 1970 Black Jack was an unincorporated part of St. Louis County. In 1969 a religious organization began planning a section 236 project "to create alternative housing opportunities for persons of low and moderate income living in the ghetto areas of St. Louis." *Id.* at 1182. Land was obtained in an area designated for multiple family construction in the county's master plan, and HUD approved the project in June 1970. Two months after that the St. Louis County Council incorporated the Black Jack area and in two more months the newly formed city council passed an ordinance prohibiting the construction of any new multiple family dwellings within Black Jack. Romney promptly termed the action "flagrantly unconstitutional," thereby embarrassing Mitchell who took over seven and a half months to bring the Black Jack case. The district court eventually ruled in Black Jack's favor, declaring that the ordinance banning apartments was a valid exercise of the police power that had no racially discriminatory effects. Finally, in January 1975, the appeals court upheld the Justice Department position and

invalidated the ordinance on the ground of its racially discriminatory effect.

65. Cornelius v. City of Parma, 374 F.Supp. 730 (Ohio, 1974).

66. Memorandum from Ruth Zack and Arthur D. Wolf, attorneys, Housing Section, to Frank E. Schwelb, chief, Housing Section, Civil Rights Division, Department of Justice, January 31, 1972.

67. U.S. Commission on Civil Rights, *Equal Opportunity in Suburbia* (Washington, D.C.: U.S. Commission on Civil Rights, 1974), p. 41.

68. *Id.* at 40–42.

69. 24 Code of Federal Regulations § 200.700, et seq. (1975), Subpart N.

70. The project selection criteria were said to represent the "first major effort by the Federal Government to consider systematically the social and environmental impact of subsidized housing on the nation's communities." Department of Housing and Urban Development, *Implementation of HUD Project Selection Criteria for Subsidized Housing: An Evaluation* (Washington, D.C.: U.S. Department of Housing and Urban Development, December 1972), Foreword. Further explaining the background of the criteria, HUD's *Evaluation* quoted Secretary Romney as follows: "[I]t seems obvious that if the nation's housing goals are to be met without further exacerbation of the problems resulting from past policies, the Federal subsidized housing of the future must be designed and located differently than has been the case in the last thirty years." *Id.* at 7.

71. U.S. Commission on Civil Rights, *Home Ownership for Lower Income Families* (Washington, D.C.: Government Printing Office, June 1971), p. 41. The reasons, as the commission staff explored them, included HUD's tacit acceptance of racially segregated patterns. Essentially HUD administered the section 235 program by waiting for real estate brokers to present it with applicants for mortgages. Nearly all brokers interviewed by the commission staff were convinced of one thing—minorities, particularly lower income minorities, did not want to move into predominantly white areas. Thus, the separate housing market for minority buyers, as perceived by brokers, led to relationships with clients and to advertising practices that fell inexorably into a segregated pattern. No HUD office visited by the commission's staff had taken any action to change that pattern. Indeed, most HUD insuring office personnel interviewed by commission staff expressed surprise that anyone should be interested in documenting the segregated buying patterns of minority and white section 235 buyers. To them the patterns were both obvious and inevitable. When commission staff discussed the possibility of affirmative action with HUD personnel, one standard answer was given: Washington had not issued any instructions. *Id.* at 47, 85.

72. *Id.* at 86.

73. 24 Code of Federal Regulations § 200.600 et seq. (1975), Subpart M.

74. Leonard S. Rubinowitz, Joel Greenfield, Jay Harris, *Affirmative Marketing of Federally Assisted Housing: Implementation in the Chicago Metropolitan Area*, A Study by the Urban-Suburban Investment Study Group, Center for Urban Affairs, (Evanston, Ill.: Northwestern University, 1974).

75. *National Journal*, December 12, 1971, p. 2433.

76. The Federal agencies that regulated housing finance institutions did virtually nothing about racial discrimination in mortgage lending. *See Report on*

Fair Lending Enforcement from the Senate Committee on Banking, Housing and Urban Affairs, H.R. 94-930, 94th Cong., 2d sess. (Washington, D.C.: Government Printing Office, June 3, 1976).

77. Golden v. Planning Board of Town of Ramapo, 285 N.E. 2d 291 (1972).

78. Taxes on the land were to be reduced to reflect its diminished value in the interim before the necessary public facilities were provided. A developer could obtain his special permit by providing facilities himself, but that would of course substantially increase the cost of his housing.

The Ramapo ordinance also limited residential zones in the unincorporated area of the township to single family housing. Since most of Ramapo's black residents lived in one of the unincorporated villages—only about 1 percent of the population of the unincorporated area was black—multifamily housing was in effect confined to the areas of black residence. (According to the 1970 census, about 4,500 of Ramapo's 76,000 odd residents were black. Bureau of the Census, *Census of Population: 1970*, Series PC(1)-C.1.)

79. Golden v. Planning Board of Town of Ramapo, 285 N.E. 2d 291 at 300.

80. *Id.* at 309.

81. *Wall Street Journal*, October 17, 1972, p. 1.

82. *New York Times*, May 20, 1973, p. 28, col. 1.

83. Board of Supervisors of Fairfax County v. DeGroff Enterprises, 198 S.E. 2d 600 (1973). For a discussion of the Fairfax County ordinance and a similar one enacted by Montgomery County, Maryland, see Leonard S. Rubinowitz, *Low-Income Housing: Suburban Strategies* (Cambridge: Ballinger, 1974), pp. 53–63.

84. Statement of George Romney before the Subcommittee on Housing of the House Committee on Banking and Currency, (Washington, D.C.: Department of Housing and Urban Development, February 22, 1972), p. 20.

85. *HUD Challenge*, April 1972, p. 26.

86. *Hearings on HUD-Space-Science-Veterans Appropriations for 1973 Before a Subcommittee of the House Committee on Appropriations.*, 92d Cong., 2d sess., pt. 3 (April 10, 1972), pp. 37 et seq.

87. *Id.*

88. *Home Ownership, supra* note 69 at 82, n. 256.

89. *National Journal*, January 1, 1972, p. 29. Senator Sparkman later said, "[T]here was never any Congressional intent to authorize local FHA offices to insure substandard housing or to accept as mortgagors the poor whose financial condition did not justify homeownership.... [The intent was] to eliminate 'redlining' in older declining urban areas...." *The Central City Problem and Urban Renewal Policy*, a study prepared by the Congressional Research Service of the Library of Congress, 93rd Cong. 1st sess. (Washington, D.C.: Government Printing Office, 1973), p. 229.

90. Just as the real estate industry played an important role in preserving the "integrity" of many white neighborhoods against blacks and other minorities, it also facilitated the turnover of neighborhoods deemed "ripe" for change. "Blockbusting," it is said, was developed into a fine art in the Bedford-Stuyvesant section of New York where, "Any time there was any possibility of stabilization, real estate men would spur on the process of change by paying Negroes to stage brawls on the street corners to frighten white residents. Nearly

every day's mail contained postcards reading, 'we have a buyer for your house.'"
Fred C. Shapiro and James W. Sullivan, *Race Riots, New York 1964*, (New
York: Thomas Y. Crowell Company, 1964), p. 109. Thereafter the art was
widely employed on the fringe of the inner city ghetto, to the enormous profit of
the industry. Brian Boyer, *Cities Destroyed for Cash: The FHA Scandal at HUD*
(Chicago: Follett Publishing Co. 1973).

91. House Committee on Banking and Currency, *Investigation and Hearings
of Abuse in Federal Low and Moderate Income Housing Program*, Staff Report
and Recommendations, 91st Cong. 2d sess. (Washington, D.C.: Government
Printing Office, December 1970), p. 1.

92. Statement of George Romney before the Legal and Monetary Affairs
Subcommittee of the House Committee on Government Operations (Washington,
D.C.: Department of Housing and Urban Development, May 3, 1972), p. 6.

93. Remarks by George Romney, *HUD News* March 6, 1972, p. 5.

94. Statement of George Romney, *supra* note 90, p. 19.

95. *National Journal*, January 1, 1972, p. 26.

96. *Hearings, supra*, note 84 at 64, 76, 93.

97. *National Journal*, July 1, 1972, p. 1079.

98. *Id.* at 1078.

99. Statement of George Romney, *supra* note 90 at 20-21.

100. *Id.* 21-23.

101. Remarks by George Romney, *HUD News*, January 28, 1972, pp. 13-14.

102. Remarks by George Romney, *HUD News*, March 6, 1972, p. 12.

103. *Public Papers of the Presidents*, January 28, 1965, p. 14.

104. *National Journal*, July 24, 1971, p. 1542.

105. *Hearings before the Subcommittee on Housing of the House Committee
on Banking and Currency*, 92d Cong., 1st sess, pt. 1 (1971), p. 70.

106. *Id.* at 75, 80-81. When subcommittee hearings resumed in the spring of
1972, Ashley's metropolitan agency proposal was twice rejected, by votes of 9-4
and 10-5. The result reflected the combined opposition of the homebuilding
industry, which viewed the metropolitan agency as another constraint on the
development of housing, and of some civil rights organizations, which still found
the proposal too weak. The basic opposition, however, was probably from suburban congressmen who wished to protect the exclusionary powers of the suburbs.
Indeed, after the defeat of the metropolitan proposal, stringent local approval
requirements were adopted instead—the subcommittee bill required local government approval even for section 235 and 236 housing, which had always been
free of such requirements, and strengthened the local veto power over public
housing by requiring local approval of the construction of a project on each
particular site. These new local approval requirements never became law only
because in September the entire housing bill was blocked by the House Rules
Committee, which voted not to permit it to go to the floor.

107. Remarks by George Romney, *HUD News*, May 23, 1972.

108. George Romney, "Accomplishments of HUD, 1969-1972," *HUD News*,
January 3, 1973.

109. Remarks by George Romney, *HUD News*, January 5, 1973.

110. *Id.*

111. *Id.*

NOTES FOR CHAPTER 3

1. Precedents of sorts existed. Early in the century Congress had expressly authorized presidents to "impound" or decline for economic reasons to spend funds it had authorized or directed to be spent. Under Franklin D. Roosevelt the practice of unilateral presidential impoundment became prevalent, particularly during World War II when congressionally authorized projects that would absorb funds needed for the war effort were often deferred. The practice continued after the war, but budgetary rather than program reasons were almost always given for expenditure deferrals. Frank Church, "Impoundment of Appropriated Funds: The Decline of Congressional Control Over Executive Discretion," 22 *Stan.L.Rev.* 124 (1970).

2. *Hearing on the Nomination of James T. Lynn Before The Senate Committee on Banking, Housing and Urban Affairs,* 93d Cong., 1st sess. (January 17, 1973), p. 3 A corporation lawyer from Cleveland, Lynn had served as general counsel and undersecretary of the Commerce Department in the first Nixon administration. *Id.* at 7. The appointment was criticized on the gound that Lynn had virtually no experience with housing and urban development problems. However, Oregon Senator Robert Packwood observed that the housing experts hadn't done very well in solving the housing problems, and he for one was happy to see an "openminded generalist" take over. *Id.* at 37.

3. President Nixon's radio address on community development, March 4, 1973, *Cong. Q. Weekly Rep.* 513; President Nixon's State of the Union Message on community development, March 8, 1973, 119 *Cong. Rec.* 13320 (1973). The "Better Communities Act" embodying the administration's proposal was soon sent to Congress. S. 1743, 93d Cong., 1st sess., 119 *Cong. Rec.* 14665 (1973).

4. *Report of the Subcommittee on Priorities and Economy in Government of the Joint Economic Committee,* 93d Cong., 1st sess., (Washington, D.C.: Government Printing Office, March 5, 1973), p. 3.

5. *Hearings on Suspension of Subsidized Housing Programs Before the Subcommittee on Housing of the House Committee on Banking and Currency,* 93d Cong., 1st sess. (March 20, 1973).

6. H.J. Res. 512, 93d Cong., 1st sess., 119 *Cong. Rec.* 16296 (1973).

7. 87 Stat. 491.

8. In July of the following year, Congress passed The Impoundment Control Act of 1974, which dealt with the impoundment issue in a responsible way. 88 Stat. 332. The new law provided that if the president did not wish to spend money Congress had appropriated, whether for program, fiscal, or other reasons, he was to send a special message to Congress requesting "recission" of the appropriation and giving his reasons and relevant information. Unless the House and Senate then passed a "recission" bill within forty-five days, the president was required to spend the money. (The president could defer an expenditure within—but not beyond—a fiscal year if, after receiving a "deferral" message, Congress failed to order that the expenditure be made without delay.) By July 1974, however, the flow of legislative activity had already carried past the point of no return to the subsidized housing programs. Although the new impoundment act assured that nothing like the unilateral termination of housing pro-

grams could happen again, the January 1973 moratorium had set the stage for the achievement of the administration's dual purposes: a shift from construction to rental subsidies in the housing laws, and a New Federalism move to more local control over community development programs.

9. Federal Housing Policy Message from the President, House Doc. No.152, September 19, 1973, 93d Cong., 1st sess., 119 *Cong. Rec.* 30261 (1973).

10. "Housing in the Seventies," Report of the Department of Housing and Urban Development, *Hearings on Housing and Community Development Legislation 1973 Before the Subcommittee on Housing of the House Committee on Banking and Currency,* 93d Cong., 1st sess. pt. 3 ((1973).

11. *The First Annual Report on Housing Goals of the President,* House Doc. No. 63, 91st Cong., 1st sess., p. 3 (1969).

12. 79 Stat. 455.

13. 84 Stat. 1777.

14. The president said that under the revised section 23 program, 200,000 units would be subsidized by July 1, 1974, of which 150,000 units were to be newly constructed and 50,000 would be leased in existing buildings. Nearly a year later only 1,719 revised section 23 units had been approved by HUD, and none were under construction. Potomac Institute Report, *The Housing Assistance Plan: A Non-Working Program for Community Improvement* (Washington, D.C., 1975), p. 35.

15. *New York Times,* October 2, 1973.

16. S. 2507, 93d Cong., 1st sess., 119 *Cong. Rec.* 32153 (1973); H.R. 10688, 93d Cong., 1st sess., 119 *Cong. Rec.* 32457 (1973).

17. S. 1744, 93d Cong., 1st sess., 119 *Cong. Rec.* 14665 (1973); S. 2182, 93d Cong., 1st sess., 119 *Cong. Rec.* 23915 (1973).

18. H.R. 10036, 93d Cong., 1st sess., 119 *Cong. Rec.* 28464 (1973).

19. *Hearings on H.R. 10036, H.R. 7277, H.R. 10688, H.R. 10689 Before the Subcommittee on Housing of the House Committee on Banking and Currency,* 93d Cong., 1st sess. pt. 1 (1973), pp. 453-54. Weaver also referred to Ashley's "innovative and creative" metropolitan measure of 1971 which, he said, was unfortunately "abandoned" before the bill left the subcommittee. Ashley thanked Weaver for his comment, but suggested "abandon" was not entirely accurate. "You do not 'abandon' your wallet," he said, "if it is being fleeced." *Id.* at 457.

20. S. 3066, 93d Cong., 2d sess., 120 *Cong. Rec.* 31, 3379 (daily ed., March 11, 1974).

21. The committee report anticipated that under the bill's provision, in the long run "we would have more housing developments which are not occupied solely by the very poor, but by a cross section of lower income households. . . ." H.R. Rep. No. 693, 93d Con., 2d sess. (1974), p. 40.

22. *Senate Committee on Banking, Housing, and Urban Affairs,* Report on S. 3066, H.R. Rep. No. 693, 93d Cong., 2d sess. (1974), p. 82 (in reference to section 807 of S. 3066).

23. H.R. 15361, 93d Cong., 2d sess., 120 *Cong. Rec.* 90, 5454 (daily ed., June 20, 1974).

24. 88 Stat. 633.

25. 42 U.S. C. § 1437f (Supp. IV 1970).

26. *Law Project Bulletin*, October 15, 1974, pp. 5–6. Desirable though the economic integration objective may have been, there was considerably irony in the new law's emphasis on helping relatively higher income people. A principal criticism in HUD's *Housing in the Seventies* study was that the older subsidized housing programs failed to focus aid exclusively on the very poor. One publication said of the new law that "the very poor have been defined out of the federal housing program." *Id.* at 7.

27. Eligible activities are listed at 42 U.S.C. 5305.

28. 42 U.S.C. 5306 (b) (1) to (4) (Supp. IV. 1970).

29. 42 U.S.C. 5304 (a) (4) (Supp. IV 1970).

30. 42 U.S.C. 5304 (a) (4) (A) to (C) (Supp. IV 1970).

31. 42 U.S.C. 5301 (d) (4) (Supp. IV 1970).

32. 42 U.S.C. § 1439 (d) (1) (Supp. IV 1975).

33. Nor was a veto power retained by a city that did not apply for community development money and therefore was not obliged to prepare a housing plan. Such a city could only "comment" on a proposal by a housing authority or private owner or developer to provide subsidized housing (section 8) within its borders, and HUD was empowered to approved such proposals regardless of the comments if it determined that there was a need for the housing.

However, under the section 235 and 236 programs, local governments had had no role at all to play in HUD's funding decisions; land use control powers had been their sole weapon. Under section 8, local governments "gained" a right to object to subsidized housing proposals viewed as inconsistent with their housing plans. Only time would tell whether the "benefit" of the formal acknowledgement of housing needs would or would not be offset by the "detriment" of the right to object to specific proposals.

34. A HUD regulation magnifies this concern. To encourage eligible families to find the cheapest housing available, the regulation offers a "shopper's incentive"—HUD will share with the assisted family the difference between the actual rent and HUD's allowable rental figure. 24 C.F.R. § 1275. 103 (n) (1975). If cheaper housing is located largely in ghetto or fringe neighborhoods, the shopper's incentive would be a disincentive for ghetto dwellers to look for section 8 housing outside such neighborhoods.

35. Personal interview with a member of the subcommittee staff. Against this background, the weakness of the linkage is a major anomaly in the history of housing legislation. After a metropolitan housing approach was deliberately abandoned as a tradeoff for linkage between housing and community development, why did the bill drafted by the subcommittee staff require only housing planning, not housing performance, as a condition of obtaining community development funds? The answer is unclear. Perhaps the subcommittee staff, and the legislators who favored linkage, decided that to require actual performance of a housing plan as a condition of obtaining community development funds would be going too far. It is of course uncertain whether a bill with such a provision could have been enacted. Nonetheless, the distinction between planning and performance was never put in issue, and a metropolitan approach to

housing was given up without a fight for what looked like a legislative mess of pottage.

36. *Housing and Development Reporter,* February 23, 1976, p. 901.

37. *New York Times,* November 19, 1975. Inquiries of HUD in the middle of 1976 disclosed that HUD had no racial data on the section 8 program at all and could not say therefore whether the program was ameliorating or perpetuating racial residential patterns.

38. *Potomac Institute Report, supra* note 14 at (i).

39. *Id.* at 24.

40. *Id.*

41. In April 1976, HUD for the first time denied a community development fund application because of inadequate performance of a housing assistance plan. The situation was an especially grievous one involving the town of Hempstead, New York. Hempstead had long ago obtained some federal land on the promise that it would build low income housing and had subsequently received a reservation for seventy-five units for that purpose. Yet it refused to take any steps after that to develop the housing, and the town supervisor repeatedly and publicly expressed his opposition to doing so. Sounding very much like a rerun of Mayor Bates in Warren, the supervisor said Hempstead would "defy any federal ultimatum" and would not place low income housing in a community that did not want it. If that meant loss of community development funds, "So be it." *Newsday,* March 31, 1976; *Housing and Development Reporter,* April 19, 1976, p. 1107; HUD telegrams to Hempstead, April 12 and April 16, 1976.

Whether HUD would act in less blatant situations remained to be seen. However, shortly before the Hempstead action, HUD Secretary Carla Hills told a Senate committee that if a community was not addressing the housing needs identified in its housing assistance plan, HUD would not provide that community with community development funds. And a HUD memorandum issued just after the Hempstead action advised HUD field offices that a housing assistance plan had to contemplate a "program of action," and that if a recipient of community development funds had failed to take actions within its control to implement its housing plan, its application for more community development funds "should receive careful attention as a possible disapproval. . . ." HUD memorandum from John B. Rhinelander, April 19, 1976.

HUD thus belatedly appeared to be finding more "linkage" between community development funding and housing assistance plans than was expressed in the statute or in its own housing assistance plan forms.

42. 42 U.S.C. §5301(a)(1)(c)(6) (Supp. IV, 1975).

43. *Hearings Before the Senate Select Committee on Equal Educational Opportunity,* 92d Cong., 2d sess., pt. 5 (1971) pp. 2757, 2782.

NOTES FOR CHAPTER 4

1. Daily v. City of Lawton, 296 F.Supp. 266 (Okl. 1969), *aff'd,* 425 F.2d 1037 (1970).

2. Kennedy Park Homes Ass'n. v. City of Lackawanna, 318 F.Supp. 669 (N.Y. 1970), aff'd, 436 F.2d 108 (1970).

3. Crow v. Brown, 332 F.Supp. 382 (Ga. 1971), affirmed, 457 F.2d 788 (1972); Banks v. Perk, 341 F.Supp. 1175 (Ohio 1972), aff'd in part and rev'd in part, 473 F.2d 910 (1973).

4. U.S. v. City of Black Jack, Missouri, 508 F.2d 1179 (1974); Metropolitan Housing Development Corp. v. Village of Arlington Hgts., 517 F.2d 409 (1975).

5. For example, the Atlanta opinion quoted the statement in the Douglas Commission report that without major changes in public policies the overwhelming majority of future nonwhite population growth was likely to be concentrated in central cities. After describing the historic concentration of public housing in Atlanta and its exclusion from suburban areas, the opinion then announced that absent supervening necessity any action *or inaction* by suburban authorities that was intended to or had the effect of perpetuating racially segregated residential conditions, or that would thwart their correction, could not be permitted to continue. Crow v. Brown, 332 F.Supp. 382 (Ga. 1971), at 391-92.

6. Gautreaux v. CHA, 296 F.Supp. 907 (1969).

7. Banks v. Perk, 341 F.Supp. 1175 (Ohio 1972) at 1185-86.

8. Mahaley v. Cuyahoga Metropolitan Housing Authority, 355 F.Supp. 1257 (Ohio 1973).

9. Southern Burlington County NAACP v. Township of Mount Laurel, 67 N.J. 151, 336 A.2d 713 (1975).

10. The result of years of successful litigation might be a few score or hundred low income units in white neighborhoods. The Black Jack case, for example, involved a four year battle to rezone a single parcel and did not assure that other developers wishing to build subsidized housing in Black Jack could avoid similar confrontations. In January 1976, it was announced that Black Jack and the developer had "settled." Since construction was no longer feasible because of high costs and interest rates and changes in federal housing programs, Black Jack would purchase the tract on which the developer's section 236 project was to be built (paying $40,000 in damages for its racially discriminatory practices, in addition to the price of the land). Black Jack officials announced that although no specific plans had been made for the site, it would not be used for apartments. *New York Times*, January 14, 1976. Under such circumstances how many developers would be willing to proceed? (Almost all of the early cases not involving public housing authorities were brought by non-profit sponsors affiliated with religious organizations rather than by commercial housing developers.)

11. Valtierra v. Housing Authority of San Jose, 313 F.Supp. 1 (Cal. 1970), rev'd, James v. Valtierra, 402 U.S. 137 (1971). In 1973, in a case involving an attack on the Texas school finance system that resulted in substantial disparities in per pupil expenditures among school districts, the Supreme Court explicitly rejected the argument that wealth discrimination alone violates the equal protection clause of the Constitution. San Antonio School District v. Rodriquez, 411 U.S. 1 (1973). The Court distinguished several cases finding a constitutional violation where a definable group of the relatively poor were absolutely deprived of some benefit on the basis of inability to pay, for example, Griffin v. Illinois,

351 U.S. 12 (1956).

The early Lackawanna opinion contained language indicating that the racial effect approach might be acceptable to the courts, as did the Cuyahoga Housing Authority case. In the latter case the lower court's finding of racial discrimination was based on little more than statistics and a demonstration of the need for low income housing throughout the country. The indication was that plaintiffs might win such cases merely by showing a need for low income housing plus statistical evidence that suburbs were nearly all-white while public housing residents were likely to be heavily black.

12. Forest City Enterprises v. City of Eastlake, 41 Ohio St. 2d 187, 324 N.E. 2d 740 (1975).

13. City of Eastlake v. Forest City Enterprises, 426 U.S. 668 (1976).

14. Mahlaley v. Cuyahoga Metropolitan Housing Authority, 500 F.2d 1087 (1974).

15. Citizens Committee for Faraday Wood v. Lindsay, 362 F.Supp. 651 (N.Y. 1973), *aff'd.* 507 F.2d 1065 (1974).

16. Joseph Skillken and Co. v. City of Toledo, 380 F.Supp. 228 (Ohio 1974, *rev'd* F.2d 867 (1975).

17. Warth v. Seldin, 442 U.S. 490 (1975).

18. Washington v. Davis, 426 U.S. 229 (1976). One pessimistic appraisal was that the Court had made problems of proof of racial discrimination "well-nigh insuperable." The Potomac Institute Inc., Metropolitan Housing Program, Memorandum 76-6, p. 7.

19. Village of Arlington Heights v. Metropolitan Housing Development Corp., U.S. ,50 L.Ed.2d 450 (1977).

20. 67 N.J. 151, at 188 n. 20 (1975).

21. As might have been expected, the use of timed development controls proliferated after Ramapo. In August 1975, that approach got another big boost from the courts in a case involving a San Francisco suburb, Petaluma, which had enacted a growth control ordinance limiting building permits to 500 per year for five years. Acknowledging that the ordinance might frustrate housing needs, the U.S. court of appeals rejected an attack on the constitutionality of Petaluma's ordinance and concluded that the concept of the public welfare was sufficiently broad to justify Petaluma's desire to preserve its small town character, open spaces, and low density population and to grow at an orderly and deliberate pace. Construction Industry Association of Sonoma County v. City of Petaluma, 522 F.2d 897, 908-909 (1975). Since Petaluma's plan called for 8–12 percent of the permitted housing, perhaps fifty units per year, to be for low and moderate income persons, the Petaluma plan would presumably meet the Mount Laurel test.

22. Report of the National Commission on Urban Problems, *Building the American City* (Washington, D.C.: Government Printing Office, 1968), p. 93.

23. 67 N.J. at 211, 208, 209-10.

24. *Id.* at 192.

25. On July 20, 1970 the district court entered an order modifying its "best efforts" judgment order of July 1, 1969 by imposing a specific timetable for the submission of proposed sites for public housing. The July 1970 order was

affirmed, Gautreaux v. CHA, 436 F.2d 306 (1971). For the later developments referred to see, Gautreaux v. Chicago Housing Authority, 342 F.Supp. 827 (Ill. 1972), *aff'd* 480 F.2d 210 (1973).

26. *Atlanta Journal*, May 3, 1973. Immediately after the Atlanta decision in 1971, the surrounding county established its own housing authority, thus divesting the Atlanta authority from jurisdiction outside the city limits. Predictably, the county authority constructed no new housing.

27. 67 N.J. at 211.

28. For a list of such cases see, The Potomac Institute, Inc., Metropolitan Housing Program, Memorandum 75-8, December 15, 1975, p. 7.

29. *Trenton Evening Times*, November 20, 1975, p. B11.

30. *Trenton Evening News*, November 19, 1975, p. B1. In June 1976, a resolution was introduced in the New Jersey Senate to amend the New Jersey Constitution in effect to reverse the *Mount Laurel* decision. Potomac Institute memorandum 76-6, *supra* note 18 at 11.

31. Crow v. Brown, 332 F.Supp. at 384.

32. 67 N.J. at 189, n. 22.

33. There is a growing tendency for the states to participate in certain types of land use decisions, for example, those having significant and widespread ecological significance. See Robert G. Healy, *Land Use and the States* (Washington, D.C.: Johns Hopkins University Press, 1976). This is of course quite different from regional zoning for low and moderate income housing.

34. City of Hartford v. Hills (D.C. Conn., C.A. H-75-258) (January 28, 1976).

35. Gautreaux v. Chicago Housing Authority, 296 F.Supp. 907 (Ill. 1969); Gautreaux v. Romney, 448 F.2d 731 (1971); Gautreaux v. Romney, 363 F.Supp. 690 (Ill. 1973), *rev'd* 503 F.2d 930 (1974).

36. Milliken v. Bradley, 418 U.S. 717 (1974). The Nixon administration had worked hard for the Milliken decision. The government first entered the case at the district court level in March 1972, six days after Nixon had sent a special message to Congress calling for a moratorium on all busing orders. Rejecting the Justice Department's motion to defer its proceedings pending possible congressional action, the district judge ruled that Detroit schools were too heavily black to permit desegregation within the city alone and ordered the consolidation of Detroit and suburban school districts. In the appeal from that order the department then opposed metropolitan relief, first in a brief filed with the court of appeals in August 1972 (the following June, by a 6–3 vote, the court of appeals upheld the district judge's metropolitan ruling), and then in a Supreme Court brief (the Supreme Court reversed the court of appeals in July 1974 by a vote of 5-4). In its Supreme Court brief the department argued that metropolitan remedies for central city school segregation were permissible only where the central city segregation had "directly altered or substantially affected" the racial composition of suburban school districts (p. 39 of the Justice Department's brief in the Supreme Court), a view the majority of the Supreme Court essentially adopted—and which prompted the dissenting judges to complain that enforcement of the federal constitutional right to equal protection of the laws could now be limited by political boundary lines drawn by the very state responsible for the constitutional violation in the first place and obligated to remedy it.

Milliken governed *Gautreaux*, the solicitor general now contended, for—contrary to the teaching of *Milliken*—ordering a metropolitan housing plan in the Chicago area would compel suburban areas to participate in remedying wrongs committee by others solely in the central city (pp. 15–28 of the Justice Department's brief in the Supreme Court).

There was more than a little irony in the fact that, in 1972, at the very time the Justice Department was opposing metropolitan remedies in Detroit, Romney was telling everyone who would listen that the fragmentation of local government was the major obstacle that stood in the way of coming to grips with the problems of the central city. He was preaching "the option process," local responsibility, and the necessity for crossing the boundary lines that produced fragmentation at precisely the moment the Justice Department was arguing that the courts ought not to require local governments to cross those lines even where unconstitutional racial discrimination had been established and needed to be remedied.

HUD's attitude was succinctly stated in a letter it sent to a civil rights group that had criticized its decision to appeal *Gautreaux*. "HUD remains committed to the principle of metropolitan wide planning, but it is also committed to the principle of voluntarism. Metropolitan planning under the coercion of court decrees cannot succeed; it is only by a continuing process of negotiation, demonstration and education that local communities can be brought to understand the significant benefits to be derived from planning on a metropolitan-wide scale." (Letter from James F. Mitchell, March 13, 1975.) Shades of Romney and TOP!

37. Hills v. Gautreaux, 425 U.S. 284 (1976).

38. One potential minor exception arose out of HUD's power under the 1974 act to administer an existing (leasing) housing program wherever local housing authorities were not organized or were unwilling to do so. Using that power HUD could itself presumably create and administer a metropolitanwide existing housing program for *Gautreaux* plaintiffs. The success of such a program would of course depend on the willingness of private suburban landlords to rent apartments to black ghetto dwellers.

39. Though it was too early to assess their ultimate effect in New Jersey, let alone elsewhere, two steps taken in New Jersey in the spring of 1976 were of great interest and potential significance. On April 2, Governor Brendan Byrne issued an executive order directing a state planning agency to formulate a state housing goal and to allocate the goal among counties in the state, and then among their constituent municipalities, in accordance with specified factors. State officials administering various state and federal grant programs were directed to "give priority where appropriate to municipalities which are meeting or are in the process of meeting a fair share of low and moderate income housing needs." (Efforts promptly began in the legislature to nullify the executive order.) The Potomac Institute, Inc., Metropolitan Housing Program, Memorandum 76-5, May 28, 1976, pp. 7-8.

The month following Governor Byrne's action, a lower court in New Jersey, relying upon *Mount Laurel*, ordered eleven municipalities in Middlesex County to revise their zoning ordinances to permit the development of nearly 19,000 low and moderate income housing units by 1985 (a figure derived from county planning board estimates) and allocated to each of the municipalities its fair share of the required total number of units. The judge held that the zoning ordinance of each municipality was invalid under the *Mount Laurel* requirement that land use regulations had to make it realistically possible for developers to satisfy prospective housing needs. Recognizing, as Justice Hall had said in *Mount Laurel*, that courts could not build housing, the Middlesex County opinion nonetheless insisted that the eleven municipalities had to do more than rezone so as not to exclude the possibility of low and moderate income housing. In the final paragraph of a thirty-five page decision, and without any specifics, the court made two suggestions. The first was that the defendant municipalities "should" impose "mandatory minimums" of low and moderate income units in giving approval to particular multifamily projects. The second was that the municipalities "should" participate in housing subsidy programs (in which connection the opinion referred to the Supreme Court's *Gautreaux* decision), although the opinion added, "it is beyond the issues in this litigation to order the expenditure of municipal funds." Urban League of Greater New Brunswick v. Burrough of Carteret, Sup. Ct. Middlesex County, Chan. Div. No. C-4122-73, May 4, 1976.

The Middlesex County decision represented a major effort to implement *Mount Laurel*. The decision remained subject to appeal, however, and, even if affirmed, it would remain to be seen whether its last paragraph precatory directives would be more effective than Justice Hall's observation that Mount Laurel had at least a moral obligation to establish a public housing authority.

40. George Edwards, Judge of the U.S. Court of Appeals for the Sixth Circuit, "Desegregation: A View from the Federal Bench" (Address delivered to the American Issues Forum Conference, Chicago, June 3, 1976).

NOTES FOR CHAPTER 5

1. The arguments in favor of a housing dispersal policy have nowhere been marshalled more comprehensively and effectively than in Anthony Downs' *Opening Up The Suburbs* (New Haven: Yale University Press, 1973). The following year, in a detailed critique, "On 'Opening Up' the Suburbs," *The Public Interest* 37 (Fall 1974), Nathan Glazer argued that Downs had exaggerated the importance of the apartheid problem. He also expressed grave doubt that the benefits Downs claimed for a dispersal policy would in fact be achieved. In Glazer's view it was therefore unwise to develop a major new housing policy to combat metropolitan apartheid; such "heroism" was not necessary. This chapter uses the Downs-Glazer exchange as a convenient format for examining some of the arguments for and against a housing dispersal policy.

2. Downs, *supra* note 1.

3. Glazer, *supra* note 1 at 89.

4. *Id.* at 93.

5. Ben J. Wattenberg and Richard M. Scammon, "Black Progress and Liberal Rhetoric," *Commentary*, April, 1973.

6. Glazer, *supra* note 1 at 97-98.

7. *Id.* at 99.

8. John F. Kain, "Effect of Housing Market Segregation on Urban Development," in Jon Pynoos, Robert Shafer, and Chester W. Hartman, ed., *Housing Urban America* (Chicago: Aldine Publishing Company, 1973), p. 253. Even the most primitive analyses, Kain says, are sufficient to raise serious doubts about poverty as the explanation. Among other things, they show that the percentage of high income blacks living in the suburbs is considerably less than the percentage of low income whites living there.

9. *Id.* at 254.

10. Karl E. Taeuber, "Demographic Perspectives on Housing and School Segregation," 21 *Wayne Law Review* 833, 840 (1975). See also, Karl E. Taeuber, "Racial Segregation: The Persisting Dilemma," *The Annuals of the American Academy of Political and Social Sciences* 422 (November 1975): 90–91.

11. Bureau of the Census, *The Social and Economic Status of the Black Population in the United States*, 1972, Current Population Reports, Series P-23, no. 46; Bureau of the Census, *Characteristics of the Low Income Population: 1972*, Series P-60, no. 88 (Washington, D.C.: Government Printing Office, June 1973); *New York Times*, July 23, 1973, p. 17, col. 7.

12. Bureau of the Census, *The Social and Economic Status of the Black Population in the United States, 1973*, Series P-23, no. 48. In 1973 the number of blacks below the poverty line dropped back down to the 1971 figure. The Census Bureau said a sampling error could have caused the 1971–73 fluctuation and that it was not clear whether the actual number below the poverty line had changed. *Chicago Daily News*, July 3, 1974. Black unemployment figures were also slightly reduced but not as much as the white figures. The two-to-one black-white jobless ratio thus actually increased. Based on statistics such as these, the Urban League concluded that the proportion of blacks who could be called middle class had not significantly increased in recent years and that the 1973-74 inflation may have brought about a decline. *New York Times*, July 31, 1974, p. 34, col. 4.

13. *Chicago Tribune*, January 29, 1976, sec. 7, p. 1.

14. *Chicago Sun-Times*, December 15, 1975.

15. Unemployment among black teenagers in central city poverty areas is particularly acute and, in terms of prospects for the future, particularly important. A Twentieth Century Fund Task Force Report on Employment Problems of Black Youth points out that at the height of the country's economic boom in 1969 more than 25 percent of nonwhite teenagers in the central cities of the twenty largest metropolitan areas were unemployed. By the second quarter of 1971 the overall black teenage unemployment rate was 35 percent, and in poverty areas it was over 39 percent. "Even so," the report continues, "the official figures do not portray the extent of the problem. An additional number of ghetto jobless are never found by the enumerators. At the very least, 100,000 young black people—a most conservative estimate—have given up hope and have stopped looking for jobs." Report of the Twentieth Century Fund Task Force on Employment Problems of Black Youth, *The Job Crisis for Black Youth*, (New York: Praeger, 1971), p. 3.

Addressing the argument that central city blacks might enter the middle class at a rapid rate, Downs made some projections of nonwhite incomes through 1983. Based on these, he estimated that at that time about two-thirds of the nonwhite population would have incomes above the poverty level, roughly the same fraction as when the projections were made in 1967. Since Downs felt nonwhites would then form a much larger share of most central city populations, he predicted that the percentage of total central city population below the poverty level would not fall very much and might actually rise slightly. Anthony Downs, "Alternate Futures for the America Ghetto," in Anthony Downs, *Urban Problems and Prospects* (Chicago: Rand McNally, 1970), p. 52.

16. Karl and Alma Taeuber are the sociologists who devised the formula most commonly used to measure the extent of residential segregation. Karl Taeuber has cautioned that some of the 1960-1970 decrease, perhaps as much as half, resulted from changes in western and southern cities that have large nonblack and nonwhite populations. William L. Taylor, Memorandum for Metropolitan School Desegregation Conference, The Center for National Policy Review (Washington, January 7, 1975), p. 2. A low index figure would be around 25 or 30, the levels computed for some European ethnic groups—certainly below 50. *Ibid.* Moreover, if many neighborhoods undergo a transition from white to black, as in the decade of the 1960s, they will be "integrated" for a period of years and produce lower segregation index figures. Reynolds Farley. "Residential Segregation and Its Implications for School Integration" (Paper dated July 1974, delivered at Metropolitan School Desegregation Conference, The Center for National Policy Review, January 1975), p. 3.

17. Albert J. Hermalin and Reynolds Farley, "The Potential for Residential Integration in Cities and Suburbs," *American Sociological Review* 38 (October 1973): 595, 599.

18. Taeuber, "Racial Segregation: The Persisting Dilemma," *supra* note 10, at 90, 95.

19. Bureau of the Census, *Statistical Abstract of the U.S.* (Washington, D.C.: Government Printing Office, 1972), p. 16.

20. Gary Orfield, "Federal Policy, Local Power, and Metropolitan Segregation," *Political Science Quarterly* 89 (Winter 1974-75): 781-82. A discussion of recent demographic trends observes that while black suburbanization is numerically greater than ever before, it remains a minor pattern in black population redistribution and evidences the same racially discriminatory patterns that characterize central cities. Taeuber, "Racial Segregation: The Persisting Dilemma," *supra* note 10.

21. The growth of segregated metropolitan patterns now tends to be self-sustaining. "Most of the young white families who will provide the future increase in white population have moved outside the city limits. . . . [Remaining white population tends to be elderly or single. . . .] On the other hand the central cities continue to be the place of residence of Negroes of all ages, including the young couples and teenagers approaching maturity who provide the potential for future population growth. Left to themselves, these population patterns can have no other effect than to swell the ghettos and further exacerbate the color dichotomy between cities and suburbs." George and Eunice Grier,

"Equality and Beyond: Housing Segregation in the Great Society," *Daedalus* 95 (1965): 87.

22. Andrew M. Greeley and Paul B. Sheatsley, "Attitudes Toward Racial Integration," *Scientific American* 225, no. 6 (December 1971): 13, 15; Thomas F. Pettigrew, "Attitudes on Race and Housing: A Social-Psychological View," in Amos H. Hawley and Vincent P. Rock, eds., *Segregation in Residential Areas* (Washington: National Academy of Sciences, 1973), p. 21.

23. Downs, *Opening up the Suburbs, supra* note 1 at 19-25.

24. Glazer, *supra* note 1 at 104-105. Glazer was not alone in his skepticism about the job mismatch, or at least about the net benefit of trying to remedy it by housing dispersal. One study of sixty-five metropolitan areas found no support for the thesis that the movement of low-skilled jobs to the suburbs had significantly affected the employment of blacks. Stanley H. Masters, "The Effect of Housing Segregation on Black-White Income Differentials" (Research Discussion Paper Institute for Research on Poverty, University of Wisconsin, Madison, 1972), p. 134. Another concluded that blacks didn't profit (although whites did) from moving to the suburbs and observed, "[O]ne cannot react . . . with anything other than the deepest pessimism about the potential effectiveness of policies for 'suburbanizing' non-whites in the urban ghetto. The known costs of such policies would be very great, and the expected benefits very small, at least in terms of employment opportunity. Bennett Harrison, *Education, Training, and the Urban Ghetto* (Baltimore: The Johns Hopkins University Press, 1972), pp. 107 and 116.

25. *New York Times*, October 15, 1972, p. 58, col. 1.

26. *New York Times*, July 21, 1974, p. 1 col. 4. Differing views about the central city job figures for the 1960-1970 decade may turn on whether one looks at some grouping of large central cities (e.g., the ten largest or all over a million) or at all central cities regardless of size. A review of the evidence for the full 1960-1970 decade and some from the early 1970s led one writer to conclude, "The redistribution of jobs within the metropolitan areas is a phenomenon of enormous proportions. The total number of jobs in suburbia has climbed dramatically, while central city jobs have remained relatively constant or declined in absolute terms. . . . [A]lmost all new metropolitan area jobs are being created in the suburbs." Leonard S. Rubinowitz, *Low-Income Housing: Suburban Strategies* (Cambridge, Mass.,: Ballinger, 1974), p. 11.

27. Edward C. Banfield asserts that employment in most large central cities increased in the 1960s because increases in service, clerical, and other white collar jobs more than made up for job losses in manufacturing. But even Banfield acknowledges that most of the new central city service jobs "are held by relatively well-trained suburbanites rather than by the low-skilled central city residents whose factory jobs have moved to the suburbs." Edward C. Banfield, *The Unheavenly City Revisited* (Boston: Little Brown, 1974), p. 39. In its analysis of the 1969-1973 figures, the *New York Times* said that the so-called postindustrial society job trends created special problems for large central cities that were trying to bring their growing minority populations into their economies because factory work, which could be learned quickly on the job, had been the traditional economic foothold for the minority poor. The poor were cut off from

many white collar job opportunities by lack of skills and low educational attainments, the *Times* said, while they could not follow manufacturing jobs to the suburbs because housing was not available to them there and many could not manage long distance automobile commuting. *New York Times*, July 21, 1974, p. 1, col. 4.

28. John F. Kain, "The Distribution and Movement of Jobs and Industry," in *The Metropolitan Enigma*, James Q. Wilson, ed. (Cambridge, Mass.: Harvard University Press, 1968); and John F. Kain, "Postwar Changes in Land Use in the American City," reprinted in *Toward an Urban Policy*, Daniel P. Moynihan, ed. (New York: Basic Books, 1970).

29. A 1971 Census Bureau study of employment in the poverty areas of fifty-one large cities showed that about 20 percent of those with jobs worked outside the city. *Census of Population: 1970*, Employment Profiles of Selected Low-Income Areas, Final Report PHC(3)-I, United States Summary—Urban Areas (Washington, D.C.: Government Printing Office, January 1972), p. 12.

30. The quotation is from George Sternlieb, *Hearings*, House Subcommittee on Appropriations, V.9-2, (April 1972), p. 41. (hearings on HUD appropriations). Sternlieb is an exponent of the loss of economic value viewpoint. George Sternlieb, "The City as Sandbox," *The Public Interest*, Fall 1971, pp. 15-19. Illustrative of the "upgrading" view is Alexander Ganz, *Our Large Cities: New Light on Their Recent Transformation: Elements of a New Development Strategy: A Prototype for Boston* (Cambridge, Mass.: MIT Laboratory for Environmental Studies, 1972), p. I-3.

31. Glazer, *supra* note 1 at 100.

32. Downs, *Opening Up the Suburbs*, *supra* note 1 at 34. Part of a steady stream of newspaper accounts of pervasively negative conditions of the sort to which Downs referred—under which, apart from all else, effective education would appear to be virtually impossible—was a news story disclosing that teachers in Gary, Indiana, had been authorized to carry guns into school. *Chicago Daily News*, October 16, 1975.

33. *Chicago Daily News*, February 3, 1975.

34. "It is well to remember that the ghetto is not simply black. It is also poor." Kain, "Effect of Housing Market Segregation on Urban Development," *supra* note 8 at 262.

35. Glazer, *supra* note 1 at 103.

36. *Federal Role in Urban Affairs*, Hearings, Subcommittee on Executive Reorganization, Senate Committee on Government Operations, 89th Cong., 2d sess. Pt. 5 (August 30, 1966), p. 1155.

37. Banfield, *supra* note 27 at 71, 72, 95.

38. Downs, *Opening Up the Suburbs*, *supra* note 1 at 29-30.

39. *Id.* at 95-97.

40. Relevant here is the view that the city can be seen as composed of groupings of residents clearly identified within a spacial location who compete for the available resources the city has to offer. The slum is the catchall for those who lose out in the competition. The more resources a group has at its command, the better able it is to control or determine what resources it will obtain from the public sector and so determine what its environment will be. Ghetto commu-

nities on this analysis tend to be relatively less able than more favored communities to have an effective impact on the provision of public resources. These resources are distributed unequally between residents within the city on a group basis, the most powerful getting the most. Slums can be defined as areas where the population lacks minimal resources needed to compete successfully against other groups and where the population lacks influence or control over the institutional channels through which such resources are distributed or could be obtained. Jack Meltzer and Joyce Whitley, "Social and Physical Planning for the Urban Slum," in Brian J.L. Berry and Jack Meltzer, eds., *Goals for Urban America*, (New York: Prentice-Hall, 1967), pp. 142-47.

41. Transcript of the American Academy Conference on the Negro American, May 14-15, 1965, *Daedalus* 95 (1965): 322.

42. Ibid.

43. Banfield says that there is a little *general* desire among slum dwellers to engage in personal or community efforts for self-improvement, and that slum dwellers *generally* are apathetic toward self-help on a community basis. This does not mean, he is quick to add, that slum dwellers are satisfied with their way of life or do not want a better way to live; it is simply that "slum apathy" tends to inhibit them from putting forth sufficient efforts to change their community—"they remain apathetic about what they could themselves do to change world." Banfield, *supra* note 27 at 71-72. "Apathy" toward the possibility of community improvement it may be called. But the description ignores the overwhelming nature of the struggle for survival in a crisis ghetto, for example, that of the slum mother who fights courageously, on a daily basis, to keep things together against what would appear to most to be impossible odds. What Banfield calls apathy might more accurately be described as a realization of the impossibility of a community self-help or "bootstrapping" operation achieving significant success within a crisis ghetto.

44. Lee Rainwater, "The Lessons of Pruitt-Igoe," *The Public Interest*, Summer 1967, p. 123.

45. Banfield *supra* note 27 at 238. A Brookings Institution study of some 4,400 metropolitan area residents concluded that the poor persons in the study had "as high life aspirations as do the nonpoor and want the same things, among them a good education and a nice place to live. This study reveals no difference between poor and nonpoor when it comes to life goals and wanting to work. . . ." Leonard Goodwin, *Do the Poor Want to Work?* (Washington, D.C.: The Brookings Institution, 1972).

46. Banfield, *supra* note 27 at 239.

47. *Id.* at 251.

48. Of course, the spectre of minighettos immediately appears when one imagines an enclave of predominantly poor black residents within a larger white middle class community. But at worst, a minighetto is better than a maxighetto. At best, the relationships with, and the institutions of, the larger community would prevent the poor black section from becoming any kind of a ghetto. Something in between the worst and best—a relatively depressed but viable, modest-sized area, physically adjacent to and having institutional contacts (schools, stores, hospitals, recreational facilities, etc.) with a middle class area—

would be a vast improvement in situational inducements and opportunities as compared with the mass enclave of crisis ghettos.

It has been pointed out that black movement into residentially segregated suburban areas has not generated much change in many of the indicia generally accepted as a measure of "living conditions," such as extent of poverty, quality of housing, and the like (although the statistics may be based largely on blacks living in big enclaves in older, inner ring suburbs, not in smaller clusters in more recently developed areas). Francine F. Rabinovitz, *Paper submitted to Subcommittee on Housing Panels*, pt. 2, Committee on Banking and Currency, House of Representatives, 92nd Cong., 1st sess. (Washington, D.C.: Government Printing Office, June 1971), p. 742. See also Bernard J. Friedman, "Blacks in Suburbia: The Myth of Better Opportunities," in *Minority Perspectives* (Baltimore, Resources for the Future, 1972).

49. Whether the same may be said of working class communities, where the level of hostility may be higher and the level of community resources lower, is perhaps open to question. Two sociology professors in Chicago, examining *Gautreaux* dispersal prospects in working class neighborhoods, concluded that giving CHA families the opportunity to move into the new neighborhoods would not ameliorate underlying human problems but would simply export social problems from one neighborhood to another. Positive results could be achieved, they thought, only if "compensatory services" such as day care and community centers were also provided in the recipient neighborhoods. Thomas M. Gannon and Morris Janowitz, "The Social Impact of Scattered Site Public Housing" (Unpublished paper, April 1974), pp. 10-11.

50. MHFA was established in 1966—though the constitutionality of the law creating it was not upheld, and hence its operations did not really begin, until 1969—to make loans to nonprofit and limited dividend developers of new or rehabilitated housing.

51. Such persons were defined by the law as families that would have to spend more than 25 percent of their incomes to pay market rate rents in MHFA developments. See p. 53, n. 25 Ch. 708, §6(b), Mass. Acts of 1966.

52. The Massachusetts Housing Finance Agency, *A Social Audit of Mixed-Income Housing* (Boston, January 24, 1974). The study was also intended to examine the feasibility of housing developments that were racially integrated as well as having an income mix. In fact, most of the minority households were concentrated in six of the sixteen developments which were viewed as the least desirable of the projects examined—they were not as well constructed or maintained as other MHFA developments, were not managed as competently, had essentially all units subsidized at either moderate or low income levels, had many more larger apartment, and were located in poorer communities. The researchers concluded that a pattern of segregation was evident in their data and that their findings did not therefore permit a very definite conclusion with respect to racial mix. They did say it was "highly probable" that any trends toward an association between racial mix and tenant dissatisfaction were accounted for by the fact that the minority families were largely living in less satisfactory developments that were characterized by a low level of tenant satisfaction generally.

53. *Id.* at 23-24.

54. *Id.* at 24. The MHFA study also contained some fascinating subsidiary data relevant to Rainwater's observation about lower class people wanting the "square" life. The researchers recognized that conventional wisdom, including most of the housing literature produced by housing and planning professionals as well as by social scientists, was that income mixing did not work. *Id.* at 3. What was the explanation for MHFA's contrary experience?, they asked. Their findings on that subject, based on their interviews, were that tenants in MHFA projects having different income levels nonetheless displayed "pretty much the same distribution of values, social attitudes, and life-styles." They guessed that the major theoretical reason for predicting difficulties from extensive income mixing—a clash in values and behavior—was probably based on misinformation (*Id.* at 22), and that the design, construction, and management of the projects, and the middle or lower class nature of the community in which the projects were located, were far more important in producing tenant satisfaction or dissatisfaction and in making a project "work" than any differences in various attitudes and life styles among income levels. *Id.* at 24.

55. Housing and Community Development Act of 1974, Section 161(a).

56. *Id.* at Section 101(c).

57. *Id.* at Section 8(a).

58. Downs, *Opening Up the Suburbs, supra* note 1 at 120.

59. *Id.* at 124–35. The following are representative of like views expressed by others:

> The ghetto has to be dispersed. In the nature of the case, efforts to make it livable as it is are doomed to failure. . . . Whether one's starting point is a humane concern for the circumstances in which children are brought up or a more hard-headed concern about the stacking of social dynamite at the cities' vital centers where the more highly valued properties are found, one must conclude that the destruction of the ghetto is imperative.

Raymond H. Wittcoff, "The Future of Cities," *The Center Magazine*, November/ December 1973, p. 69.

> Wiping out the ghetto is essential to the future of the Negro and of the city itself. . . . The long run life of the city itself depends upon the Negro being able to live where he chooses, in any part of the metropolitan area. . . .

Robert F. Kennedy, "Policies to Combat Negro Poverty," in *Goals for Urban America, supra* note 40 at 116.

Kain says that "the first requirement is devising methods of opening suburban housing to blacks. If the growth of the ghetto could be arrested, he continues, programs aimed at making the central city attractive to middle income families might have a chance. Otherwise the expectation that the city will become a lower class slum will persist and there is "no way" present trends could be reversed. Kain, "Effect of Housing Market Segregation on Urban Development," *supra* note 8 at 266.

60. Downs, *Opening Up the Suburbs, supra* note 1 at 127. Downs suggests that "non-capital enrichment," by which he means raising the incomes of ghetto residents to middle class levels through income maintenance and jobs programs (something Downs says would cost far more than we have ever been willing to spend on such matters), would result in the departure of large numbers of ghetto residents, for households with incomes high enough to be considered middle class will not voluntarily remain in crisis ghettos. Large scale physical improvements—"capital enrichment"—could not be carried out without major displacement of existing residents or prior abandonment by them. *Id.* at 125-27.

61. Even the rehabilitation of ghetto dwellings—let alone of ghetto neighborhoods—has proved to be elusive. The Kaiser Committee report explained why thoroughgoing housing rehabilitation efforts may be more complicated and time consuming than new construction, The Report of the President's Committee on Urban Housing, *A Decent Home* (Washington, D.C.: Government Printing Office, 1969), p. 108, and a recent examination of some specific rehabilitation projects is not encouraging. Chester W. Hartman, *Housing and Social Policy* (Englewood Cliffs, N.J.: Prentice-Hall, 1975), pp. 70-72.

62. The Twentieth Century Fund, *Community Development Corporations: New Hope for the Inner City,* (New York, 1971), p. 10.

63. Charles E. Schultze et al., *Setting National Priorities—The 1974 Budget* (Washington, D.C.: The Brookings Institution, 1973), p. 144.

64. Revenue Sharing Clearinghouse, November/December, 1974.

65. *Annual Report of the Office of Revenue Sharing* (Washington, D.C.: Department of the Treasury, March 1, 1975), p. 16.

66. City of Chicago Community Development Plan (March 1975), p. 25. See Donald H. Haider, "Fiscal Scarcity: A New Urban Perspective," in Louis H. Masotti and Robert T. Lineberry, eds. *The New Urban Politics* (Cambridge, Mass.: Ballinger, 1976), p. 179.

67. Banfield suggests that if we wait long enough, deteriorating inner city neighborhoods will become so completely depopulated that land values will drop sufficiently to permit private redevelopment in a "natural" economic cycle. Banfield, *supra* note 26 at 44. Probably so, but the ghetto will not have vanished; it will simply have moved to adjacent neighborhoods.

68. Frances Fox Piven and Richard Cloward, "The Case Against Urban Desegregation," in *Housing Urban America, supra* note 8 at 97, 101-102.

69. Frank S. Kristof, "The 1970 Census of Housing: Does it Meet Data Needs for Housing Programs and Policy," quoted in Banfield, *supra* note 27 at 38. A similar observation appeared in HUD's housing policy study of 1973: "[T]here is clearly a disproportionate concentration of poverty within the central cities. Therefore, improvements in the physical condition of their housing by sudsidized new construction in these areas or by other means only solves part of the problem. Indeed, it may worsen the situation by reducing the migration of the poor out of an unsuitable environment." Department of Housing and Urban Development, *Housing in the Seventies* (Washington, D.C.: Government Printing Office, 1973) p. 6-21.

70. *National Journal,* October 17, 1970, p. 2262.

71. Comment, "Public Housing and Urban Policy: Gautreaux v. Chicago

Housing Authority," 79 *Yale Law Journal* 712 (1970). The late Senator Robert F. Kennedy is quoted as having said that the majority of new housing should go into the ghetto because sensitivity must be shown to the aspirations of minorities who would build their own communities to achieve "comparability of housing and full employment that are the keys to free movement and to the establishment of a society in which each man has a real opportunity to choose whom he will call neighbor." *Hearings on S.3029 Before the Subcommittee on Housing and Urban Affairs of the Senate Banking and Currency Committee,* 90th Cong., 2d sess. (1968).

72. George Lefcoe, "From Capitol Hill: The Impact of Civil Rights Integration on HUD Policy," 4 *Urban Lawyer* 119 (Winter 1972). This argument presents an interesting reversal of roles in relation to a common criticism of white liberals. Normally the white liberal is criticized for presuming to know what is best for the black community or at least what that community wants, namely, integration. Here Lefcoe's attribution of a preference for "black community life" (read, stay in the ghetto) illustrates the same supposed error. Since the effect of government housing policy for a generation has been to "presume" a black preference to stay in the ghetto and to deny a choice or option to those blacks, if any, who would prefer to move out, fundamental fair play would seem to suggest that government should now redress the past policy by affording poor blacks a housing choice so that they may make their own decisions about where to live instead of having government continue to make that decision for them.

73. Gary Orfield, "Federal Policy, Local Powers, and Metropolitan Segregation," *Political Supreme Quarterly* 89 (Winter 1974-75): 782.

74. *National Journal,* November 27, 1971, p. 2347.

75. Downs, "Alternative Futures for the American Ghetto," *supra,* note 15 at 60. A variant of the black power argument is that dispersal would attract the most upwardly mobile of the ghetto population, leaving those who remained even worse off than before. But it would hardly do, of course, to oppose a dispersal policy because some blacks might take advantage of it. Another asserted disadvantage is that dispersal would funnel resources to relatively better off neighborhoods rather than to the ghetto neighborhoods in dire need, thus reversing the proper priority. The likelihood that "enrichment" without dispersal would not succeed seems a sufficient rejoinder.

76. National Commission on the Causes and Prevention of Violence, *To Establish Justice, To Insure Domestic Tranquility* (Washington, D.C.: Government Printing Office, 1969). The commission's report said: "If the racial situation remains inflammatory and the conditions perpetuating poverty remain unchanged, and if vast numbers of our young see no hope for improvement in the quality of their lives, then this country will remain in danger. Violence will not go away because we will it. . . ." *Id.* at 118. See also, Downs, "Alternative Futures for the American Ghetto," *supra* note 15 at 51-52. Recent revelations disclose that the urban violence of the 1960s triggered illegal surveillance and harrassment activities, and even burglaries, by the FBI and local police forces that constituted significant inroads upon the personal freedom of thousands of Americans.

77. George Edwards, "Desegregation: A View from the Federal Bench"

(speech before the American Issues Form Conference, Chicago, June 3, 1976).
78. There is little doubt that virulent anger seethes beneath the surface. In mid-1976, a sudden Chicago thunderstorm flooded the streets and stranded some white motorists in the black part of town. There were immediately set upon by gangs of black youths and clubbed and shot. *Chicago Daily News*, June 14, 1976, p. 1.
79. *Time*, June 30, 1975, pp. 11-12.
80. *Id.* at 17.
81. *Id.* at 12.
82. Banfield, *supra* note 7 at 12.
83. Glazer, *supra* note 6 at 106.

NOTES FOR CHAPTER 6

1. *President's Sixth Annual Report on National Housing Goals*, House Doc. No. 94-18, 94th Cong., 1st sess. (1975), p. 26.
2. Department of Housing and Urban Development, *Housing in the Seventies* (Washington, D.C.: Government Printing Office, 1973), pp. 2120, 2137.
3. *Report of the Subcommittee on Priorities and Economy in Government of the Joint Economic Committee*, 93d Cong., 1 sess. (March 5, 1973), p. 4.
4. *Report of the Committee on Banking and Currency*, No. 93-1114, 93d Cong., 2d sess. (June 17, 1974), p. 193.
5. *President's Fourth Annual Report on Housing Goals*, House Doc. 92-319, 92d Cong., 2d sess. (1972), p. 30. A congressional report said,

> Great care has to be exercised in trying to sort out what actually happened when the various insured mortgage programs were utilized in inner city areas during the years 1968-72. . . . A popular belief was established that most of the inner city homes foreclosed had been financed under the Section 235 subsidized homeownership program. A record of what actually happened showed that most of the foreclosed homes had been financed under the nonsubsidized . . . programs.

An Analysis of the Section 235 and 236 programs, printed for the Senate Committee on Banking, Housing, and Urban Affairs, May 24, 1973, p. 21.
6. Analysis of the Section 235 and 236 Programs, *supra* note 5 at 15-22, 25-26.
7. Report of the General Accounting Office on §235 and §236 programs; and Office of Audit, Department of Housing and Urban Development, Audit Nos. 05-2-2001-4900, December 10, 1971 (section 235 program), and 05-02-2001-5000, January 29, 1972 (section 236 program). One aspect of the mismanagement was insufficient HUD staff. In 1972, after he had finally gotten the president to agree to a staff increase, Romney indicated that he had been trying to see the president for that purpose for months.
8. Irving H. Welfeld, *America's Housing Problem* (Washington D.C.: American Enterprise Institute for Public Policy Research, 1973), pp. 20-25.

9. *Id.* at 20.

10. *Id.* at 25-26.

11. United States v. Chester, 144 F.2d 415 (1944).

12. Charles Abrams, "The Housing Problem and the Negro," *Daedalus*, Winter, 1966, pp. 64, 74.

13. *Building the American City* (Washington, D.C.: Government Printing Office, 1968), p. 192; *A Decent Home* (Washington, D.C.: Government Printing Office, 1969), p. 36.

14. Herbert M. Franklin, "The Federal Government as 'Houser of Last Resort': A Policy for Democratic Growth," *Urban Law Annual* (1972), p. 23.

15. The case is U.S. v. Certain Lands in Louisville, 9 F. Supp. 137 (Ky. 1935), and is discussed in Chapter One.

16. The Uniform Relocation Assistance and Land Acquisition Policy Act of 1970, 84 Stat. 1894.

17. See, for example, Herbert M. Franklin, "Federal Power and Subsidized Housing," *Urban Lawyer*, Winter, 1971, p. 61. Franklin says that a sensible pattern would be to create consolidated mortgage banking and community development agencies at the state or metropolitan level that could not only receive federal funds as though they were local housing authorities but could also receive federal loans to enable them to act as development lenders. Both private (but governmentally financed) and public construction could proceed simultaneously.

18. There is considerable discussion in the literature of the fiscal cost to a community of accepting subsidized housing for the poor and minorities. Although some dispute the contention, it is a widely accepted view that the cost of providing public services to additional poor families, particularly those with children, is considerable, and that the prospect of the increased local taxes required to pay for the services, rather than discrimination, is behind a great deal of the opposition to dispersal of subsidized housing. This has led to suggestions that communities in which subsidized housing is to be located be "compensated" for the additional burdens to be imposed on them. See, for example, Anthony Downs, *Opening Up the Suburbs* (New Haven: Yale University Press, 1973), p. 163. Full payment of local real estate taxes or the equivalent on subsidized housing seems appropriate. Beyond this, however, Herbert Franklin and others have questioned "financial gimmickry tied to housing programs." Herbert M. Franklin, "Urban Growth Policy in the Courts: The Quest for New Ground Rules" (Paper delivered to the 1971 National Planning Conference, American Society of Planning Officials, March 30, 1971), p. 17. Franklin argues that people, as people, place demands on municipal services, and questions whether redressing the historical imbalance created by allowing communities to wall themselves off from the poor should lead us now to "pay" suburban communities to do what certain cities have for generations been doing without payment. *Id.* p. 15. The resolution of this "incentive" question is important, but the essential federal houser of last resort capability could be provided with or without such incentive arrangements.

19. Miami Valley Regional Planning Commission, *A Housing Plan for the Miami Valley* (Dayton, O.: Miami Valley Regional Planning Commission 1970).

For an analysis see Leonard S. Rubinowitz, *Low-Income Housing: Suburban Strategies* (Cambridge, Mass: Ballinger, 1974), p. 267. As first authorized by the Housing Act of 1954, HUD provides a substantial part of the funding for regional planning agencies. 40 U.S.C. §461. Indeed, most of these agencies depend upon federal dollars for survival. In 1968, Congress added a requirement that planning carried out with HUD financial assistance include a "housing element." 40 U.S.C. §461(a). The law called for planning that "adequately covered" housing needs of the region and local communities, existing and prospective. In administering the new law, HUD asked planning agencies not merely to identify housing needs but also to "define strategies and specific steps by which housing needs, and . . . related public services and facilities, can be met through responsive governmental programs and private action." "Comprehensive Planning Assistance Requirements and Guidelines for a Grant," HUD Handbook 1, CPM 6041.1A, ch. 4, §5, March 1972.

20. Mary E. Brooks, *Lower Income Housing: the Planners Response* (Chicago: American Society of Planning Officials, 1972), p. 20.

21. See Rubinowitz, *supra* note 19 at 267.

22. Determining how to allocate scarce housing subsidy dollars *among* rather than *within* metropolitan areas—in effect determining the relative housing needs of metropolitan areas—is in principle the type of task Congress has already assigned to HUD. Under §213 of the Housing and Community Development Act of 1974 HUD is directed to allocate section 8 funding on a geographic basis in accordance with a few general criteria—"population, poverty, housing overcrowding, housing vacancies, amount of substandard housing, or other objectively measurable conditions. . . ."

23. The supremacy clause is Article VI, Clause 2, of the Constitution. During World War II the federal government's power to acquire land and build temporary housing for defense plant workers was upheld as an exercise of the war power, and local zoning was said to be inapplicable by virtue of the supremacy clause. United States v. Chester, 144 F.2d 415 (1944).

24. Following its grant of extensive legislative powers to Congress, including the power to "provide for the . . . general welfare of the United States," the Constitution adds that Congress shall have the additional power to make all laws "necessary and proper for carrying into execution . . ." the specifically granted powers. Article 1, Section 8. In addition, to the extent that a housing dispersal program was explicitly said to be a means of combating racial discrimination in housing the federal power could also be rested on the Thirteenth and Fourteenth Amendments.

There is perhaps less certainty that the courts would uphold a zoning override power and a federal building code employed on behalf of private builders who, on the sections 235 and 236 models, would own the subsidized housing they built. The case for a compelling public interest in housing dispersal is so strong, however, that it is likely that such a law would be sustained. Even if it were not, the government could itself first condemn the land, exercise the zoning override power and then involve private developers either by selling the land to them for subsidized housing construction (a close analogy to the way many urban renewal programs worked) or, if that were held impermissible, by long-term leases.

25. This bears a possibly ironic resemblance to an early effort by William Safire, then one of Nixon's speech writers, to define New Federalism. Safire said his purpose was to come to grips with a paradox—the need for both national unity and local diversity.

Step one in coming to grips with the unity-diversity paradox is to begin to decentralize administration: to say that barriers previously used to stymie social progress—the former obstacle of 'states rights'—have now become 'rights of first refusal.' Local authority will now regain the capacity to meet local needs itself, and gain an additional right to federal financial help—but it has given up the right it once had to neglect the needs of its citizens. Result: 'National localism,' not much more local power in deciding *what* to do, but considerably more power in deciding *how* to do it so as to fit the differing needs of different communities.

William Safire, *Before the Fall* (Garden City, N.Y.: Doubleday and Co., 1975), p. 222. New Jersey Governor Byrnne's executive order, described in note 39 to Chapter Four, illustrates the kind of local action that might be stimulated by the existence of the federal powers suggested in the text.

26. As noted earlier, poverty areas are those in which at least one fifth of the residents have incomes at or below the poverty level.

27. White tenants in a virtually all white San Francisco housing development sued to halt racially discriminatory rental practices by their landlord that kept blacks out, contending that they were being denied the "social benefits" of integrated living. In upholding the right of the whites to bring such a suit under the 1968 act, a unanimous Supreme Court, quoting a Senate sponsor of the legislation, said that one of the purposes of the 1968 act was to replace the ghettos by intergrated and balanced living patterns. Trafficante v. Metropolitan Life Ins. Co., 409 U.S. 205 (1972).

28. Gautreaux v. CHA, 304 F.Supp. 736 (1969).

29. As noted earlier, HUD entered into just such a contract with the Leadership Council for Metropolitan Open Communities following the Supreme Court decision in *Gautreaux*.

30. Special efforts could also be made with suburban employers whose work forces contained a number of "reverse" commuters who desired housing closer to their jobs.

31. Swann v. Charlotte Mecklenburg Bd. of Education, 402 U.S. 1, 25 (1970).

32. Otero v. New York City Housing Authority, 484 F.2d 1122 (1973).

33. Daniel Bell, "On Meritocracy and Equality," *The Public Interest*, Fall 1972, p. 38. For a detailed discussion of racial quotas, particularly in housing, see Bruce L. Ackerman, "Integration for Subsidized Housing and the Question of Racial Occupancy Controls," *Stanford Law Review* 26 (1974): 245. Ackerman argues for the use of quotas in federally subsidized housing projects. The issue of "reverse discrimination" has gained sufficient currency to merit cover treatment in a magazine such as *U.S. News & World Report* (March 29, 1976).

34. A partial yet significant first step in the suggested direction, but falling far short of full houser of last resort powers, would be to require regional planning agencies to include not just a "housing element" in their plans but a full-fledged metropolitan housing dispersal program, and also to require that, as a condition of receipt of community development funds under the Housing and Community Development Act of 1974, recipient communities (1) prepare housing assistance plans that meshed with the metropolitan plan and (2) implement their plans through public agencies if private developers failed to do so. Although this would remedy two of the major housing deficiencies in the 1974 act, the failure to require metropolitan planning and to put teeth in the linkage between housing and community development, it would still be an inadequate step because it stops short of assuring that a metropolitan dispersal plan would be carried out. (Communities could avoid participation by foregoing community development funds, and in this sensitive area coercion based on the threat of withheld federal dollars is more likely to produce Warren type confrontations than housing.) What is required is that Congress express a national will that metropolitanwide housing dispersal is necessary and will be accomplished, leaving a simple choice to localities, without moral or punitive connotations, to decide whether the planning and implementation is to be done locally or federally.

35. Eli Ginzberg and Robert M. Solow, "Some Lessons of the 1960's," *The Public Interest* 34, (Winter 1974): 211.

36. Edward C. Banfield, "Why Government Cannot Solve the Urban Problems," *Daedalus*, Fall 1968, pp. 1231, 1233.

37. Edward C. Banfield, *The Unheavenly City Revisited* (Boston: Little, Brown, 1974), pp. 96-97.

38. Nathan Glazer, "The Limits of Social Policy," *Commentary* 52 (September 1971): 51.

39. *Id.* at 54.

40. *Id.* at 57.

NOTES FOR CHAPTER 7

1. Nathan Glazer, "On 'Opening Up' the Suburbs," *The Public Interest* 37 (Fall 1974): 111.

2. Bureau of Census, *Current Population Reports*, Consumer Income Series P-60, no. 77, May 7, 1971, p. 6. The largest number and percentage of the poor are thus found in nonmetropolitan areas. But the concern here is with the problem of the poor in the cities; whatever its pathos and inequity, rural poverty is not destroying America's cities. From the housing point of view, rural poverty also presents a different aspect than urban poverty. Whereas the bulk of substandard housing is in rural areas, only a relatively modest fraction of poor rural households pay more than 25 percent of income for rent. In urban areas only a relatively small percentage of the poor live in substandard units, but many pay a very large percentage of their income for housing. Oversimplifying, the rural poor live cheaply in substandard housing, while the urban poor pay dearly for

standard housing. Charles L. Schultze et al. *Setting National Priorities—The 1972 Budget* (Washington, D.C.: Brookings Institution, 1971), pp. 290-92.

3. Anthony Downs, *Opening Up the Suburbs* (New Haven: Yale University Press, 1973), p. 154.

4. *Id.* at 154-59. Downs says his estimates are not intended to be precise but are designed merely to illustrate the orders of magnitude involved in a dispersal policy at a significant scale—i.e., a scale large enough to be likely to have a measurable impact on central city concentrations of poverty.

5. HUD has argued that this pump primer view is incorrect because it fails to consider what could or would happen in the absence of the subsidized programs. "Presumably, other Federal expenditures would have been made, taxes reduced, or less debt issued. . . . All of these alternatives would also have stimulated economic activity and, therefore, there need be no net increase or net decrease in national income simply because the Government chose to subsidize or not to subsidize housing." Hearings before the Subcommittee on Housing of the Committee on Banking and Currency, House, 93d Cong., 1st sess., *Housing in the Seventies* (Washington, D.C.: Government Printing Office, 1973), p. 2181. Some economists point out, however, that cyclical variations in housing tend to be much greater than in industrial production, and the multiplier effect of declines in housing construction may be unusually large. See, Henry B. Schecter, "Housing's Disastrous Roller Coaster," *AFL-CIO American Federationist*, January 1975, pp. 6-7. Leon Keyserling, speaking of the "intimate connection" between housing production and the state of the general economy, attributes our recurrent periods of economic stagnation and recession in part to a "serious long-term relative and absolute lag in the growth of investment in residential and commercial construction." Leon H. Keyserling, *The Coming Crisis in Housing* (Washington, D.C.: Conference on Economic Progress, 1972), pp. 1, 3.

6. Helpful analyses of budgetary decisions and their policy implications are to be found in an annual series of Brookings Institution publications that have examined each proposed federal budget since 1971. A recent volume in the series, *Setting National Priorities—The 1974 Budget*, says the federal budget reflects choices in at least four dimensions: (1) among objectives—the relative importance of the things the federal government is trying to accomplish; (2) about means—how the government should act in pursuit of its objectives; (3) about distribution—who should benefit from federal programs and who should pay for them; and (4) about the overall size of the federal budget—how big a share of national output should go to federal government activities. Charles L. Schultze et al., *Setting National Priorities—The 1974 Budget* (Washington, D.C.: Brookings Institution, 1973), pp. 3-4.

7. *President's Second Annual Report on National Housing Goals*, House Document No. 91-292, 91st Cong., 2d sess. (1970), p. 28.

8. *Id.* at 29.

9. *Id.* at 28. The Brookings Institution estimated that to reach the 1968 act goal of twenty-six million new and rehabilitated housing units (subsidized and unsubsidized) during the decade 1969-1978 would require the yearly fraction of gross national product devoted to residential construction to rise from 3.5 percent to slightly more than 4 percent. Charles L. Schultze, et al., *Setting National Priorities—The 1971 Budget* (Washington, D.C.: The Brookings Institution,

1970), p. 85. In recent years the percentage has ranged from a low of 3.2 percent (1967) to a high of 4.1 percent (1965 and 1971). The post-World War II high was 5.5 percent in 1950. These figures are roughly comparable, perhaps slightly on the low side, to the fraction of gross national product devoted to housing in other industrialized nations. Anthony Downs, *Federal Housing Subsidies: How Are They Working?* (Lexington, Mass.: Heath, 1973), pp. 92-93.

10. Downs, *Opening Up the Suburbs, supra* note 3 at 158.

11. *President's Third Annual Report on National Housing Goals*, House Doc. No. 92-136, 92d Cong., 1st sess. (1971), p. 22.

12. The Report of the President's Committee on Urban Housing, *A Decent Home* (Washington, D.C.: Government Printing Office, 1969), pp. 49-50.

13. The housing subsidy figures are exclusive of Department of Agriculture subsidies for rural housing and other public facilities of $578 million in fiscal 1970, $327 million in 1971, and $877 million in 1972. *Cong. Quarterly*, February 5, 1971, p. 294; January 29, 1972, p. 170; and February 3, 1973, p. 218. Even when these Department of Agriculture figures are added to HUD's, annual expenditures for housing subsidies are only about 1 percent of total federal expenditures for fiscal years 1970, 1971, and 1972. Budgetary expenditures do not of course include tax policy housing subsidies, such as deductibility of mortgage interest and property taxes, which "appear" in the budget only in the form of reduced revenue and are the largest housing subsidy items.

14. The estimate was probably about right. Cautioning that reliable estimates of such future costs are inherently uncertain, Downs estimated that the 1978 housing subsidy payment bill if the six million goal had then been met would be between $5 and $7.8 billion. Downs, *Federal Housing Subsidies, supra* note 9 at 58.

15. *New York Times*, February 4, 1975, p. 20 col. 1. Attention must be paid, of course, to the large fixed costs in the budget (the "uncontrollables") and to the relative inflexibility of some defense and other expenditures which, taken together, leave little room for "play" in any given year.

16. "The 1975 Budget: An Advance Look," A Staff Study for the Subcommittee on Priorities and Economy in Government of the Joint Economic Committee, 93d Cong., 1st sess. (December 27, 1973), p. 31.

17. Downs, *Federal Housing Subsidies, supra* note 9 at 93.

18. *Id.* at 23-24.

19. *Housing in the Seventies, supra* note 5 at 2097. None of the figures under discussion include any portion of welfare payments that may be used for housing. In 1972 the federal government provided about $4.6 billion to state welfare programs. Data on the portion used for housing is very inadequate, but HEW estimated that perhaps $2.6 of the $4.6 billion was used for housing purposes. *Id.* at 2011-12.

20. Downs, *Federal Housing Subsidies, supra* note 9 at 90-91.

21. Housing allowance proposals date back to the early days of public housing when they were advanced by real estate industry spokesmen as an alternative to "socialistic" public housing. In 1968, the Kaiser Committee recommended an experimental housing allowance program. In 1969 HUD authorized two small-scale experiments to be conducted in Kansas City and Wilmington with Model Cities program funds. The Housing and Urban Development Act of 1970 autho-

rized HUD to carry out a major housing allowance experiment. After preliminary work, HUD scheduled three separate types of projects in a dozen cities around the country (to run two, three, and five years, respectively), involving nearly 20,000 families at an estimated cost of over $150 million. The experiments were collectively described by the comptroller general of the United States as one of the largest social experiments ever undertaken in the United States.

The core of the housing allowance concept is the promise of cash assistance to help pay the rent if a low income family finds a home or apartment that the owner is willing to lease and that meets HUD standards for physical condition and maximum permissible rent. Housing allowance payments are thus "attached" to the qualifying family, not to a particular housing unit. The advantages of housing allowances are said to include expanded consumer choice (for recipients are not limited to government-subsidized projects); improvement of the existing housing stock, including a reduction in abandonment (for landlords would presumably have more rent revenue to spend on maintenance); and reduced administrative costs as compared with the administrative costs of a construction subsidy system.

22. Downs, *Federal Housing Subsidies*, supra note 9 at 19.

23. 119 *Congressional Record* 30261.

24. The lack of "equity" in the new construction approach—i.e., providing a small fraction of eligible families with new housing and most with no housing subsidy at all—was another major argument against it, and in favor of housing allowances, in the Nixon statements of 1973 and in *Housing in the Seventies*. As discussed in the text following, exclusive reliance on housing allowances would purchase "equity" at the cost of abandoning any effort to use housing subsidies to ameliorate residential apartheid. The section 8 program of the 1974 Housing and Community Development Act, like subsidies for new construction, provides subsidies for a limited number of units, not for all families who are theoretically eligible on the basis of income.

25. Report of the National Commission on Urban Problems, *Building The American City* (Washington, D.C.: Government Printing Office, 1968), p. 59.

26. See, for example, Chester W. Hartman, *Housing and Social Policy* (Englewood Cliffs, N.J.: Prentice-Hall, 1975), p. 156, concluding that without construction subsidies or rent control housing allowances would benefit landlords far more than low income families. In an incisive and telling analysis entitled "Housing Allowances: The Grand Delusion," Hartman has ably noted other concerns as well, pointing out, for example, that empirical evidence does not support the hypothesis of housing allowance advocates that landlords will correct code violations upon receiving increased rent revenues. *Id.* at 157. He also suggests that the experience of welfare recipients should be viewed as instructive, for although welfare families receive a lump sum payment under the welfare program, a specified portion is earmarked for housing, an arrangement quite similar to some forms of a housing allowance. Yet, Hartman says, welfare recipients have "just about the worst housing conditions of any group in the society." *Id.* at 158.

27. Observations on Housing Allowances and the Experimental Housing Allowance Program," Report of the Comptroller General, March 18, 1974, p. 28.

28. Quoted in *Law Project Bulletin*, publication of the Earl Warren Institute

(December 15, 1972), p. 4, from an interview in the Kansas City Star.

29. Department of Housing and Urban Development, *Housing Allowances: The 1976 Report to Congress* (Washington, D.C.: U.S. Department of Housing and Urban Development, February 1976), p. 7.

30. Downs, *Federal Housing Subsidies, supra* note 9 at 59.

31. Irving H. Welfeld, *America's Housing Problem* (Washington, D.C.: American Enterprise Institute for Public Policy Research, 1973), p. 33.

32. Following the Supreme Court decision in the *Gautreaux* case and pursuant to an agreement with the plaintiffs' counsel, HUD contracted with the Leadership Council for Metropolitan Open Communities to provide such services to members of the *Gautreaux* plaintiff class as part of a demonstration, metropolitanwide program.

33. *The 1974 Budget, supra* note 6 at 41. Rainwater argues that it is *relative* poverty that creates the "underclass" that inhabits American ghettos.

> The nation has a poverty problem because too many families and too many individuals do not have enough money. What is "enough money?" To answer in terms of an income sufficient to live at some subsistence level defined as adequate has been the major error of the traditional approach to American poverty. Very few American families and individuals have so little income that they cannot meet their minimal needs.
>
> The problem of poverty is a problem of relative deprivation. A family is poor when it does not have enough money to live in the conventional style of the average American, when its low income does not allow it to buy the products, and services that Americans need. These needs are social needs; they are needs for the housing, furniture, clothes, food and services we all regard as reasonable and expected for the American family. Those who live below the going standard of American affluence form a kind of under class.

Lee Rainwater, *Behind Ghetto Walls* (Chicago: Aldine Publishing Co. 1970), p. 402.

34. The authors of *The 1974 Budget* list three ways in which the government can affect the distribution of cash among people: (1) paying cash (e.g., social security or welfare checks); (2) collecting taxes; and (3) subsidizing employment. *The 1974 Budget, supra* note 6 at 45-100. Only the first of the three methods is discussed here. Reform of the tax system offers considerable potential for helping to relieve poverty, but only if a system of cash payments is included as part of the tax reform package. *Id.* at 45-63. As previously discussed, the present tax system is particularly generous in subsidizing relatively well-off homeowners. Although unemployment may be the chief cause of poverty (most of the poor are employable, not aged or disabled) and it would therefore seem logical to try to combat poverty by providing jobs to those without them, the most credible studies seem to conclude that public employment programs present so many troublesome issues that they are useful as complements to, not substitutes for, cash payment programs. (See, e.g., *Income Security for Americans: Recommendations of the Public Welfare Study*, Report of the Sub-

committee on Fiscal Policy of the Joint Economic Committee, 93d Cong. 2d sess. (Washington, D.C.: Government Printing Office, December 5, 1974), pp. 149-152; *The 1974 Budget, supra* note 6 at 90-100.

35. *Income Security for Americans, supra* note 34 at 2.

36. The $91 billion consists only of cash payments to individuals and is exclusive of an additional $36 billion spent by federal, state, and local governments for goods and services under health, education, housing, food stamps, job training, and other social services programs. $77 billion of the cash payments and $31 billion of the goods and services expenditures were made by the federal government. *Id.* pp. 23-28.

37. *The 1974 Budget, supra* note 6 at 43-45.

38. Gilbert Y. Steiner, *The State of Welfare* (Washington, D.C.: The Brookings Institution, 1971), pp. 32-33.

39. The 1960s were good economic times; gross national product rose from $520 billion in 1961 to $932 billion in 1969. As a Brookings Institution study says, "One of the things not expected to rise under those prosperous conditions was payments to relief recipients. Yet . . . it is roughly accurate to say that during the 1960's the unemployment rate was halved, AFDC recipients increased by almost two-thirds, and AFDC money payments doubled." *Id.* at 32-33.

40. Theodore Marmor, "On Comparing Income Maintenance Alternatives," *The American Political Science Review* (March 1971), p. 85. See *The 1974 Budget, supra* note 6 at Ch. 3.

41. *Income Security for Americans, supra* note 34 at 12.

42. Rainwater, *supra* note 33 at 402.

43. Few social scientists, at any rate, believe that they would. See, for example, James S. Coleman, *Resources for Social Change: Race in the United States* (New York: Wiley, 1971), p. 68.

NOTES FOR CHAPTER 8

1. Harold Wolman, *Politics of Federal Housing* (New York: Dodd Mead, 1971), pp. 181-82

2. *New York Times*, October 28, 1972, p. 35, col. 6.

3. *New York Times*, April 7, 1976, p. 1, col. 7.

4. *New York Times*, April 9, 1976, p. 1, col. 1.

5. Daniel P. Moynihan, *The Politics of a Guaranteed Income* (New York: Vintage Books, 1973), pp. 8-9.

6. *Id.* at 9.

7. *Id.* at 544.

8. *Id.* at 7.

9. *Id.* at 10.

10. Quoted, *Id.* at 12.

11. *Id.* at 10-11.

12. *New York Times*, April 12, 1976, p. 1, col. 6.

13. For example, the aggregate 1973 income of those who moved into central cities between 1970 and 1974 was almost $30 billion less than the annual income

of those who moved out. *New York Times*, February 13, 1976, p. 1, col. 1. New York City's fiscal crisis is widely perceived to be a harbinger of like crises for other cities. Donald H. Haider, *"Fiscal Scarcity: A New Urban Perspective,"* in Louis H. Masotti and Robert L. Lineberry, eds., *The New Urban Politics* (Cambridge, Mass.: Ballinger, 1976).

14. Second Biennial Report of the President on National Growth and Development (Washington, D.C.: Government Printing Office 1974), pp. 30, 32.

15. *Id.* at 2; see also, Haider, *supra* note 13.

16. For evidence that it might have been, see Thomas Sewell, "Minorities and the City," in *The Future of the Metropolis: People, Jobs, Income*, Eli Ginzberg, ed. (Salt Lake City: Olympus, 1974), p. 112.

17. Edith Elmer Wood, *Slums and Blighted Areas in the U.S.*, Administration of Public Works, Housing Division Bulletin, no. 1 (Washington, D.C., 1935), p. 19.

18. Sewell, *supra* note 16 at 118-24.

19. See Haider, *supra* note 13.

20. Karl Taeuber makes the following observation about the contrast between the immigrant and black experiences:

Studies of the residential segregation of . . . European groups show that they were never as segregated from others of the same ethnic group or from the native whites as are blacks from whites. In fact, 60 to 70 years ago, black-white segregation was less than it is now, and was roughly comparable to the segregation of European groups. In the following years, especially from 1910 to 1930, black-white segregation increased, and European ethnic group segregation decreased. This occurred despite the fact that every major black organization favored integration whereas many European groups sought to preserve their neighborhoods, their foreign-language church services, and ethnic businesses.

Karl E. Taeuber, "Demographic Perspectives on Housing and School Segregation," *Wayne Law Review* 21 (March 1975): 839. See also Report of the National Commission on Urban Problems, *Building the American City* (Washington, D.C.: Government Printing Office, 1968), pp. 2, 52.

21. Wilbur R. Thompson, "Emergency Issues in Metropolitan Economics," in *The Future of the Metropolis: People, Jobs, Income*, Eli Ginzberg, ed. (Salt Lake City: Olympus, 1974), p. 28.

22. Karl E. Taeuber, "Racial Segregation: The Persisting Dilemma," *The Annals of the American Academy of Political and Social Sciences* 422 (November 1975).

23. *New York Times*, April 1, 1976. A study prepared by the Congressional Research Service of the Library of Congress states:

Although the problems of the central cities are most acute in those which are in the largest and oldest metropolitan areas (SMSA's), data from other cities indicate that the problem is national. The 12 largest SMSA's, each with 2 million or more populations in 1970, contain one-fourth of the U.S. population. During the sixties, 11 out of 12 were characterized by massive net-outmigrations from the central city of middle-class whites and immigrations of lower-income Negroes. Populations in 10 of the 12 central cities declined during the last decade. The next group of 21 SMSA's, with populations of 1 to 2 million each, are approaching the age and size of the largest and many of them have been experiencing the same sort of population changes. The data suggest that the national significance of the central city problem is growing.

The Central City Problem and Urban Renewal Policy, Study prepared for the Subcommittee on Housing and Urban Affairs of the Committee on Banking, Housing and Urban Affairs of the Senate (Washington, D.C.: Government Printing Office, 1973), p. 3.

24. Edward C. Banfield, *The Unheavenly City Revisited* (Boston: Little, Brown, 1974).

25. *Chicago Sun-Times*, August 25, 1974, p. 36.

26. *Id.*

27. *New York Times*, April 5, 1976.

28. Joel L. Fleishman, "Goals and Strategies of a National Housing and Urban Growth Policy," in *Papers Submitted to Subcommittee on Housing Panels, House Committee on Banking and Currency*, 92d Cong. 1st sess. (June 1971), p. 712. The pattern may well be that the central city will simply become one specialized center among a number of centers of economic activity in the metropolitan area, what has been described as a loose federation of a small number of centers and surrounding rings, "'suburbs' that process materials and produce goods ringing 'central cities' that process information and deliver services." Thompson, *supra* note 21 at 29. Such a pattern, if it develops, would not make it less important to ameliorate the metropolitan apartheid condition in our present central cities or to prevent a like condition from developing in the emerging outlying economic centers.

29. In the early 1960s and 1970s school segregation decreased dramatically in the South, but the story was quite different in the large northern and western cities. An examination of the fourteen largest northern and western districts enrolling at least 15 percent black students showed that segregation grew worse in nine systems in the year following 1968, with only one district showing more than a slight improvement. In 1970 Chicago had only 3 percent of its black students in predominantly white schools, and Philadelphia had only 7.4 percent. The next fall, Los Angeles and Detroit had fewer than 7 percent in majority white schools, and Milwaukee and Boston had less than 15 percent. Even school districts with relatively small percentages of black enrollment tended to be highly segregated. Gary Orfield, "Federal Policy, Local Power and Metropolitan Segregation," *Political Science Quarterly* 89 (Winter 1974-75): 780-81.

30. *Hearings before the Subcommittee on Housing and Urban Affairs of the Committee on Banking, Housing and Urban Affairs*, 92d Cong., 1st sess. (September 16, 1971), p. 996.

31. Lord Bryce, *The American Commonwealth* (New York: G.P. Putnam, 1959).

32. Arnold Rogow, *The Dying of the Light* (New York: G.P. Putnam's Sons, 1975).

33. Richard Goodwin, Review of The Dying of the Light, *New York Times Magazine* (February 8, 1976), p. 5.

34. *New York Times*, November 11, 1975, p. 31, col. 1.

NOTES TO APPENDIX

1. Letter to Robert C. Weaver from West Side Federation, August 26, 1965.

2. Public Housing Administration Low-Rent Housing Manual, §205.1 (September 1965).

3. Letter from Marie C. McGuire, commissioner, Public Housing Administration, to Reverend S. Jerome Hall, chairman, West Side Federation, October 14, 1965.

4. In addition to the author, volunteer lawyers who worked on the case at various times included Milton Shadur, Charles Markels, Bernard Weisberg, Merrill Freed, Cecil Butler, Robert Vollen, and Roger Pascal. Shadur and the author took on the primary responsibility, although in the beginning, major decisions were generally made collectively.

5. *Gautreaux v. CHA*, 265 F. Supp. 582 (Ill. 1967).

6. *Gautreaux v. CHA*, 296 F. Supp. 907, 912-13 (Ill. 1969).

7. *Id.* at 913.

8. *Id.* at 907.

9. *Id.* at 912.

10. *Id.* at 915.

11. *Chicago Daily News*, February 11, 1969.

12. *Chicago Daily News*, February 12, 1969.

13. *Chicago Daily News*, February 14, 1969.

14. Civil Rights Commission, letter of June 2, 1969.

15. *Gautreaux v. CHA*, 304 F. Supp. 736, 741 (Ill. 1969).

16. *Chicago Daily News*, July 3, 1969.

17. Chicago *Sun-Times*, July 5, 1969.

18. *Chicago Tribune* editorial, July 2, 1969.

19. *Time* magazine, July 14, 1969, p. 74.

20. *Chicago Daily News*, July 2, 1969.

21. *Chicago Sun-Times*, March 6, 1971, p. 7.

22. *Chicago Today*, March 9, 1971.

23. *Chicago Tribune*, March 11, 1971.

24. Gautreaux v. Romney, 448 F.2d at 731.

25. The case against HUD, which had been filed simultaneously with the one against CHA, had not been decided at the time of the 1969 CHA decision because Judge Austin said that he wanted first to dispose of the case against CHA before considering HUD's liability.

26. Unpublished transcript of court proceedings.

27. For an article describing the early operation of the demonstration program, see Barbara Garland, "Cabrini-Green to Willow Creek," *Chicago* (June 1977).

28. *Chicago Daily News*, August 5, 1977, p. 1.

Index

About the Author

Alexander Polikoff is a lawyer who in 1970 left private practice to become executive director of BPI (Business and Professional People for the Public Interest), a public interest law center in Chicago. He was chief counsel in the *Gautreaux* case, a housing desegregation suit which led to a significant 8–0 decision by the United States Supreme Court in 1976. Mr. Polikoff holds degrees in both literature and law from the University of Chicago and is the author of a number of articles on environmental and urban issues.

C2